Research Methods in
Early Childhood

Education at SAGE

SAGE is a leading international publisher of journals, books, and electronic media for academic, educational, and professional markets.

Our education publishing includes:

- accessible and comprehensive texts for aspiring education professionals and practitioners looking to further their careers through continuing professional development

- inspirational advice and guidance for the classroom

- authoritative state of the art reference from the leading authors in the field

Find out more at: **www.sagepub.co.uk/education**

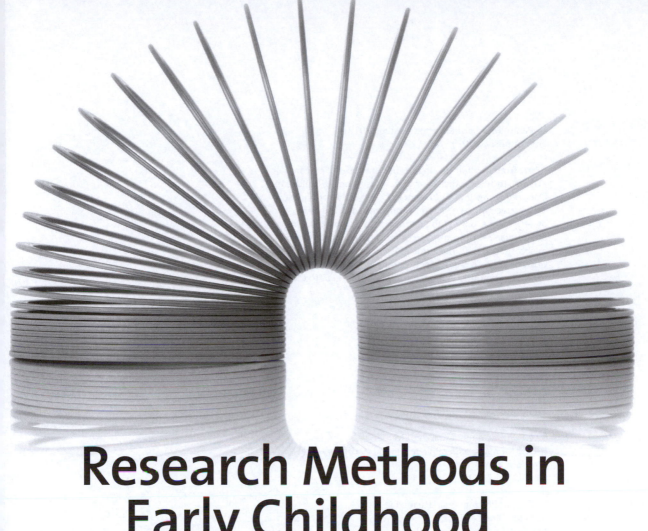

Research Methods in Early Childhood

An Introductory Guide

Penny Mukherji and Deborah Albon

SAGE

Los Angeles | London | New Delhi
Singapore | Washington DC

SAGE Publications Ltd
1 Oliver's Yard
55 City Road
London EC1Y 1SP

SAGE Publications Inc.
2455 Teller Road
Thousand Oaks, California 91320

SAGE Publications India Pvt Ltd
B 1/I 1 Mohan Cooperative Industrial Area
Mathura Road
New Delhi 110 044

SAGE Publications Asia-Pacific Pte Ltd
33 Pekin Street #02–01
Far East Square
Singapore 048763

Library of Congress Control Number: 2009926698
British Library Cataloguing in Publication data

A catalogue record for this book is available from the
British Library

ISBN 978-1-84787-523-5
ISBN 978-1-84787-524-2 (pbk)

Typeset by Dorwyn, Wells, Somerset
Printed in Great Britain by T.J. International Ltd, Padstow, Cornwall
Printed on paper from sustainable resources

CONTENTS

ACKNOWLEDGEMENTS

First and foremost, we wish to acknowledge the huge contribution our partners Dave and Ashu have made to this project – without their constant support it would not have been possible.

Many thanks to all the students who inspire us and continue to inspire us with their research projects. Particular thanks go to former students Abby Gumbrell and Yolande Bruzon for permission to refer to their work in this book.

In addition to this, we would like to thank Panayiotis Angelides and Antonia Michaelidou and the children in their research for their permissions to use drawings published in their paper: Angelides, P. and Michaelidou, A. (2009) 'The deafening silence: discussing children's drawings for understanding and addressing marginalisation', *Journal of Early Childhood Research*, 7(1): 27–45.

Also, many thanks to Stephen Kemmis and Robin McTaggart for their permission to use a diagram of the action research spiral, published in the paper: Kemmis, S. and McTaggart, R. (2005) 'Participatory action research: Communicative action and the public sphere', in N.K. Denzin and Y.S. Lincoln (eds), *The SAGE Handbook of Qualitative Research*. 3rd edn. London: SAGE.

Finally, we would like to acknowledge the huge support we have had from the team at SAGE – especially Jude – and the reviewers for their helpful suggestions.

ABOUT THE AUTHORS

Penny Mukherji has been involved in educating students in the field of early childhood for over 20 years and during this time has developed a deep understanding into how to support students on their learning journeys. At present Penny is a Senior Lecturer in Early Childhood Studies at London Metropolitan University, where an important part of her teaching involves supporting both undergraduate and postgraduate students as they complete their research projects. With a background in health and psychology, Penny is an established author, with a special interest in the health and well-being of young children.

Deborah Albon worked as a nursery nurse, teacher and manager in a range of early childhood settings for nearly 20 years. Her research interests are primarily around food and drink provisioning and play in early childhood settings. Deborah has published a range of articles in this area and with Penny Mukherji has co-written *Food and Health in Early Childhood*. She now works as a Senior Lecturer in Early Childhood Studies at London Metropolitan University, where she has considerable experience teaching research methods to both undergraduate and postgraduate students.

FOREWORD

Researching early childhood issues is notoriously difficult. Not only is it extremely difficult to conduct robust research in an area that is relatively subjective, but researching anything to do with young children has enormous ethical issues which are often underplayed. How I wish I'd had a book like this when I first started my career as a researcher into early years education and care! Not only do the writers outline very clearly the various methods and methodology feasible in early childhood contexts but they explain and explore critical issues like ethics when researching young children and their experiences.

One vital issue that I've always found so challenging is that of power relationships between children and adults, especially as an adult researcher: how do we make children 'equals' in the research process? How do we ensure that children's own voices are heard? When one embarks on research in early years settings one is immediately and potentially in a 'power' situation in respect of children: they tend to see adults as 'all powerful' – they who must be obeyed! – and, therefore, when asked questions will respond in ways that 'please' the adults. This book explores these issues openly and honestly and provides clear guidance on how to make children, as far as possible, joint and parallel researchers within a carefully conceived project, however young.

Another strength of the book for me is in outlining with clarity and cohesiveness the major challenges and strengths of various types of methods for conducting research and the underpinning methodologies available to researchers. The writers explain unambiguously the difference between methods – the tools of research – and methodologies – the way research is conducted, which will be of considerable help to new researchers, especially those undertaking masters and doctoral studies. These people, in my experience, often misjudge and misrepresent the differences between methods and methodologies: they will be in no doubt after reading this excellent book.

It is worth pointing out that the book is not only extremely readable but is very well referenced, important for those who want to read further into the issues raised. All references are up-to-date and, within the text, are vital to exploring the various challenges and concerns outlined.

Where we often think of 'meaningful' experiences for young children as paramount to their developing understanding of various concepts, as researchers we often forget the meaningfulness issues when it comes to children and our own researches. This book reminds us powerfully of the need for our research, whatever its overall focus, to make sense to children if they – and their parents – are to consent to involvement and remain involved over a period of time. It is clear that the writers both feel that the child as participant is a vital aspect of research and of this book: the writers are both sensitive to children's involvement and clearly feel that listening to children is a crucial part of all early childhood research. They are also clear that 'listening' involves not only researchers' ears but their eyes as well, in that children's body language and actions are often just as telling – sometimes more – in research terms, as their oral contributions. In other words, what a child does is just as important as what a young child says – or doesn't say!

An essential area covered in the book is the difference between undertaking primary and secondary research and the importance in both contexts of critiquing the research of others. This may be through literature reviews or other forms of textual analysis, for example, or action research into what policies appear to be effective in practice. Various different examples of research projects are interrogated and evaluated in terms of how they help us to understand research into practice and policy in early childhood. The reported empirical research within the book and the various outcomes will be a great support for all who are seeking to conduct their own research and are unsure of the challenges and issues that are likely to confront them. There is practical support, too, for observation which is one of the major ways in which practitioners and researchers are likely to interpret and analyse many aspects of early childhood practice and experiences.

In my experience, most students have great difficulty in developing their own research – where to start, what to focus on, how the analysis should be conducted, what they are likely to find and such like – are all extremely difficult areas for inexperienced researchers. All these aspects are covered with thoroughness and thoughtfulness in this excellent book. There's something for everyone at whatever level they embark on their research. The writing is not only extremely clear and concise, but the examples make it very interesting and informative.

The real underpinning of the book is its major strength: the role of children in supporting researchers to understand more about children's experiences of life in early years environments. The book is highly creative in terms of ensuring that readers must think through various issues and challenges if they are to conduct effective, robust and worthwhile early childhood research. Much of the research with young children will be subjective and interpretive in nature: other studies will involve positivist research where numerical data is collected. Both issues are covered with clarity and integrity in this book and the differences, advantages and disadvantages of both are explored and explained in ways which will support readers at both undergraduate and post-graduate levels. The structure of the book, in itself, is most supportive and considerate to its readers: a bonus for all those researching early childhood.

The book is bold and not afraid to cover difficult issues such as those involved in analysing and interpreting the data collected either through positivist or interpretivist methodologies whilst still putting young children at the heart of the process. In summary, this book is a model of clarity for all those involved, or intending to be involved, in early childhood research. I wholeheartedly commend it to those embarking upon, or wishing to extend their knowledge of, early childhood research.

Professor Emeritus Janet Moyles
Early Years and Play Consultant

KEY FOR ICONS

Chapter objectives

Case study

Reflection point

Research in focus

Glossary Ⓖ

Key points from the chapter 🔑

Further reading 📖

INTRODUCTION

WHAT DO WE MEAN BY 'RESEARCH'?

Research can sometimes appear daunting to a new researcher. We can recall a student telling us that the key difference between writing an essay and carrying out a piece of research is the 'venture into the unknown' or onus on the *student* to conduct the inquiry as opposed to having to write about the work of others. This, she suggested, was scary.

Yet we carry out research all the time. In reading this book you will have made the decision to do this based on a range of information; the recommendation of a tutor or student; a whim based on the cover of the book; or by thoroughly examining a range of research methods' texts in person. Similarly, when deciding what school to send their child to, parents might ask for the opinions of other families that use the school, they might visit the school themselves and talk to the staff and observe what happens on a typical day. Alternatively, they might prefer to examine what they view as more 'objective' evidence such as school league tables. These examples could be regarded as 'research' and demonstrate that we are being 'researchers' a lot of the time. Young children and babies are also carrying out 'research', it could be argued, when they explore the possibilities of a particular object using all of their senses. It would seem, then, that to answer the questions that we pose for ourselves it is necessary to collect information, analyse it and interpret it in some way (Kumar, 2005) and this is a process we engage in at different points and for a variety of reasons throughout our lives.

But there is a clear distinction between this kind of 'kitchen sink' research and academic research. To qualify as *academic* research, there needs to be an understanding of the paradigm and methodological approach that underpins the research. The terms 'paradigm' and 'methodology' are ones that you will come across throughout the book, but especially in Chapters 1 and 2, and relate to the philosophy that underpins the research and the rules associated with producing knowledge within that paradigm respectively. The researcher needs to be able to argue the position they take with regard to this as well as the methods chosen in order to undertake their research. This is because *academic* research is open to greater scrutiny. An example would be the need to subject research that is put forward for publication to a rigorous process of peer review (Kumar, 2005). 'Kitchen sink' research is not subject to such scrutiny. Decisions made in relation to academic research need to be justified carefully in the same way as one would draw upon published work to support the points made in an academic essay. This would not be required in less formal writing, such as a text sent to a friend, for instance. But we should remember that knowledge and skills in relation to *research*, like essay writing, are something that can be developed and improved upon.

The exact purpose of the research will determine the type of research study that is undertaken. Johnson and Christensen (2008) identify five different kinds of research undertaken with or about children: basic research, applied research, evaluation research action research and orientational research. We will look at these briefly in turn:

1. **Basic research.** This is research that is aimed at finding out the fundamentals about scientific and human processes. In the sphere of early childhood there is much fundamental research being under-taken to discover underlying brain mechanisms. For example, in 2007 it was reported that Gallo et al. had discovered new information about processes involved in the repair of white matter in the brain. Gallo comments that 'By understanding the fundamental mechanisms of brain development, we get closer to finding clear instructions to repairing developmental brain disorders and injuries' (Darte, 2007: 1). Often it is not immediately apparent how the information discovered in basic research will help us in everyday life, but it is upon these fundamental discoveries that applied research is based, which can lead to advances in practical applications of basic knowledge.

2. **Applied research**. This is research that is focused on answering or finding solutions to 'real life' questions. Applied research may draw upon the findings of basic research to point the way to solutions. This is the type of research that early childhood practitioners and students of early childhood studies are most likely to be involved with.

Basic research and applied research can be considered to be two ends of a continuum, as often, research projects have elements of both, in varying proportions.

3. **Evaluation research.** This type of research, a form of applied research, is undertaken when a new intervention or project has been implemented and is designed to evaluate the effectiveness of the initiative. Evaluation research projects are often undertaken to see if the new programme should be rolled out for wider participation. There are many examples of evaluation studies in the field of early childhood, perhaps one of the largest being the ongoing evaluation study into the effectiveness of the Sure Start programme. The programme, started in 1999, aimed at giving children and families from deprived areas, intensive support in the children's earliest years. Although the programme has now evolved into the nationwide provision of children's centres, the evaluation programme contin-ues. In 2008 the team reported positive effects for three-year-olds in the programme, who showed better social development and higher levels of social behaviour and independent self-regulation than children who were not part of a Sure Start scheme (NESS, 2008).

4. **Action research.** This is research based in the workplace, and is another example of applied research. It arises out of the identification of a problem or need within the workplace and the prac-titioners within the setting design and implement the research study. The objective is to arrive at a solution or intervention that can be implemented and evaluated by the staff team. Action research is looked at in more detail in Chapter 8 of this book.

5. **Orientational research (critical theory research).** This is research that aims to collect information to help strengthen the argument of those who wish to promote a particular ideology or political posi-tion, with the intention of improving society (Johnson and Christensen, 2008). Orientational researchers aim to promote the most disadvantaged sections of society and focus on social inequal-ities, and, therefore make their ideology (orientation) explicit.

AIMS AND SCOPE OF THIS BOOK

Our aims in writing this book are many. We hope that students who are new to early childhood research will learn about some of the main paradigms, methodologies and methods that are used in early childhood research. Of course many of these might relate to research in general, but our aim throughout is to write a research methods' text with *early childhood studies* at its heart.

Therefore, in recognition of the multidisciplinary nature of early childhood studies, we draw upon research from a variety of theoretical and professional fields. We will be looking at research from health studies, psychology, anthropological studies, education and such like. In doing this, we will be reflecting upon small-scale and large-scale studies as well as studies that are longitudinal or provide a snapshot of an issue. Some of the research we will be referring to may already be known to you, some is likely to be new to you. As previously noted, the guiding principle has been to include reference to research in the field of 'early childhood' or that has clear relevance to this area.

By 'early childhood research' we are referring to research that has been carried out with or about children from birth to eight years and related issues, such as those relating to practitioners that work with this age group or parents of children in this age group. As many of you are probably aware, some of the research that falls within the 'early childhood' umbrella might actually be carried out with adults, especially parents and practitioners rather than *directly* involving young children. In addition, as you will see in Part 3 of the book, early childhood research might involve looking at documents that are pertinent to the field, such as diaries and other forms of 'text'.

We hope that reading this book will equip you with some of the knowledge that will enable you to critique the research of others. In doing this, though, we wish to stress that no research lies outside the possibility of criticism. There are always possibilities and limitations with *any* research design and, as new researchers in particular, you should aim at being tentative and considered when critiquing the work of others as opposed to merely declaring them as 'wrong' or 'flawed' in some way. This is another skill to develop in becoming an early childhood researcher. You will notice that in this book, each chapter will outline the possibilities and limitations of the paradigm, methodology, approach or method discussed in the chapter. Sometimes this is in the form of a distinct section towards the end of the chapter, and on other occasions this discussion is threaded throughout the chapter.

Greig et al. (2007) point out that a key difference between training to be a professional, such as a teacher or nursery nurse, and learning how to be a researcher is that the trainee professional usually has an opportunity to observe the skills of other, more experienced practitioners. They also have an opportunity to reflect on their professional training experiences with other student practitioners and their lecturers at college. Such opportunities are often not replicated for the novice researcher. We hope that in this book, by reflecting upon early childhood research in our 'research in focus' sections and reading about the experiences of people who have embarked upon their own research projects in the 'case study' sections, you will be afforded such opportunities. Certainly the development of the 'Research Methods in Early Childhood' module on the degree course that we are both involved in came about as a result of the need to support students in developing knowledge and skills in relation to research on the course, especially as they prepare for their final dissertations or projects.

HOW THE BOOK IS ORGANISED

The book is divided into four parts. At the beginning of the book we look at paradigms and principles that underpin early childhood research. We think about positivism and then the growth in interpretivist and post-structuralist research. Within these first two chapters we also discuss methodological approaches. We will show how the positivist paradigm has a tendency to employ a quantitative methodological approach, whereas the interpretivist and especially the post-structuralist paradigms tend to embrace a qualitative methodological approach. You will also find that we thread discussion about research paradigms and methodology throughout this book.

The third chapter focuses upon ethics and the fourth, listening to young children in research. These appear in the first part of the book owing to our belief that ethical principles should underpin any piece of research. We draw upon Lahman's (2008: 285) notion of the *'competent* yet *vulnerable* child' in Chapters 3 and 4 to highlight the way that one's view of the 'child' underpins a research project. By emphasising the child as *competent*, we wish to highlight the potential of seeing the child as a participant in research – as opposed to the object of research. By recognising the child as *vulnerable* we are highlighting the necessity of keeping the needs of young children firmly in mind when carrying out research. This is in recognition that research that directly involves very young children and babies, in particular, is likely to be different to research carried out with children of secondary school age, for instance. However, in saying this, we believe that *everyone* is vulnerable in some sense in research and it is important that researchers keep this in mind.

Part 2 of this book looks at some approaches that are used in early childhood research. We look at surveys, ethnography, case studies and action research. These approaches might draw upon a range of different methods and it is these 'tools' or methods of research that we discuss in Part 3 of the book. Here, we look at observation; interviewing; questionnaires; using documents and other visual 'texts'; journaling and creative methods for involving children in research.

The final part of this book, Part 4, outlines some of the key things someone new to early childhood research needs to know in relation to designing a small-scale research project, analysing data and writing up a piece of research. Chapter 17, which looks at analysing and presenting data is a lengthy chapter in comparison with others, owing to the volume of information we wished to cover. Part 4 also includes a chapter on writing a literature review as all research needs to position itself in relation to the research that has been carried out in a similar area or using a similar methodological approach previously – a key role for this chapter in a piece of written up research.

Inevitably, when writing a text such as this, decisions as to where to place different topics have sometimes been difficult to make. Other writers may have placed the chapter on research design at the beginning of the book, for instance. We decided to organise the book in the way that we have so that the reader is introduced to some of the key ideas about paradigms, methodology and ethics early on in the book as they underpin research practice. The second part of the book, which looks at approaches such as surveys and action research, is located next because it seems to follow on logically and needs to be discussed before Part 3, which deals with specific research methods. We decided to position the chapters relating to designing, carrying out and writing up a research project in Part 4 of the book because we want the reader to draw upon the knowledge they have gained about early childhood research in order to support their decision-making.

We hope that as you read through the book you will have developed some understanding of paradigms, methodologies, principles, approaches to research as well as methods themselves that will help you in planning your own research project. The boxed research in focus sections, Case studies, Reflection points and Activities aim to encourage you to think further about a point that has been raised or provide an exemplar from a piece of published research or student project. Some of the activities will involve you in accessing particular websites. If these prove difficult to open, try shortening the web address to its main page. For example, if the British Psychological Society's code of conduct is difficult to access on the following website: (http://www.bps.org.uk/the-society/code-of-conduct/code-of-conduct_home.cfm), you could shorten the web address to http://www.bps.org.uk and carry out a search within their particular website. Occasionally you will see a word in **bold** and the symbol Ⓖ in the margin. This tells you that this word is further explained in the glossary.

Finally, in reading this book, we hope that you will develop knowledge and skills in relation to *early childhood* research. We especially hope that you will have the confidence and enthusiasm to undertake your own piece of research, in an area that you feel *passionate* about. In doing this, whether you are carrying out research aiming at instigating a change in practice, developing a greater understanding of an issue or suchlike, you will be contributing to a body of knowledge that enriches our understandings of young children and the many factors that impact upon their lives.

PART 1
PARADIGMS AND PRINCIPLES

If you have read the introduction to the main part of the text, you will know that we have carefully organised the chapters into four parts and that these parts have a logical order. This first part of the book, entitled 'Paradigms and principles' contains information that will underpin the decisions you will be making if you are planning to carry out early childhood research. We strongly recommend that you look at this part of the book before reading further.

Chapters 1 and 2 look at paradigms that guide early childhood research, positivism and, as a reaction to this way of conceptualising the world, interpretivism and post-structuralism. These paradigms reflect our underpinning assumptions about the nature of knowledge and the best ways of understanding the world around us. Positivism is an approach to research that is founded on the underlying assumption that there are 'truths' to be uncovered, and that the best way to uncover these 'truths' is to use scientific methods. This approach guides research in subjects such as physics, chemistry and biology. Any paradigm that we hold not only frames what we believe to be the nature of knowledge, but also underpins the methodology we will use to investigate this knowledge. Hughes (2001a: 32) defines methodology as 'what to investigate, how to investigate it, what to measure or assess and how to do so'. Positivism tends to use *quantitative* methodology that aims to produce information, or data, in numerical form that can be analysed by using statistics. In Chapter 1, we will look at how this approach has been applied to early childhood research. We will, however, discover that there are limitations to this approach, which have led to the increasing prominence of the interpretivist paradigm. Interpretivism is an approach that, far from assuming that it is possible to reveal 'the truth' by the strict application of scientific methodology, accepts that 'the truth' varies according to the perspectives of those involved and the context within which research is located. Interpretivism uses *qualitative* methodology, which focuses more on words and meanings than quantitative methodology.

Whatever the paradigm that is guiding researchers' thinking, researchers have to ensure that their research conforms to the highest *ethical* standards. In the same way that the paradigm we hold will steer decisions about the research we undertake, our 'moral philosophy or set of moral principles' define our ethical stance, which in turn will decide how we conduct our research (Aubrey et al., 2000: 156). It could be considered that the paradigm we hold has a direct influence on the ethical stance that we take, as, within a positivist paradigm, children may be seen as *objects* to be studied, as opposed to children being seen as *active participants* in the research process. Chapter 3 looks broadly at ethics in relation to early childhood research and Chapter 4 examines issues relating to *listening* to children. We include these chapters in the first part of the book owing to our belief that they are important principles in research.

In Chapter 4, we discuss how the way we 'see' children influences the degree to which we consider children's voices should be heard. We will argue that there has been a shift away from researchers thinking that children are not competent enough to join in the research process, that they are passive and powerless, to an increasing emphasis on children's abilities to be active participants in research. This, as we will see, has ethical implications.

POSITIVIST RESEARCH

Chapter objectives
- To develop an understanding of the positivist research paradigm
- To consider the relationship between positivist research, quantitative methodology and experimental methods
- To outline the possibilities and limitations of positivist research

In this chapter, we will look at what is meant by *positivist* research, and consider how a positivist approach to research leads to the use of experimental and **quantitative** methods. We will also be introducing you to the idea of research **paradigms**. This is important because carrying out research involves an understanding of the philosophy that underpins the research – or 'paradigm' – because this, in turn, determines the methodological approach taken. Positivism tends to underpin quantitative methodological approaches to research as we will see.

FINDING OUT ABOUT THE WORLD AROUND US

By the time we reach adulthood we know a lot of things, not only facts about the world around us, such as how to peel a banana and the age that children usually begin to walk, but we also have ideas and opinions on many topics. The branch of philosophy that looks at what knowledge is (its nature), the source of knowledge and the **validity** of knowledge, is called **epistemology**. Johnson and Christensen (2008) identify three sources of knowledge: experience, expert opinion and reasoning.

Experience

This is the first way that babies begin to learn about the world around them, as they explore the world via their senses. The idea that knowledge comes from experience is known as **empiricism** (Atkinson et al., 1996) and according to this way of thinking only the knowledge that we obtain through our senses can be said to be true. From this concept is derived the word 'empirical', the idea that a statement can be proved or disproved by observation, experiment or experience (Johnson and Christensen, 2008). Later on in the chapter we will see that positivist **methodology** relies on the collection of empirical

Ⓖ **data**; facts or information that has been derived by observation or experiment.

Expert opinion

The sum total of human knowledge would not grow very fast if we had to formulate our knowledge and understanding of the world by 'first principles' all the time. Much of our knowledge has been passed down to us from others. Among the sources of information are our parents, other family members, friends, educators and 'experts'. It is difficult to turn on the television or read a newspaper without encountering the ideas of experts. As we grow older we come to realise that not everything that we are told by experts is true or helpful. We learn to practise discernment and realise that sometimes expert advice can be contradictory. Nevertheless, learning from others remains an important source of information about the world around us.

Reasoning

Whereas empiricists argue that the only valid way to find out about the world around us is by observation, experiment and experience, adherents of rationalism consider that *reason* is the primary source of knowledge (Johnson and Christensen, 2008). Through the processes of thinking and reasoning, rationalists believe that it is possible to develop an understanding of a subject, without actually directly observing a phenomenon.

Atkinson et al. (1996) identify two main types of reasoning; deductive reasoning and inductive reasoning.

- *Deductive reasoning* is the process of drawing conclusions about something on the basis of prior knowledge known to be true. For example, one may agree that the following statement (premise) is true: 'Newborn babies cannot talk.' Then, given another statement, 'Baby John can say "DaDa"', it is possible to deduce that John cannot be a newborn baby. Deductive reasoning is only successful if the first premise is true.
- *Inductive reasoning* is when one draws conclusions about something on the balance of probability that a statement is true, based on what has previously occurred. For example, you may have noticed that every cat you have seen has a furry coat and from this you reason that it is probably true that all cats have furry coats. However, when using inductive reasoning it is always possible that the exception to the rule may come along, which will disprove the theory.

WHAT DO WE MEAN BY A 'PARADIGM'?

Research is about asking questions and seeking information to answer the questions that we pose. Influencing the questions that we ask and underpinning the research approach we eventually take are our ideas and conceptions about childhood and children. This understanding of children and childhood ultimately influences the research paradigm that we use.

It is worth taking some time to discuss what a paradigm is as it is a term that will be used frequently in this book. In common usage, a paradigm is an exemplar or a model. However the term has come to mean something more specific when used in relation to research, mainly because of the work of Thomas Khun in the 1960s and 1970s (Hammersley, 2007). According to Mackenzie and Knipe (2006) a paradigm is a theoretical framework. They cite Bogdan and Biklen (1998: 22) as defining a paradigm as 'a loose collection of logically related assumptions, concepts and propositions that orient thinking and research'. Hughes (2001a: 31) describes a paradigm as a way of seeing the world that 'frames a research topic' and influences the way that we think about the topic. Similarly, Fraser and Robinson (2004: 59) describe it as a 'set of beliefs about the way in which particular problems exist and a set of agreements on how such problems can be investigated'. From this, it is clear that our choice of paradigm is important in influencing the methodology we choose, but it also shapes our perceptions of children and childhood as we will see.

Hughes (2001b) illustrates the connection between underlying beliefs and research methodology when he looked at a number of research studies into the influence and significance of the media in children's lives. He concludes that the way that the various research studies were conducted reflects the *model of childhood* held by the researchers, and that this underlying model influenced the research that was conducted. For example, researchers who held the underlying belief that children are like 'little sponges', uncritically absorbing messages from the media, asked the question 'what does the media do to children?' Researchers who saw children as more active, discriminating consumers tended to ask the question 'what do children do with the media?' (Hughes, 2001b: 356).

Although various authors (Hughes, 2001a; 2001b; Mackenzie and Knipe, 2006) have identified a number of paradigms that underpin research into children, Kumar (2005) suggests that the two main paradigms that form the basis of research in the social sciences are the *positivist approach* and the *naturalistic (interpretivist) approach* and it is these two paradigms (as well as post-structuralism) that we will be looking at in more detail in both this chapter and the next.

THE MEANING AND ORIGINS OF POSITIVISM

The positivist paradigm is one that has its roots in physical science. It uses a systematic, scientific approach to research. Hughes (2001a) explains that the positivist paradigm sees the world as being based on unchanging, universal laws and the view that everything that occurs around us can be explained by knowledge of these universal laws. To understand these universal laws we need to observe and record events and phenomena around us in a systematic way and then work out the underlying principle that has 'caused' the event to occur. An example of this process in action is the story of Sir Isaac Newton and the apple. It is said that Isaac Newton was walking in an apple orchard and saw an apple fall straight down to the ground. He started wondering about how far above the Earth the force of gravity had an effect and began to develop his theory of gravity. In this example the observed event was the falling apple and the underlying universal law was that of gravity (Keesing, 2008).

Scientific discoveries have been made since ancient times, for example as early as 4800 BC there is evidence that standing stones were being used for astronomical calculations in an area of Africa near the Sudanese border with Egypt (Lee, 2008). The positivist paradigm, however, is not just associated with scientific discovery; it involves the application of scientific methodology. The development of the scientific method as a means of exploring the world around us probably emerged around the time of the European Renaissance (fifteenth and sixteenth centuries) and the Enlightenment (eighteenth century) (Fraser and Robinson, 2004).

THE SCIENTIFIC METHOD

In the section above we outlined that positivist researchers in the field of early childhood, and indeed other subject areas, have to make a basic assumption that what is being studied is subject to underlying, unchanging, universal laws. Johnson and Christensen (2008: 17) point out that positivist researchers also have to make other assumptions, including that they should operate within agreed norms and practices as well as the idea that it is possible to distinguish between more and less plausible claims and that science cannot provide all the answers.

The key features of the scientific method include:

1. Observation and collecting data
2. Looking for patterns and developing a theory
Ⓖ 3. Forming a **hypothesis** to test the theory
4. Conducting research to test the hypothesis
5. Support or adjustment of the theory (Coolican, 2004).

These steps are often represented as a cycle or wheel (see Figure 1.1).

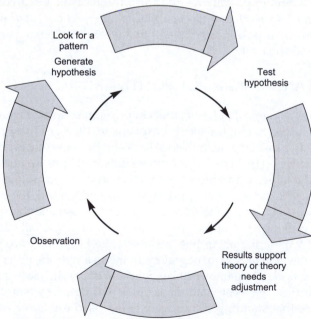

Figure 1.1 The research wheel

Within this framework Johnson and Christensen (2008) identify two different approaches: an *exploratory* approach and a *confirmatory* approach.

- The *exploratory approach* starts with the researcher making observations and searching for a pattern. If a pattern is found then the researcher puts forward a theory or idea about why this pattern occurs. This approach is sometimes known as the *inductive* method.
- The *confirmatory approach* is where a researcher starts with a theory about why a particular phenomenon is occurring and develops a hypothesis (a prediction) based on the theory. The next stage of this approach is when the researcher conducts an empirical investigation to test the hypothesis. If the data upholds the hypothesis then this supports the underlying theory. This approach is sometimes known as the *deductive* method.

You may find it helpful to look at the section on 'reasoning' earlier on in this chapter to remind yourself about inductive and deductive reasoning.

In reality these two approaches often work hand in hand with each other, as the following research in focus will show.

 Research in focus

Ili et al. (2001) reported the findings of a longitudinal cohort study into the relationship between the number of respiratory infections children have and asthma. Previously, it had been observed that children from larger families and those who attended group day care seem to have a lower incidence of asthma. This led to the theory that children who were exposed to more infections as infants (from siblings or peers in nursery) were protected from acquiring asthma as they got older (Kelan and Weiss, 2001). From this theory, Ili et al. developed the hypothesis that the more upper respiratory tract infections (colds) that children had, the less likely they were to develop asthma. This hypothesis was tested by following up 1,374 children from birth until the age of seven years and recording the number of upper respiratory infections that they had before the age of three and whether or not they had been diagnosed with asthma by the age of seven. The findings confirmed the hypothesis.

This report contains elements of both the exploratory approach and the confirmatory approach. The initial observations about the link between respiratory infections could be said to be exploratory in approach, while the follow-up study of 1,374 children could be said to be confirmatory.

Can we use science to study children?

Before concluding this discussion on the scientific method, it is important to consider whether it is possible or desirable to use science to study children in the same way that science is used to study the physical world.

Up until the eighteenth century, children and childhood were not considered to be topics for scientific study, but from the time of Rousseau there is evidence that children were subject to observation, although it was not until the late nineteenth and twentieth centuries that systematic, scientific observation of children took place. Chapter 9 of this book looks at the historical origins of child observation in more detail. The application of scientific methodology to social and psychological phenomena has, and continues to be, passionately debated. Whereas it is possible to use scientific methods to research the *biology* and *physiology* of children, as in the Ili et al. study, it is harder to see how these methods can be employed to investigate attitudes and feelings and the social world in general. This is a key criticism of positivist research.

Greig et al. (2007) consider the question as to whether we can legitimately use scientific methods to study children to be a pseudo debate. They point out that children are complex individuals in whom there is a highly sophisticated interplay between physical, biological, chemical characteristics and 'psychological' characteristics. In addition the environment does not act passively upon children, they are active agents able both to adapt to and alter their environment. The complexity of children and childhood is such that no single approach will be wholly satisfactory, and scientific methodology should be viewed as part of an eclectic approach to research about and with children (Greig et al., 2007). The scientific method is an especially important approach in research into children's physiology – after all, in testing a new treatment to be used on young children, it is vital that it has gone through a rigorous scientific process.

POSITIVISM AND THE QUANTITATIVE METHODOLOGICAL APPROACH

As we have seen previously, the positivist paradigm leads to a scientific, systematic approach to research and as such lends itself to the use of quantitative methodology. Researchers using a quantitative methodological approach usually (but not always) concentrate on the *confirmatory* stages of the research cycle, that is, the formulation of a hypothesis and the collection of numerical data to test this hypothesis. Thus, quantitative methodology aims to measure, quantify or find the extent of a phenomenon, as opposed to **qualitative** methodology, which is usually more concerned with describing experiences, emphasising meaning and exploring the nature of an issue (Coolican, 2004). Kumar (2005) describes the quantitative methodological approach as being a *structured* approach, in which all aspects of the research process are decided upon before data collection begins. The qualitative methodological approach is seen to be more *unstructured* with aspects of the research process subject to change in response to events as they occur. Qualitative methodology will be looked at in more detail in Chapter 2.

Characteristics of quantitative research

Johnson and Christensen (2008: 34) outline the characteristics of quantitative research as follows:

- The confirmatory part of the research cycle is emphasised.
- Behaviour is seen to be predictable and regular.
- Common aims of research are to explain and predict.

- The researcher is interested in understanding general laws that apply to whole **populations** rather than particular groups.
- There is an attempt to study behaviour under controlled conditions with an attempt to isolate the effect of single variables.
- An objective approach is taken, that is, different observers should be able to agree to what is being observed.
- Data is based upon precise measurement using structured and validated data collection instruments.
- Data analysis aims to look at statistical relationships.

EXPERIMENTAL METHOD

We have seen that the confirmatory stage of the research cycle involves the testing of a hypothesis, an investigation of cause and effect. One way of doing this is by conducting an experiment. An experiment is a way of testing a hypothesis by precisely controlling the variables involved. It is very unlikely that students of early childhood will use an experiment in *their* research, but we will describe this method here as it will help you interpret the research findings of others.

Variables

Consider this imaginary piece of research. Members of staff in a local reception class have noted that children who come to them from one particular children's centre (centre A) appear to have attained a higher level of language development than children from another children's centre (centre B). Observations and records of children's language skills over a period of several years seem to support this view. The staff concludes that the difference is attributable to the higher quality of language interaction between the staff and children in centre A.

> ### ⩗ Reflection point
>
> Thinking about the conclusion made about the two children's centres in the above scenario, do you consider that the conclusion is appropriate? What other factors might be involved?

There has been a flaw in the reasoning behind the conclusion made, because the findings may have nothing to do with the quality of language interaction at all. It may be that one centre drew children who come from an area of higher social disadvantage than the other. The children may have entered centre B with very poor language development compared with the children entering centre A. In fact, the quality of interaction in centre B may be better than centre A as the gap in language skills between the two groups of children may have actually closed while they were attending centre B. Factors that may affect the outcome of research in this way are called variables, and for appropriate conclusions to be drawn the variables have to be controlled. In this case, one would have had to look at the language development of the children on entry to the two children's centres as well as when they arrived in the reception class to have any chance of reaching a sensible conclusion. Even then, controlling for variables in 'real-life' situations such as this is near to impossible.

Atkinson et al. (1996: 17) define a variable as 'something that can occur with different values', so time, age, social class, gender, for instance, are all examples of variables. In an experiment, the researcher takes control over the variables that may affect the outcome of the research, and it is the *precise control* of variables that distinguishes an experiment from other scientific methods of enquiry.

For example, a teacher has a theory that children learn better in the morning when they are 'fresh'. She decides to conduct an experiment to find out if this is true. Before she starts her experiment she needs to make several decisions.

- *How will she measure 'learning'?* In this case the teacher decides that her measure will be the number of spellings remembered after 24 hours from a list of five spellings.
- *What will her hypothesis be?* In this case she decides that her hypothesis will be 'Children learning a list of five spellings in the morning will remember more spellings 24 hours later than children who learn a list of five spellings in the afternoon'. The number of spellings remembered is called the **dependent variable** because this is what is being measured and the hypothesis is that the number of spellings learned is dependent on the time of day. The time of day is known as the **independent variable** as it is not under the control of (independent of) the participant; it is manipulated by the experimenter.
- *What other variables need to be taken into account and how will they be controlled?* The teacher comes up with the following ideas.

Table 1.1 Showing possible sources of variation and how these will be controlled

Variable	How it can be controlled
Age of child	Children will be chosen between the ages of 6 years and 6 years 3 months
Gender of child	Half the children will be boys, half will be girls
Health of child	Only children who are fit and well will be tested
Language	Children whose first language is not English and who are not yet fluent will be excluded
Hunger	Efforts will be made to test the children approximately two hours after they have had either breakfast or lunch
Environment	The children will be tested in the same room, with noise levels kept to a minimum
The spelling list	The list will be the same for all children

〰 **Reflection point**

Do you think the ability to remember spellings is the best way to measure *learning*? Are there *other* ways that you can think of that would enable this teacher to test her theory that children learn best in the mornings?

The key feature of an *experiment* is that the researcher tries to control as many variables as possible while only altering the independent variable.

Experimental design

The design of an experiment is the actual way that the experiment is put together. The simplest designs are similar to the one that we have just outlined; that is, there is one independent variable and one dependent variable (Atkinson et al., 1996).

In the hypothetical experiment outlined previously, the teacher decides that she will choose two groups of eight children, four girls and four boys, who fit in with the criteria outlined above. She gives one group the spellings in the morning, giving them 15 minutes to learn them. She tests them 24 hours later. She gives the spellings to the other group in the afternoon, again with 15 minutes to learn them and tests them 24 hours later. She makes sure that she gives both groups exactly the same instructions. This is known as an independent sample design; that is, that there are two different groups being tested under similar conditions (Coolican, 2004). The advantage of an independent design is that you can use the same 'test'. In this case, the same list of spellings was used, reducing the variance that could occur with different words. The disadvantage is that having two groups introduces other sources of variance, because individuals can differ according to a variety of dimensions such as personality, learning style, class, and culture. These variables, for which the researcher has not controlled, are sometimes called confounding variables (Johnson and Christensen, 2008).

The alternative to the independent sample design, which controls for individual differences, is the repeated measure design, where the same group is tested under different conditions (Field, 2009). In our example this would involve using a different set of spellings, which would introduce a source of variance.

One solution to the disadvantages to both of these designs is the matched pair design (Cardwell et al., 1996). In this design two groups of participants are used, but each participant in one group is matched as far as possible with someone from the other group, according to relevant variables. So in the hypothetical example we are discussing, each child would be partnered with another and matched according to variables such as level of mother's education, social class of the family and cultural background. Identical twins are often used as participants involving this sort of design because they are natural matched pairs.

Types of experiment

When we think of scientific experiments, we often think about laboratories and, indeed, many experiments in the field of child development have been undertaken in a laboratory situation, but experiments can be conducted in other ways. Coolican (2004) outlines the following experimental situations.

- **Laboratory experiments**. It is easier to control variables in a laboratory and some notable examples of research with children, such as Bandura et al.'s (1963) research on aggression have been undertaken in laboratories. Laboratory experiments have, however, been criticised because of the narrowness of the situations being investigated and the artificiality of the situation. Children, in particular, are unlikely to react the same way in 'real life' as they do in controlled laboratory situations.

Research in focus

Piaget (1896–1980) famously conducted a series of laboratory-based experiments designed to show that the way children think and reason is different from adults. Robson (2006) describes an experiment conducted by Piaget to demonstrate that young children under about the age of 7 find it very difficult to see things from another's point of view. The experiment involved a model of three mountains that was placed on a table top. The three mountains were different in colour and were easy to tell apart because one had a house on its summit, one had a cross and another was covered by snow. A toy doll was placed looking towards the mountains, with the child being 'tested' being placed looking at the model, but at an angle to the doll. The child was asked 'What can the doll see'? and given photographs of the three mountains taken from a variety of positions. Children of different ages were tested under the same conditions and it was found the children under 7 typically chose the photograph that represented the view that they could see. This was taken as confirmation that young children were egocentric, and cannot 'decentre' (Cardwell et al., 1996).

- **Field experiments**. These are carried out in naturalistic surroundings. In the memory experiment that we were discussing previously, the experiment would have been carried out in the children's school. Obviously, children react more naturally in a field situation, but it is more difficult to control sources of variance.
- **Natural experiments**. Sometimes it is possible to exploit a naturally occurring event for research purposes. For example, a nursery may introduce a key person approach and it may be possible to compare the time taken for new children to settle before and after the change. Coolican (2004) points out that this is a 'quasi' experiment as the researcher has no control over the independent variable (the change in policy).

CORRELATIONAL METHOD

Experiments are not the only way to conduct scientific research. Other non-experimental approaches that can be included within the positivist paradigm include correlational studies (Field, 2009). Correlational studies are used in situations when it is difficult, or impossible to use experiments, but the researcher wants to see if there is a relationship between two variables.

Consider this imaginary scenario. A researcher has a theory that childhood obesity is related to the amount of 'fast food' that a child consumes. It would be unethical to conduct an experiment where two groups of children are fed a diet consisting only of 'fast food', and the other group of children were not allowed to eat any 'fast food' at all. More indirect ways of looking at this issue need to be used so the researcher formulates a hypothesis that the more fast-food outlets there are in a town or city, per head of population, the higher will be the levels of childhood obesity.

In this study the independent variable is the number of fast-food outlets and the dependent variable is the percentage of overweight children (as recorded on school entry as part of the National Child Measurement Programme [DoH, 2008] for instance). An important difference between a correlational study and an experiment is that the researcher does not manipulate the independent variable, but just measures it. In this example, the hypothesis is that there will be a positive **correlation** between the two variables, that is, the more fast-food outlets there are per head of population, the higher will be the percentage of childhood obesity. A negative correlation would involve one variable increasing as the other decreases. In this case there would be a negative correlation if the levels of obesity reduced as the number of 'fast-food' outlets increased. To conduct a correlational study, one needs to have variables that can be measured on a scale or counted, interval data, rather than data that describes categories such as male/female, hair colour and suchlike (Coolican, 2004).

It is important to note that, even if a positive correlation is found, this does not *prove* cause and effect. In the example we are using a positive correlation suggests an association between the number of 'fast-food' outlets and obesity, but does not prove that 'fast food' causes obesity. It may be that there is an intervening variable; for instance, there may be more 'fast-food' outlets in poorer areas, and that there are higher levels of obesity in areas of disadvantage.

VALIDITY AND RELIABILITY

Scientific method, with its rigorous control of variables, aims to produce findings that are valid and reliable. Validity, according to Blaxter et al. (1996: 200) 'has to do with whether your methods, approaches and techniques actually relate to, or measure, the issues you have been exploring'. **Reliability** relates to how well research has been carried out. Findings are said to be reliable if other researchers can replicate the findings of a study by using the same methods (Blaxter et al., 1996).

The positivist paradigm starts with an assumption that 'the truth is out there'. Quantitative methodology, which derives from this, aims to improve *validity* by 'careful **sampling**, appropriate instrumentation and appropriate statistical treatments of data' (Cohen et al., 2000: 105). Reliability, using quantitative methods involves choosing measures that demonstrate 'consistency and replicability over time, over instruments and over groups of respondents' (Cohen et al., 2000: 117).

However, not everyone agrees that there is a universal truth, waiting to be discovered. An alternative viewpoint is that each individual interprets and understands the world around them differently, influenced by their social and cultural context and that there may be multiple explanations for actions (Hughes, 2001a). This point of view belongs to the interpretivist paradigm that is outlined in Chapter 2. Cohen et al. (2000) point out that discussions about reliability and validity should be framed by the paradigm and methodological approach taken. Thus, reliability, when using a qualitative methodological approach, involves trying to ensure that different researchers are consistent in the way that they interpret or categorise observations or interviews, or that the same researcher will show consistency over time (Silverman, 2005). Validity in qualitative research tends to relate to the extent that the research provides an authentic account of the participants' voices (Hughes, 2001a) as well as a reflexive account of the researcher's own role in the production of the data (Coffey, 1999). Validity and reliability are key concepts in research and are revisited throughout this book.

THE POSSIBILITIES AND LIMITATIONS OF POSITIVIST RESEARCH

In reading this chapter, we can see that positivism is an important paradigm in research. The positivist approach has led to advances in our understanding about children and childhood, particularly in the area of biology. We conclude this chapter by summarising the key possibilities and limitations of positivist research and the quantitative methodological approach that is informed by this paradigm.

Possibilities

- There is recognition that children and childhood are legitimate subjects for scientific study and this has led to real advances in our understanding, especially in the field of physiology and medicine.
- By applying highly controlled procedures and quantifying variables it is possible to obtain results that can help to refine theory.
- Because of the rigid control of variables, findings are generalisable, that is, the findings from the participants under study can be applied to a wider population (Robson, 1993).
- The emphasis on the strict application of scientific method and the control of variables means that the findings are seen as valid and able to be replicated by others.
- Positivism gives rise to quantitative methodology and the use of statistical analysis. In early childhood this approach has been valuable as the basis for the large cohort studies of children (see Chapter 5).

Limitations

- Because of the need to control variables, research on children is often undertaken out of context, so the holistic nature of children and childhood is lost (James, 2007). This is especially true if children are investigated under laboratory conditions, as their behaviour may be very different than in everyday, naturalistic situations.
- The need to control variables often leads to very small units of human behaviour being studied, for example, memory, attention and attachment, without regard for how all these aspects work together in an individual.
- Scientific methods, such as the use of highly structured questionnaires, may produce superficial information. If you *really* want to find out about the complexity of children and childhood(s) you need to use methods that delve deeper.
- Strict scientific method requires the researcher to be objective, but in 'real life' one does not find out about other individuals by remaining distant (Coffey, 1999).
- Objectivity may be an illusion anyway. As we will see in the next chapter, it is impossible to remove the influence of the researcher in the data-gathering process (Coffey, 1999).
- *Some* scientific research entails a degree of deception, with the participant not being told the real reason for the research. This raises ethical concerns, which will be discussed in Chapter 3.
- Scientific methods often put the researcher in a more dominant, powerful position than the participant. Coolican (2004) comments that the participants' behaviour may mirror this and adversely influence findings.

The next chapter will pick up further on some of these criticisms as we will be discussing interpretivism and then post-structuralism as paradigms that have developed as a response to positivism.

Key points from the chapter 🔑

- The decisions we make about the research process depend upon the paradigm we hold. A paradigm is a set of beliefs about the way in which particular problems exist and a set of agreements on how such problems can be investigated.
- A positivist paradigm is one that assumes that early childhood can be studied using the same scientific methodology as one would when studying the physical world, and that the subject being studied is subject to the same universal laws that govern the universe.
- Scientific method involves a cycle of investigation including the following stages: observation, identification of underlying patterns and generating a theory, forming a hypothesis, conducting research to test the hypothesis, and accepting or rejecting the theory.
- Positivism gives rise to quantitative methodology. This is methodology that involves the collection of 'scientific' data that is precise and based on measurement and is often analysed using statistics with the intention that the findings can be generalisable.
- One method used in positivist research is the experiment. The key feature of an experiment is that the researcher tries to control as many variables as possible while only altering the independent variable.
- Correlational studies are another scientific approach where the researcher looks for an association between two variables, but the independent variable is not manipulated.
- However, positivist research is not without criticism. It could be regarded as being very narrow and unable to demonstrate the holistic nature of children and childhood. The findings from positivist studies are often superficial and fail to contribute to a deep understanding of an issue. Finally, by applying research principles about the natural world to the social world of human beings, positivist research seems to ignore the complexity of human life and the difficulty of the researcher remaining objective and detached from the people with whom s/he is carrying out research.

Further reading 📖

Coolican, H. (2004) *Research Methods and Statistics in Psychology.* 4th edn. London: Hodder Arnold. This book is helpful in describing experimental methods used in research.

Hughes, P. (2001a) 'Paradigms, methods and knowledge', in G. MacNaughton, S. Rolfe, I. Siraj-Blatchford (eds), *Doing Early Childhood Research: International Perspectives on Theory and Practice.* Maidenhead: Open University Press. This is a very useful chapter in outlining the major paradigms and associated methodological approaches that inform early childhood research.

2 INTERPRETIVISM AND POST-STRUCTURALISM

Chapter objectives

- To develop an understanding of interpretivism and post-structuralism as key paradigms in research
- To consider the significance of interpretivism and post-structuralism within *early childhood* research
- To develop an understanding of qualitative methodological approaches to research
- To reflect on the possibilities and limitations of qualitative research
- To consider how quantitative and qualitative research methods can be combined

This chapter discusses another key **paradigm** in research; interpretivism, which arose out of criticisms of positivist research. It later moves on to a brief discussion of post-structuralism, which is also developed further in later chapters. As noted in the first chapter, all research falls within a particular paradigm – in other words, all research is underpinned by a particular philosophy or way of seeing the world and making sense of it (Hughes, 2001a). In reading the chapter you will see that interpretivist and post-structuralist researchers tend to favour a **qualitative** methodological approach to their work. Thus, we also include a discussion of what is meant by qualitative research and the kinds of methods that fall within this methodological approach.

WHAT DO WE MEAN BY INTERPRETIVISM?

As noted previously, any piece of research has a philosophical basis, which links to the way knowledge is viewed and appropriate methodologies to use in research. The previous chapter discussed positivism, which has a longer history when compared with interpretivism. Positivism, you may recall, is characterised by the use of the **quantitative** methodological approach, which emphasises the need to make generalisations about the world and the need for accurate measurement. It is underpinned by a belief that the 'truth' is possible to discover and often involves the

setting out of a **hypothesis** with the aim of proving or disproving it. In addition,   Ⓖ
positivist research is concerned with maximising objectivity – in other words,
minimising the effect of the researcher on the research subjects and/or research
context.

Aubrey et al. (2000: 33) trace the development of qualitative research, which can be
viewed as located primarily within the interpretivist paradigm, as arising from a
'fundamental disquiet at the logico-positivist position which claimed a single,
objective and value-free reality that could be deduced through experimental
methods.' Similarly, Scheurich (1997) equates positivist research within the **modernist**   Ⓖ
tradition, which believes it is possible to construct universal generalisations about the
world. He argues that uncertainty and ambiguity as well as the complexity of the real
world are seen as needing to be *erased* from such an approach, something he sees as
impossible and undesirable. Crucially, positivist research is criticised for its belief that
the social world can be interpreted and categorised in a similar way to the natural
world through the application of scientific theories and principles in the hands of the
researcher (Hughes, 2001a).

It should be noted here that research that falls within the interpretivist paradigm
tends to be qualitative as opposed to quantitative in nature. This, as we will see,
means the research tends to focus more on *words* than numbers and is smaller scale in
focus. However, interpretivist researchers and positivist researchers *may* employ both
qualitative and quantitative methods (Roberts-Holmes, 2005).

Sometimes 'qualitative research' is used synonymously with ethnography, which
means a 'description of people or cultures' (Denscombe, 2003: 84). Ethnography is an
approach that has developed primarily from the anthropological tradition. The terminology associated with research **methodology** and methods can be a little confusing but   Ⓖ
on the whole, 'qualitative' and 'ethnographic' approaches are similar in their philosophical underpinnings. While we recognise that research that could be described as
'ethnographic' is diverse (Jenks, 2000), it is important to note that the term is traditionally employed in relation to research with a high component of observation in terms of
gathering **data** and is carried out over a period time; indeed sometimes a long period of   Ⓖ
time is spent 'in the field' (Denscombe, 2003). You will find out more about ethnography
in Chapter 6.

By way of contrast to positivist approaches to research, interpretivism is a position
that emphasises gaining a detailed insight into an issue as opposed to being concerned
with being able to make generalisations about the world. Furthermore, interpretivist
research acknowledges that there may be multiple explanations for actions. Hughes
(2001a: 35–6) states,

> Interpretivists argue that rather than simply perceiving our particular social and material cir-
> cumstances, each person continually makes sense of them within a cultural framework of
> socially constructed and shared meanings, and that our interpretation of the world influ-
> ences our place in it.

> ### 〰 Reflection point
>
> Before thinking about the characteristics of qualitative research let us look closely at what is being said in the quotation taken from Hughes (2001a). There are some complex ideas being expressed here:
>
> - the idea that culture impacts on the way we view the world
> - the idea that within this cultural framework we develop understandings of the world *with other people*
> - the idea that these understandings that we have developed about the world actually impact upon the world.
>
> Therefore, a key idea that is being expressed is that there is not one way of understanding the world; there may be multiple interpretations of a given thing. This can be further exemplified if you think about the following questions:
>
> - How should practitioners assess learning in the early years?
> - Should young children be encouraged to play with their food?
> - How should practitioners support war and weapon play in the early years (if at all)?
> - Should babies and young children be given dummies (pacifiers)? Is there a 'right age' when they should stop using them?
>
> We are sure that you are familiar with at least one of these questions either from your professional work or from your own personal background. People come to a view on questions such as these based on cultural, political and socio-economic context, personal background, historical moment, professional training and suchlike. Furthermore, how they might answer these questions may well change – we are sure your own views on some of these questions are likely to change, as do the ideas of the early childhood community itself, over time in the light of new knowledge and experience.
>
> As you can see, this is far removed from the idea that there is one truth waiting to be discovered that remains the same for all time, as in the positivist paradigm.

As noted previously, interpretivist research draws primarily on qualitative methodology and associated methods. We will now look at this in some more detail as we discuss the characteristics of qualitative research.

Characteristics of qualitative research

Ⓖ
- The focus is on gaining detailed information often about a small **population** as opposed to being able to make generalisations about large numbers of people or phenomena. Densombe (2003) uses the analogy of torchlight, which we think is a useful one. If you shine a torch up close to something, you see a small area in great detail. Alternatively, if you shine a torch some distance away, you will cover more area but you will not capture the same degree of detail. The torchlight metaphor is useful in thinking about the key differences between qualitative and quantitative research respectively.
- There is usually a focus on *words* and/or *images* as opposed to numbers (Denscombe, 2003).
- Arguably there is more of a concern for the people whose experiences the researcher is attempting
Ⓖ to represent than present in quantitative **research design** (Edwards, 2001).

- There is often an emphasis on the research being carried out in a naturalistic setting as opposed to a more experimental situation as used in positivist research. This is especially important in early childhood research as we will see in the next section.
- There is an emphasis on the different *meanings* people attribute to different phenomena and actions (Denzin and Lincoln, 2005; Greene and Hill, 2005). In other words, as in the boxed reflection point earlier in the chapter, there is acknowledgement of diversity of viewpoints.
- The research *process* is sometimes seen as important as its outcomes.
- Ethnographic researchers, in particular, tend to describe their research as providing 'thick description' – a term first used by Gilbert Ryle (Geertz, 1973). In addition, they might aim for making the familiar *strange* (Barbour, 2008), which is useful as it encourages a questioning of taken-for-granted practices and assumptions. We will see this, in particular, when we look at ethnography in Chapter 6.
- It tends to be based on inductive reasoning as opposed to deductive reasoning (see previous chapter). For example, themes are likely to be developed *from* data collected as opposed to themes being identified a priori or *before the research has been conducted* – as in the case of experimental research designs, which test hypotheses.
- Finally, and importantly, there is an acknowledgement of the *self* of the researcher (Barbour, 2008) and how this impacts upon the research as well as how the research itself impacts upon the researcher. In research methods literature this is known as **reflexivity**.

The notion of reflexivity is a very important one in research that falls within the umbrella of qualitative research. Fine et al. (2000: 108) argue that, 'There has long been a tendency to view the self of the social science observer as a potential contaminant, something to be separated out, neutralised, minimised, standardised and controlled'.

Rather than a fixed self engaged in research, Lincoln and Guba (2000) argue that the self is fluid in the research setting and is also *created* in the process of the research. Reflexivity, they argue, can be linked to a process of coming to know oneself better within a research project. Reinharz (1997: 5) argues that the many selves the researcher brings to the field come into three broad categories: *research-based selves*; *brought selves* (our personal and historical baggage); and our *situationally-created selves*. The following case study aims to develop your understanding of this further, but we will continue to think about the self of the researcher in later chapters.

> ### 🗁 Case study
>
> Caitlin, an early childhood studies' student, carried out a piece of research looking at how nursery nurses working in school settings perceive their role. She had both a personal and professional interest in the subject matter as she too had been a nursery nurse in both nursery and reception classes in a school for many years prior to going to university. This was the 'brought self', to use Reinharz's (1997) category that Caitlin bought to the research.
>
> Caitlin recognised that she had 'inside' knowledge of the role that gave her a degree of status and familiarity with the nursery nurses in the study that would not have been there had she not shared their professional background. While this familiarity was useful as the nursery nurses in the study seemed to be comfortable in opening up to Caitlin when being interviewed about their work, Caitlin also recognised that there was exploitative potential in
>
> *Continued*

Continued

their shared professional background. She felt that there were occasions when the nursery nurses were less guarded than they might have been with another researcher and noted that some of the nursery nurses in the study used phrases such as 'of course, you know what it's like too' that demonstrated a shared sense of solidarity. On some occasions she found it very difficult to maintain a degree of objectivity because she related to many of the stories told about their professional work. In carrying out research, employing her skills as an interviewer, Caitlin bought her 'research-based self' (Reinharz, 1997) to the research.

In writing up the study, Caitlin acknowledged her shared professional background and reflected on the impact it made on the research. She also acknowledged the way that the research had encouraged her to think in new ways about her previous work as a nursery nurse in a school and indeed her subsequent career in early childhood. During and after the research, Caitlin herself changed, which could be linked to Reinharz's (1997) notion of a 'situationally-created self'. As Lincoln and Guba (2000) observe, she came to know herself *better* through the process of the research.

HOW DOES INTERPRETIVISM RELATE TO EARLY CHILDHOOD RESEARCH?

In terms of early childhood studies, increasingly research is being carried out that falls within the interpretivist paradigm. The previous section noted that one of the important aspects of this is the tendency for interpretivist research to be carried out in a naturalistic setting. But what do we mean by a *naturalistic setting* and why might this be especially important in early childhood research?

Dunn's (2005) research looks at young children in the context of their home environment. Unlike the experimental conditions set up by theorists such as Piaget, for instance, which took children away from the environment in which they were familiar in order to conduct the tests, Dunn (2005: 87) emphasises the following:

- the need to carry out research that acknowledges how children grow and develop in complex social worlds
- the need to carry out research in situations that have emotional significance for young children
- the need to observe children in the context of their everyday lives as opposed to studying their responses to experimental situations.

These three aspects of her work would be impossible to replicate in strictly experimental conditions. While Dunn's research has sometimes involved observing children within the home, there are other contexts that could be described within the umbrella of a 'naturalistic setting'. These might include the nursery a child attends regularly for instance. Crucially, the child or group of children are not asked to deviate too much from the place(s) they are used to, what they usually do or who they are usually with. This is because the researcher tries, as far as is possible, not to disturb the setting. Inevitably, however, researchers do impact upon research settings, as the earlier discussion about reflexivity encouraged you to consider. Those of you who have carried out observations in a nursery know that your presence probably has some impact on the children's behaviour. This impact might take the form of some of the following examples:

- The children may stop what they are doing and come and talk with you.
- The children may move away from the area.
- The children may appear to be self-conscious in their play, looking over at you for approval.
- The children may become highly interested in the way you are recording your observations, for example, making notes or using a video.

There are many factors at work here, not least the degree of familiarity the children have with you as a researcher. If you are a *practitioner* in the setting, then the children are likely to be very familiar with you making observational notes on individuals and groups of children. Researchers who are external to a setting will often visit a nursery, for example, many times in order that the children become familiar with their presence and thus, their presence does not unduly affect the play observed.

 Research in focus

Let us now think about the importance of carrying out research in naturalistic settings in relation to early childhood research. We will also consider the limitations of doing this.

The work of Mary Ainsworth in relation to attachment is characterised by the need for controlling variables and standardisation with regards to conducting the research (Ainsworth and Bell, 1970; Ainsworth et al., 1978). The research involved introducing babies to a 'strange situation', which involved the following:

- A 20-minute session in which a mother and a baby were introduced to a researcher and a playroom (one they are unfamiliar with in order that it is the same for each baby and mother).
- Then, the mother is asked to leave the room for 3 minutes and the baby is left with the researcher. The mother then comes back into the playroom.
- When the mother returns and is reunited with their baby, the mother and the researcher both leave the room at the same time.
- Then, the mother and baby are reunited.

This process is taped and the baby's responses are given a rating. Ainsworth identified four main patterns of response:

- secure attachment
- insecure-avoidant
- insecure-ambivalent (insecure-resistant)
- insecure-disorganised.

Holmes's (1993) book provides a useful summary of the research for those of you that wish to read further. In addition, Woodhead and Faulkner (2008) provide a thought-provoking

Continued

Continued

critique of the research in terms of ethics. They question whether carrying out research where a baby is placed in a strange room, then left with a stranger (the researcher) and then left on their own is ethical. They also question the ethics of the researcher(s) dispassionately measuring the responses of the baby during what is possibly a distressing experience. We look at ethics in research in some detail in the next chapter.

Hatch (1995) believes that qualitative researchers would approach research in the area of attachment in a very different way to Ainsworth, studying the interactions between caregivers and children in naturalistic settings such as nurseries, homes, or maternity wards, for instance. Their approach would be more likely to focus on the shared meanings young children and their caregivers construct together within a particular environment. Hatch (1995: 125) states: 'The best contexts for research that takes seriously the study of childhood as a social construction are settings in which naturally occurring social behaviour is observed in natural surroundings.'

In this 'research in focus' section we can see that researchers working within the positivist and interpretivist paradigms are likely to approach research on attachment in different ways. The former, as in the Ainsworth research, are likely to be keen to be able to control any variables in the research, for example, the environment (the playroom), the length of time the mother leaves the baby, the effect of the researcher, the sequence of the research and suchlike. This is useful in enabling others to replicate the research conditions and may be regarded as more reliable than a more qualitatively based research methodology.

Alternatively, the approach that might be taken by qualitative researchers is one that is likely to prefer a naturalistic setting – a setting that the baby feels comfortable in and that reflects the unpredictability of everyday life. We might regard this approach as more ethical as it is likely to involve less distress to the baby. Moreover, we might view the resulting data as more reflective of everyday attachment behaviour owing to the research being carried out in an everyday context. In this sense, it too could be regarded as valid and reliable research, albeit in a different way. It should be noted, that for interpretivists, authenticity is gained when the 'true' voice of the research participants shines through (Hughes, 2001a).

Another argument in favour of interpretivism in relation to early childhood research is that it is more in keeping with what is sometimes known as 'the new childhood studies' (Mayall, 1999). This is a perspective that sees children as social actors with their own experiences and understandings of childhood (Farrell et al., 2002). As we have noted in this chapter, interpretivist researchers focus on the meanings people ascribe to their experiences and to phenomena. But more than this is the criticism interpretivists might level at the positivist or quantitative tradition, which has tended to emphasise children's 'otherness' and developmental immaturity (James et al., 1998). Chapters 3 and 4 of this book look at this issue in more depth.

QUALITATIVE RESEARCH APPROACHES AND METHODS

In Chapter 1, we argued that the researcher's choice of paradigm underpins the method-ological approach taken in the research and this in turn, influences the methods they choose to use in their research. Earlier in this chapter, we noted some of the key charac-teristics of qualitative research. We noted that interpretivist researchers tend to use primarily *qualitative* research approaches and methods. Edwards (2001) warns us not to consider qualitative research as a 'soft' or 'easy' option. She maintains that *all* qualitative research will involve the researcher in 'getting to grips with the complexities of the social world of early childhood' (p. 117). Parts 2 and 3 of this book look at approaches to research and methods in more depth but here we want to highlight a few of those most used within the qualitative research tradition. These can be summarised as follows.

Action research

Action research may employ both quantitative and qualitative methods in tandem. Action research usually involves participants as researchers, such as a group of nursery staff working together in order to make *improvements* to an area of their practice. These participants will often be led by a member of the team or possibly an outside researcher working with them. The key, however, is on facilitating change in a particular setting and often within the participants themselves and in this sense it is usually *small scale* in focus with no aim at making generalisations about the world.

Ethnography

Ethnographic research involves spending a long period of time immersed in a particular setting such as a nursery in order to gain detailed insights about the research partici-pants' lives. In order to carry out ethnographic research, the researcher often becomes a participant in the setting in order to become a familiar face, able to observe people's behaviour in as naturalistic a setting as possible.

Case studies

Case study research, as the name suggests, focuses on a case or a series of cases. A 'case' might be a family, a children's centre, a child, a local authority and suchlike. Crucially, the emphasis is on developing a detailed understanding of the 'case' under study.

Observation

Research methods such as observation may also fall within the umbrella of qualitative research, although not exclusively. Observation may involve an element of number crunch-ing, such as counting the number of children who visit the book area in a given day. However, narrative observation, which focuses on the 'rich description' is *qualitative* in nature.

Interviewing

Like observation, there are different types of interviewing. If interviewing a subject with a set of highly structured questions, which allow for little or no deviation beyond yes/no answers coupled with a large number of respondents, then this research may well be described as quantitative in nature, thus falling within the positivist paradigm. Usually, interviews that are carried out face to face are semi-structured or sometimes unstructured, in order that the researcher captures as much detail as possible.

Activity

What differences can you see between the qualitative approaches to research discussed here and the experimental designs outlined in Chapter 1? Form your own table, outlining the possibilities and limitations of qualitative approaches to research.

COMBINING QUALITATIVE AND QUANTITATIVE RESEARCH METHODS

So far the first two chapters of this book may have given the impression that **qualitative** and quantitative research cannot be combined owing to their bases in different philosophical positions: positivism and interpretivism. There are different viewpoints on this as this section aims to demonstrate.

Aubrey et al. (2000) argue that quantitative and qualitative research should not be viewed as in opposition with each other (see also Clough and Nutbrown, 2007). They believe that they are *complementary* to one another or might be indicative of *different stages* in the process of conducting a piece of research. Thus, some research involves a combination of quantitative methods such as a structured questionnaire and qualitative methods such as semi-structured interviews. Using more than one method to obtain information is known as **triangulation**, whereby the strengths of one method compensate for the weaknesses of another. However, it can mean far more than this. Kasunic (2005: 15) describes the purpose of triangulation as being to 'obtain confirmation of findings through convergence of different perspectives. The point at which the perspectives converge is seen to represent reality'. This might be done through using more than one researcher; more than one theory; or more than one methodological approach (Denzin, cited in Edwards, 2001).

There is a range of ways that combining quantitative and qualitative methods might be useful:

- Carrying out a detailed, small-scale pilot study, for example, to see how successful a new reading scheme is, then later, extending this to a large scale and carrying out a quantitative analysis to assess how successful it has been with a larger group.
- Conducting a large-scale survey, for example, to gain some general information about parents' views on paediatric services in a hospital or local primary care trust (PCT) and then carrying out some focus group interviews with small groups of parents to ascertain their views in more detail.

- In a piece of action research, for example, looking at improving the use of the block play area in a nursery class, the researcher might carry out some detailed narrative observations as well as something more quantitative, for example, counting the number of children who use the block play area during a week in comparison to other areas of the nursery room.

So far in this section, we have shown how qualitative and quantitative approaches might be combined. But before concluding this chapter, it is important to note that not all writers believe it is advisable or even *possible* to combine methods from the quantitative and qualitative traditions successfully. For Denzin and Lincoln (2005), this is owing to the differences inherent in their underpinning philosophies and the greater status sometimes attributed to quantitative research methods. As you may recall, positivism and the quantitative research tradition has its basis in the idea that research can uncover *truths* about the world, that is, that the world is knowable and can be measured and categorised, with findings generalised to a large population. Interpretivism, as this chapter has shown, has its basis in the belief that there are multiple 'truths' and ways of seeing the world and that these are specific to particular people in particular places (Hughes, 2001a).

Finally here, it is important to note that interpretivism is but one key philosophical position that underpins qualitative research. Denzin and Lincoln's (2005) edited work is a good example of this. Under the title 'qualitative research', they highlight writing from a range of positions such as post-structuralism that employ qualitative approaches to research. Although we only provide a very brief outline of this paradigm here, we will be referring to post-structuralism and postmodernism in this book, especially in Chapters 8 and 13. Very simply – and it is not a simple theory – post-structuralism problematises the idea that the 'truth' is knowable; indeed, it often seeks to disrupt commonly held understandings of what is 'normal' and 'true' (Brown and Jones, 2001). In terms of research, the idea that the researcher can 'capture' data and arrive at the truth in some way is impossible as ideas are ever changing and knowledge is uncertain. Thus, *triangulation* – the idea that through using a range of data, researchers and methodological approaches, a fixed point can be arrived at – is a difficult one to accept. Richardson and Adams St Pierre (2005), for instance, employ a metaphor of a crystal as crystals have many facets; they are changeable and light refracts as it shines through them. Applied to a research context, this means that there are multiple ways of viewing reality and these depend on the position from which we look – a position that is ever changing.

Key points from the chapter 🗝

- Interpretivism developed as a response to positivism, which was criticised for its belief that we can make generalisations about the world.
- By way of contrast, interpretivism is a position that tends to focus on the meanings people attribute to phenomena and actions.
- The interpretivist position lends itself to qualitative research approaches and methods, which tend to focus on gaining a detailed understanding of a small sample or case and often emphasises the need to carry out research in *naturalistic* settings as opposed to *experimental* conditions.

- The *self* of the researcher is viewed as important in interpretivist research, which can be contrasted with positivism, which tends to aim at neutralising out what is commonly referred to as 'researcher effect'. This is also a concern in post-structuralist research.
- The researcher's choice of paradigm impacts on the methodology and methods they use in their research. In qualitative research, for instance, observations (especially narrative observation) and interviewing are often employed.
- Quantitative and qualitative approaches to research may be combined successfully in order to enhance a research project – gaining 'the best of both worlds'. Triangulation is a term used to denote the way that combining methodologies, methods, different researchers, and different theories can help the researcher to arrive at a reasonably clear understanding of their research area (Denzin, cited in Edwards, 2001).
- Post-structuralist researchers, on the other hand, also employ a qualitative methodological approach to research but are sceptical about the idea that research can arrive at any 'truths' with certainty.

Further reading

Greene, S. and Hill, M. (2005) 'Researching children's experience: methods and methodological issues', in S. Greene and D. Hogan (eds), *Researching Children's Experience: Approaches and Methods*. London: Sage. A useful overview of a range of issues relating to research methodology as it relates to research with children.

Reinharz, S. (1997) 'Who am I? The need for a variety of selves in the field', in R. Hertz (ed.) *Reflexivity and Voice*. London: Sage. This is a very interesting chapter that looks at the issue of reflexivity in some depth.

3 ETHICS

Chapter objectives

- To develop an understanding of ethics and why a consideration of ethics is important in research
- To consider ethics in early childhood research, in particular the notion of 'informed consent'
- To develop an understanding of how ethical considerations need to be thought through in relation to the whole research process
- To consider professional and legal guidelines in relation to ethics

This chapter examines a crucial aspect of research: ethics. *All* research involves a consideration of ethics and early childhood research, it could be argued, needs to be particularly mindful of ethics owing to the age and vulnerability of children from birth to eight years. This said, alongside consideration for the vulnerability of young children, we also want to stress children's competence and ability to participate in research – something we focus on in more depth in Chapter 4. This chapter comes in the first section of this book owing to our belief that a careful consideration of ethical issues is of *central* importance to any research project.

WHAT DO WE MEAN BY 'ETHICS'?

Many of you reading this book will have heard the word 'ethics' used in relation to a wide range of contexts. You may have read about medical ethics' debates in areas such as embryo technology, euthanasia and human cell cloning. You may also have thought about ethics in relation to other issues such as testing products on animals or the responsibility human beings have in relation to exacerbating global warming.

Reality television programmes may also have encouraged you to think about ethics. There are occasions when participants in programmes such as these are put in positions of extreme stress in the particular situations they find themselves in. This might include physical stress, such as having little food, or mental stress, such as being ridiculed or being compelled to take part in activities seemingly against their better judgement. In addition to this, the participants are being filmed and observed – sometimes 24 hours a day – by a large watching public. While programme-makers might argue that people give their consent to being a participant on one of these shows and are fully informed about what might happen and possibly even screened for mental illness, it is questionable whether everyone comes away from the experience unscathed.

For those of you that work or have worked directly with young children and families, you may think about ethics in relation to your professional work. Indeed Aubrey et al. (2000) argue that teachers – and we would broaden this to all early years practitioners – are making decisions every day, moment by moment, that have ethical considerations at their heart. As you can see, 'ethics' is a term that is used across a broad range of contexts.

Activity

Reflect on the work of an early childhood practitioner working with young children and families. Construct a list of the ethical issues with which they are confronted on a regular basis. Here are a few ideas to start you off:

- storing information about families carefully in order to preserve confidentiality
- ensuring the practice in the nursery is anti-discriminatory
- listening and acting upon *children's* ideas about what they would like to do.

But our concern in this book is with *research*. So what does 'ethics' mean in relation to research? Aubrey et al. (2000: 156) define ethics as, 'The moral philosophy or set of moral principles underpinning a project'.

Over time, ethical considerations in research have become more important. Clearly, research with human and animal subjects needs to involve acting in a moral way. As Greig et al. (2007) note, the label 'researcher' does not mean we can act in ways considered not moral or ethical. Yet abuses have occurred in the name of 'research' and these have led to greater regulation over what is ethical or not in research practice. A clear example of this can be seen in the Nazi experimentation on twins in which 1,500 sets of twins, some of them children, were subjected to horrific experiments with the aim of seeing if the Aryan race, which was considered superior by the Nazis, could multiply more quickly. Many twins died in the process of this research and many more were subjected to torturous experiments. Experimentation such as this came under scrutiny during the Nuremberg Trials that followed the Second World War from 1946 to 1949. There was public shock and condemnation at what had occurred in the name of 'research' and the Nuremberg Code was developed to make clear the legal, moral and ethical principles that should govern *any* research involving human beings (Greig et al., 2007).

But despite the Nuremberg Code and other subsequent legislation, such as the Helsinki Declaration in 1964, research still comes under the spotlight and raises questions about ethics to the present day (Greig et al., 2007). Infamous studies have drawn wider attention to the issue of ethics.

> ### 🔍 Research in focus
>
> Miligram's experiments, carried out between 1963 and 1974, have gained a level of notoriety in relation to ethics. His research looks at the issue of obedience to authority. Individuals were asked to act one at a time as 'teachers' to another person, who was, in fact, someone working with the research team unbeknown to them. The 'teachers' were required to administer an electric shock to their 'students' if they did not respond correctly to their verbal learning tasks. The electric shocks increased with severity throughout the experiment as 'wrong' answers were given. More than 1,000 'teachers' from various backgrounds took part in the research and Miligram reports how 67 per cent administered the most severe electric shock to their 'students' during the experiments, despite being told how dangerous it was. For Miligram, this meant that people have a tendency to obey authority even if that means doing something that is regarded as wrong. The research is reported in many research methods texts such as Cohen et al. (2000).
>
> Of course the electric shocks administered were not real, but the 'teachers', that is, the research subjects did not know this – indeed, the 'students' acted as if they were in pain when the shocks were administered. As you read on, consider the ethical implications of a study like this and why it has become infamous in its disregard for the people who acted as research subjects.

Robson (1993: 33) encourages the reader to reflect upon 10 questionable practices in social research. These are as follows:

- Involving people without their knowledge or consent
- Coercing them to participate
- Withholding information about the true nature of the research
- Otherwise deceiving the participant
- Inducing them to commit acts diminishing their self-esteem
- Violating rights of self-determination (e.g. in studies seeking to promote individual change)
- Exposing participants to physical or mental stress
- Invading their privacy
- Withholding benefits from some participants (e.g. in comparison groups)
- Not treating participants fairly, or with consideration, or with respect.

Some of these 10 questionable practices can be applied to the research discussed in the previous 'research in focus' section. The research participants did not know the true nature of the research; they were deceived about who the other research participants were, that is, they did not know they were actors and that they were acting feeling in pain; and the research is very likely to have diminished the participants' sense of self-esteem because after the research was over they had to live with themselves in the knowledge that they were capable of following orders to the extent that they might inflict pain on others (Barbour, 2008; Cohen et al., 2000).

While the example discussed so far involves adults, we can apply Robson's (1993) 10 questionable practices to *early childhood* research. In doing this, we will be reflecting upon conceptualisations and the subsequent status of young children.

WHY IS A CONSIDERATION OF ETHICS IMPORTANT IN EARLY CHILDHOOD RESEARCH?

Greig et al. (2007) maintain that inexperienced researchers are able to practise designing research instruments such as questionnaires and interview schedules. However, they go on to argue that ethics is an area that should never be learned in practice. While it is important that researchers think carefully about the ethical issues that relate to their topic, research has a tendency to be more 'messy' than this suggests (Greig et al., 2007).

Researchers also need to be especially heedful of young children's vulnerability. With this in mind, Coady (2001: 64) states that children are 'heavily represented among victims of research'. Even well-meaning researchers can cause harm to child subjects of research. An infamous example of this, cited by Coady, is that of 'Genie', a 13-year-old child from Los Angeles, who was found to have been deprived of any human contact for most of her life. This lack of human contact meant that her language skills were severely restricted. For some researchers, this meant that 'Genie' was an 'ideal' subject for research into whether there is a sensitive period for learning a language. When the grant for the research ran out and the researchers had got what they wanted – furthering their own careers in the process – 'Genie' was returned to poor care arrangements. Thus, the principle of beneficence to the research participants was overtaken by a concern for the research itself.

Activity

Investigate the website below as you can find out more about how the research was conducted, and what happened subsequently to Genie.
www.ling.udel.edu/simyong/ling101/2005s/lecturenotes/genie.pdf

---

It would seem that the vulnerability and 'otherness' associated with being younger, less experienced, and physically smaller can also result in a view of young children as an *object* of research as opposed to a feeling *subject*. Woodhead and Faulkner (2008) seem to be implying this in relation to the research carried out by Mary Ainsworth in relation to attachment, which we discussed in Chapter 2. Coady (2001) relates this lack of consideration for research participants to research carried out on indigenous peoples in the nineteenth century, in which they were viewed as less human or as objects in some way. Thus, while the relative positionings of adult and child are not universal and are constantly changing (Connolly, 2008), what is important to foreground here is the powerful position held by adult researchers as 'experts' in the study of young children (Woodhead and Faulkner, 2008). In addition to this, Lahman (2008: 282) argues that such power imbalances are further accentuated by 'intersecting marginalities', which are present when white, able-bodied, adult researchers, for example, carry out research on young, Black and minority-ethnic children or children with disabilities.

Although this discussion has so far focused on the vulnerability of children, we also want to stress a view of the child as *competent*, something we explore in more depth in the next chapter, where we will be arguing that the researcher's perception of the child underpins the extent to which s/he believes they are able to fully participate in research. Lahman

(2008: 285) sums up the idea that researchers can hold a view of the child as both vulnerable and competent at the same time by stating, 'I believe both the notions of competent and vulnerable, worded as *competent yet vulnerable child* may be held simultaneously as a way of considering the unique position of children' (original emphasis).

This section has encouraged you to begin to think about how conceptualisations of the child impact upon research. In particular, it has focused on the relative power of adults in relation to children. One of the ways that this imbalance of power can be seen is in the notion of informed consent.

WHAT DOES 'INFORMED CONSENT' MEAN IN THE CONTEXT OF EARLY CHILDHOOD RESEARCH?

A key term in research ethics is 'informed consent'. This means that the participants in the research give their consent to the research and fully understand the following:

- what the purposes of the research are
- why they have been asked to take part in the research
- how their involvement fits in to the research as a whole
- what they will be asked to do, for example, be part of a focus group interview as well as how long this commitment is for; for instance, in a case study it may be for a few months, whereas in a one-off interview it may be for half an hour
- their right for information about the research before, during and following the **data** collection
- that all names of individuals and institutions will remain anonymous
- their right to withdraw from the research at any point
- how the data will be recorded
- where the data will be stored and how
- who will see the data – what it will be used for

Initially, researchers will often do this in the form of a letter, which they ask the participants in the study to sign. The assumption that underpins this is that everyone that has signed their consent fully understands the information on the form they have signed. Robson (1993) maintains that there are particular ethical problems in relation to informed consent when working with vulnerable groups such as children, particularly very young children. This is because it may be difficult for them to fully understand every aspect of the research. For Robson (1993: 32) the issue relates to whether they can 'rationally, knowingly and freely give informed consent'. While we would argue that children are far more competent than this suggests, especially if adults take the trouble to ensure they explain things in a clear and understandable way, *very* young children and babies are not in a position to *sign* a consent form. Furthermore, they are unlikely to understand many aspects of the research in advance of it actually happening.

For this reason, researchers working with children and babies have to ask the children's parents or guardians for written permission to carry out the research. In addition, if the research is to be carried out in a school or hospital or similar, permission will usually have to be granted by someone or a group of people in a position of power, who act to protect the individuals within their institutions.

Increasingly, researchers have to get their proposal agreed by an ethics' committee, such as at the university where they are studying. The people who have the power to say 'yes' or 'no' in relation to whether research with children should go ahead or not – be they parents or professionals – are often called 'gatekeepers'.

Although it is important to gain the consent of key adults or 'gatekeepers' for research to be carried out and older children may be able to understand and sign to demonstrate they consent to research being carried out, it is important to be clear that we *do* think young children's direct consent should be sought. Many research texts, when they talk about gaining the direct consent of children, do not seem to consider what this issue means for research with *very* young children and babies. Inevitably, in practice it means something different when compared to research with children of secondary school age for instance.

Langston et al. (2004) demonstrate that very young children and babies are able to give or withdraw their consent to research. They might do this in a variety of ways, such as:

- refusing to engage with the researcher
- becoming abnormally quiet
- turning away and crying (or sounding distressed)
- refusing to engage with any materials used in the study.

Therefore the researcher needs to be sensitive to the moment in order to pick up on the child's cues. If engaged in research somewhere where the children do not know the researcher, it is important that the insights of parents, carers and practitioners who work there are taken into account. This is because their greater knowledge of the children is crucial in monitoring any changes in the child's behaviour. In this sense, negotiating consent with babies and young children should happen on a *moment-by-moment* basis (Langston et al., 2004). Researchers also need to be mindful that children are sometimes keen to please adults and may not obviously look as if they are distressed. Again, the insights of adults and children who know the child better are invaluable. Therefore, informed consent could be regarded as an *ongoing achievement* as opposed to something that is agreed to purely in advance.

〰️ Reflection point

We should also remember that it is not only young children that are vulnerable in early childhood research. Many adults are vulnerable too and they may well be participants in a piece of early childhood research. Reflect on the issue of informed consent in a study in which a nursery manager asks the following individuals for their views on the quality of care for babies in the nursery:

- a parent who is an asylum seeker
- a mother who is in prison
- an early years practitioner working in the setting where the research is being carried out
- a 16-year-old woman who has just given birth to her first baby and has come in to the nursery for a few 'drop ins'
- a father who has had three children come through the nursery over the last few years.

In reflecting on the issues raised in the reflection point you may have thought of similar points to those that we will highlight here. A parent who is an asylum seeker may be worried that if they say 'no' to participating in the research, the nursery place for their baby may be taken away from them (especially if they have had poor experiences in their former country of residence). A mother who is in prison is quite literally captive and it may be very difficult to say 'no' to a study when so many of her other freedoms have been taken away from her. A different issue is presented by the early years practitioner who is working in the setting. In this instance, the practitioner might feel unable to say 'no' to participating in the research because it is her line manager who is carrying out the research – it would be easier to say 'no' to an outside researcher. The 16-year-old woman who has just given birth to her first baby might be vulnerable owing to issues of relative age difference. Furthermore, in a similar way to the first example, if she did not consent to the research, she may be concerned that she appears as uncooperative before she even begins to access the nursery's services regularly. Finally, the father who has had a few children come through the nursery may find it difficult to say 'no' because he feels he owes the nursery something – after all, three of his children have attended the nursery.

A common denominator in all five examples is the issue of power, that is, the differentials in power between the researcher and the research participants. This is something to reflect upon in any research project. However, remember too, that people are often very happy to participate in a piece of research, especially if they are confident that you have their best interests at heart and that in some way their participation will make a positive contribution to something they view as important. The issue of research being of some *positive* benefit is sometimes called 'beneficence' and is an important principle to hold on to in research.

We should remember that vulnerability also extends to the *researcher*. In carrying out research, it is important to take care *who* you are going to see and *where* you will see them. If interviewing a person that is completely unknown to you, it might be wise to conduct the interview in a public space where there are other people nearby rather than privately in the person's own accommodation. This, however, might impact on how comfortable a person feels during an interview and the type of data that might be obtained. Nevertheless, we raise the issue of researcher vulnerability because personal safety is also an ethical concern.

Before moving on to consider how ethical issues should be considered throughout the research process, we want to point out that gaining consent can raise a number of dilemmas for the researcher. Warming (2005) argues that in her research, which involved participant observation of young children in a nursery, she felt it was important, as a *principle*, that the children knew that she was a researcher, who was carrying out a particular research project. But in *practice*, she came to the conclusion that she would inform children as and when they asked who she was and what she was doing. In this way, she felt she would be responding to the children's individual needs and interests in a more ethical way than by informing them as a group – the underpinning assumption being that the children would be as interested in the research as the researcher. Warming (2005: 62) discusses her dilemma, saying 'the most ethical practice might turn out to be unethical'.

Research in focus

An example of Warming's notion of responding to children's individual needs and interests in relation to research can be seen in Debbie Albon's (2007; 2009) research looking at food and eating in early childhood settings.

Debbie has spent a few years now carrying out observations in four early childhood settings. In one setting, a child of 3 years whom we will call Avleen became very interested in the observational notes she was making. Here is an extract of conversation held between them:

Avleen: 'Are you writing again?' (*she had often observed me writing*)
Debbie: 'Yes – I'm writing about what I see in the home corner again.' (*I have been coming to the setting for two terms*)
Avleen: 'Did you write about me yesterday?'
Debbie: 'Well … not really – not like this. To write observations of what you are actually doing I have to be able to see you.'
Avleen: 'What does that say?' (*pointing to my writing*)
Debbie: 'It says "K … says 'I'll go and have my drink now'".'
Avleen: 'K … just said that.'
Debbie: 'I know. I found it interesting, so I wrote it down … here.' (*Avleen looks intently at the observational notes made*)

Debbie wrote about this extensively in her research journal. Here is one of many extracts that relate to this from her journal:

> Avleen asked about lots of other notes in my fieldwork book and borrowed my pen to write her own notes on my pages. I must share this observation of her interest in writing with practitioners and her mum. She has shown a lot of interest in the research process and seeks me out to ask me about it – other children are keen to play with me e.g. in the home corner but are not so bothered about what I am writing and why – even though I do this very openly. Children, like adults, will be more drawn to some things than others and research is no different.

ETHICAL CONSIDERATIONS THROUGHOUT THE RESEARCH PROCESS

This section aims to demonstrate that a consideration of ethics is important at every stage of the research process. In thinking about this, we will be encouraging you to think about the following:

 • research **paradigm**
- planning the research
- data gathering
- analysing the data and writing up.

We will go through each of these in turn.

Research paradigm

Aubrey et al. (2000) argue that because early childhood research has a tendency to involve human interactions, with all the complexity associated with this, it is almost impossible to predict and iron out *all* potential errors and misunderstandings. They go on to suggest that a researcher's choice of paradigm impacts upon their understanding of ethics. Chapters 1 and 2 of this book looked at positivism and interpretivism as key paradigms in research. Positivist researchers, you may recall, aim at neutralising out the effect of the researcher. In a hypothetical study in which the researcher is concerned with observing young children and practitioner interactions in a nursery, the researcher is likely to try to eradicate the effect of their presence on the children and the practitioners. They might do this by quietly sitting back and taking field notes, trying to avoid doing anything that will impact upon what they are observing. By not 'spoiling the field', the positivist researcher might view their research as ethical.

Conversely, interpretivist researchers may see the positivist researcher's approach as unethical. This is because they would regard it as important to gain a range of explanations and views of the interactions taking place in the nursery. They are likely to want to elicit the views of the practitioners and the children and possibly parents too on the interactions taking place. Aubrey et al. (2000: 158) state that they might possibly view the positivist approach as constituting 'a disregard for the humanity, the "inner life", of the people involved, treating them as if they are observable and measurable, data-generating machines'. In wanting to listen to the perspectives of a range of people on the interactions they have observed, the interpretivist researcher is also acknowledging that their view is one of possibly many perspectives.

Whatever paradigm the researcher locates their work within, there needs to be a discussion of the ethical considerations that underpin the study. Even a seemingly 'hands-off', positivist approach to research such as a structured, self-completion questionnaire involves ethical considerations. These might include:

- The questionnaire needs to be well-presented as this shows respect for the respondent.
- The questions should be straightforward and free of jargon. Respondents should not be made to feel stupid because they do not understand what the questions are getting at. That would be the fault of the researcher who designed the questionnaire.
- It should not take too long to complete.
- The questionnaire should not require people to spend money to return it.

The points raised here are also important to keep in mind in order to maximise the response to the research. After all, a poorly presented self-completion questionnaire that is difficult to fill in, that takes a long time to complete and needs the respondent to spend their own money to return it, is probably going to end up in the bin. You will find out more about questionnaire design in Chapter 11 of this book.

Planning the research

In planning any research project, the researcher needs to think about the initial question they develop. Clough and Nutbrown (2007) develop a range of ways to critique such questions, including the Goldilocks test. At one point in the story 'Goldilocks and the

Three Bears' you may recall that Goldilocks tries the porridge left by the bears when they go on their walk, and in the case of father bear's porridge, declares it to be 'too hot'. Clough and Nutbrown apply the idea of 'too hot' to research. An example of a question that is 'too hot' might be: 'Which practitioner is most successful in settling children in at the beginning of a session?'

A question like this focuses on individuals and implies that the research is about judging people against each other. It would be far better to focus the question on the characteristics of good practice in the area of settling children at the beginning of sessions. In this way, the focus is not on *who* does something successfully but on *what* people do, implying that we can all develop our practice in this area. In addition, by focusing on the individual in this example of a 'hot' question, the research places practitioners outside of the structures and routines of the setting, that is, it is likely that there are organisational factors rather than purely individual traits that impact on the beginnings of sessions. These might include allowing parents to stay as long as needed at the beginning of sessions, not expecting children to sit for a formal registration period, and so on. These would not be individual decisions but would reflect the ethos of the institution as a whole.

Data gathering

The methods for collecting data used in any research project will raise particular ethical issues. As was noted under 'research paradigm', questionnaires – a method that may on the surface seem free from ethical concerns – have ethical implications that need to be considered. However, methods that require a greater level of face-to-face encounters inevitably carry with them a higher potential for harm.

In face-to-face interviewing, for instance, researchers need to consider where and when interviews are conducted and the general comfort of the interviewee. Furthermore, the structure and questions asked during the interview should help to put the interviewee at ease.

But we should be mindful of Oakley's (1981) criticisms of interviewing as a research tool when she states that some of the strategies designed to put the interviewee at ease are, in fact, tactics designed to manipulate them. As Fontana and Frey (2000) observe, although researchers may appear friendly and courteous, actually they are expected to remain emotionally neutral, keeping their feelings and opinions to themselves – unlike in a normal conversation.

This is an interesting point to reflect upon and is an issue raised by feminist researchers in particular. It can also be linked to the debates raised in Chapters 1 and 2 about the self of the researcher. You may recall that positivist researchers aim for objectivity, so would try to neutralise the impact of their views and feelings on the research. Conversely, researchers working within other research paradigms – and in particular, feminist researchers – are likely to acknowledge their own subjectivities. In other words, they are more likely to share information about themselves with participants in an attempt to make the research relationship more equal and responsive.

When interviewing young children, should they disclose anything that indicates abuse, it is important that the researcher shares this information with the appropriate adults – be they parents or professionals. Although it is usual to maintain anonymity in most studies, the welfare of a child who is potentially in danger must *always* take precedence. Thus, it is important not to make false promises about confidentiality in case information needs to be shared.

Observation too is not without ethical difficulties. Earlier in the chapter we highlighted the importance of informed consent, but also noted the potential difficulties Warming (2005) sees as presenting themselves when observing children at play over time. As a general principle, people who are being observed should know what is being looked at, and in the case of young children, their parents and other relevant gatekeepers should also have agreed to this. It is good practice, we would argue, to share any observations with a setting or a family, assuming the research involves observation. Not only does this make it clear what the researcher is recording and his or her reflections on it, but the people that know the child(ren) best, that is, parents and practitioners can also add their insights. This point is picked up in the next section.

Analysing the data and writing up

Analysing data and writing it up is also an area that needs thinking through in relation to ethics. Here are some ethical questions that might be raised by this:

- Do research participants feel the same about the way I have analysed the data gathered? What are their interpretations of the data?
- Can research participants be involved in the data analysis and if so how?
- Who is going to see the research once written up?
- Is the research written in a way that is respectful of participants?
- How can I 'give something back' to the research participants at the end of the research that is meaningful to them?

These questions are explored in further depth in the final two chapters of this book, but are raised here to encourage you to view ethical considerations as part of the research process as a whole.

ETHICAL GUIDELINES AND LEGAL CONSIDERATIONS

Research is carried out in virtually all academic disciplines and each will have codes that are especially applicable to them. In early childhood research, the most relevant codes of ethics to refer to come from the following groups:

- the British Psychological Society (www.bps.org.uk/the-society/code-of-conduct/code-of-conduct_home.cfm)
- the British Sociological Society (www.sociology.org.uk/as4bsoce.pdf)
- the British Educational Research Association (http://bera.ac.uk).

Universities will also have their own ethics committees, which govern the types of research that are given the go-ahead under the auspices of the university. This would include research undertaken by people employed by the university and research students. Not to abide by these guidelines can be a disciplinary offence and, at worst, a criminal offence. This is an expression of how seriously ethical issues need to be taken. It is not just universities that have ethical committees. For those of you who are embarking on student research projects, it is important to talk through ethical issues with your supervising tutor *from the outset*. This person will help to advise you about your choice of topic, the method(s) chosen to gather data and the data analysis and writing up. You should note that individual colleges and universities may have slightly different ways of doing this. In addition to colleges and universities, individual institutions or local authorities may require the researcher to have their research agreed by a group or committee.

Finally here, the Data Protection Act 1998 (see website address at the end of this section) provides a legislative backdrop to some of the ethical issues raised in this chapter. In particular, the Data Protection Act legislates that researchers must do the following:

• store data securely (including electronic storage)
• ensure research participants know how the data will be used and who will see it
• ensure data is not used beyond the life of a given research project unless express permission has been granted from participants for this.

You can look at the Data Protection Act yourself online at the website for the Office of Public Sector Information (OPSI): www.opsi.gov.uk

Key points from the chapter 🔑

• Ethical considerations should underpin *every* research project.
• Early childhood research raises particular ethical issues owing to the age and vulnerability of young children, but at the same time young children should be viewed as competent. We particularly like Lahman's (2008: 285) conceptualisation of the '*competent yet vulnerable child*' here.
• Power is an important issue to reflect upon in research, for example, the relative power of a young child in relation to an adult, or a parent whose child attends a nursery in relation to a practitioner-researcher.
• The issue of informed consent is of key importance in any research project. In early childhood research, adults usually act as 'gatekeepers' to children's involvement.
• Older children in the early childhood age range, that is, children up to the age of 8, are likely to be able to give prior and possibly written consent to research in a meaningful way. However, in research with very young children and babies, informed consent might mean negotiating access on a moment-by-moment basis as their signed consent is impossible or likely to be meaningless.
• Ethical issues are present throughout the research process, in the choice of paradigm, the planning of the research, the data gathering, the data analysis and the writing up of the research.
• Finally, there are societies and research associations that have ethical guidelines that researchers working within those disciplines should be working to. Universities will also have codes of ethics that they expect researchers employed within the university and research students to abide by.

Further reading

Farrell, A. (ed.) (2005) *Ethical Research with Children*. Maidenhead: Open University Press. A collection of chapters on the subject of ethics for those of you that want an in-depth look at the topic. Alderson's chapter on ethics in research design is especially useful.

Lahman, M. (2008) 'Always othered: ethical research with children', *Journal of Early Childhood Research*, 6(3): 281–300. This is an excellent article that looks at the position of children in early childhood research.

4   LISTENING TO YOUNG CHILDREN

Chapter objectives

- To consider the growth in research involving listening to young children
- To link this to the emergence of children's rights' perspectives
- To reflect on ethical issues relating to involving young children in research

An emerging principle that underpins research is one of listening to young children. Building on the previous chapter, where we thought through some of the ethical issues relating to research with young children, this chapter looks more specifically at how the early childhood researcher might develop creative ways of listening to young children and including them as *participants* in research. The former chapter on ethics looked at Lahman's (2008: 285) notion of the *'competent yet vulnerable child'* in research. Like Lahman, we believe these are two conceptualisations of the child that are possible to hold simultaneously. In particular, the former chapter looked at young children's protective rights in relation to research, whereas this chapter's focus is on their participatory rights – although inevitably, as the notion of the *'competent but vulnerable child'* implies, these are interwoven.

THE DEVELOPMENT OF INTEREST IN LISTENING TO YOUNG CHILDREN

Moss et al. (2005) maintain that the development in interest around listening to children can be the linked to the growth in the children's rights' perspective across the globe. This perspective is one that embraces children's participation and recognises that children have their own views of what affects them directly as well as their own perspectives of the world around them (Taylor, 2000).

The United Nations Convention on the Rights of the Child (UNCRC), which was adopted by the United Nations (UN) in 1989 and has been ratified by 192 countries including the UK, champions this principle of participation alongside enshrining the need to protect children. The notion of participation can be seen most clearly in articles 12 and 13:

> Parties shall assure to the child who is capable of forming his or her own views the right to express those views freely in all matters affecting the child, the views of the child being given due weight in accordance with the age and maturity of the child ...

> The child shall have the right to freedom of expression; this right shall include freedom to seek, receive and impart information and ideas of all kinds, regardless of frontiers, either orally, in writing or in print, in the form of art, or through any other media of the child's choice. (UNCRC articles 12 and 13, quoted in Moss et al., 2005: 2)

We will return to the issue of capability of 'forming his or her own views' as well as the issue of age and maturity later in the chapter. It is important to acknowledge that in the UK, prior to the UNCRC, the 1989 Children Act had begun to enshrine the importance of listening to children in their own right. Prior to the 1980s, international and national legislation had a tendency to view children – especially young children – as the property of their parents as well as being incapable of expressing an opinion on matters affecting them. Thus, children were viewed as unable to form or express a view about matters affecting their lives (Taylor, 2000). This position is changing.

Underpinning the children's rights' perspective is a view that children are persons in their own right – not human 'becomings' but human beings (Qvortrup, 1994). Thus, in some of the literature, children, as a group, are considered as being in a similar position to other minority or marginalised groups such as women, Black and minority ethnic groups or people with disabilities; groups that have tended to be, 'at best underrepresented, more generally ignored and at worst exploited and manipulated' (Cook and Hess, 2007: 30). Thus, we might conceptualise the burgeoning interest in children's perspectives within a broader umbrella of research, which actively seeks the perspectives of people from marginalised groups (Greene and Hill, 2005).

Also underpinning this perspective is a view that recognises that there is a variety of different experiences of childhood according to whether the child is able bodied or has a disability, is a girl or a boy, is living in poverty, or comes from a minority ethnic group. Other differences might relate to children's experiences of family life or whether they live in a rural or urban area, which may affect their access to early childhood services, or indeed there may be a mixture of these such as a white boy, living in an urban area who has a disability, for instance. We should recognise, then, that there is no one, universal 'child' that stands for all children (James and Prout, 1990) and that children's experiences are multiple and varied (Greene and Hill, 2005).

Increasingly, the response from public policy-makers is one of developing approaches that involve listening to children, such as reports from the Office of the Children's Rights Commissioner for London (for example, Hood, 2001). This, as previously stated, is because children are viewed as having the right to participate in decision-making that has an impact upon their lives (Taylor, 2000).

Activity

Find out about the ways in which local government in your area attempts to gain the perspectives of children and young people about services that affect them. What areas are they interested in finding out about? What strategies are used to elicit children's views? How old are the children who are consulted – is there evidence of children under 5 years being consulted?

It is important at this point to be cautious in thinking that developments in the area of listening to children are applied equally to very young children and older children. Hyder (2002: 311) reports on the way a listening to children project was caricatured as 'Babies consulted about council policy' in the local newspaper. This highlights the way young children are often viewed; as incapable of forming and expressing opinions about matters that affect them owing to their young age and immaturity.

 Reflection point

Reflect on what we might mean by 'listening' to babies and young children. Does it have to involve speech? How do babies and young children communicate to us about what they like and dislike?

It might be useful here to think of a practical example such as meal times. Babies will often use their mouth and tongue to push out a teat or small spoon or draw it in using a sucking action. They may also move their head towards or away from a teat or spoon when being fed or change body position in a way that tells the person feeding them what they want to do. The baby's facial expressions are also indicative of whether the experience is enjoyable or not and as the baby gets older, increasingly, their use of hands and early speech are important in communicating their feelings. If we add in the close relationship the child's parent or carer has with the baby, then minute changes in the above examples are likely to be noticed and acted upon. In other words, in tuning into babies in a sensitive way we are 'listening' to them – 'listening' not only with our ears, but with our eyes, whole bodies and minds too.

What does this mean for research?

The growth in the children's rights' perspective and its increasing impact on public policy making has its parallels in a widening range of research. Cook and Hess (2007) note that since the late 1980s there has been a move away from seeing adults as speaking for children in research contexts towards one that seeks to listen to children's viewpoints and experiences. Crucially, adults are seen as not necessarily in the best position to represent children's viewpoints and experiences fully because children themselves have a unique perspective on their own lives. Thus, Greene and Hill (2005: 3) argue that,

> The researcher who values children's perspectives and wishes to understand their lived experience will be motivated to find out more about how children understand and interpret, negotiate and feel about their daily lives

Such a perspective is a shift in thinking about children in research. This is because traditionally, research has been carried out *on* children rather than *with* them. For Westcott and Littleton (2005), this links to the idea of the child being passive and powerless, with the focus of the research being on adults *revealing* children's understandings as opposed to *creating* understandings with children. While this undoubtedly still happens, since the mid-1990s researchers have increasingly been developing participatory and inclusive research strategies in which the child, viewed as a social actor, is at the centre (Barker and Weller, 2003). Underpinning this movement in thinking about children is the criticism of developmental psychology as confining children to a position of being consistently 'less able' than adults because of their supposed location in lower developmental stages. Since the mid-1990s, writers that are sometimes known collectively as embracing the 'new sociology of childhood' have criticised this view of children as 'other' to adults and the idea of developmental stages per se and this has lead to new ways of conceptualising children and childhood in research (James et al., 1998). In short, we have begun to talk about children as being more capable than we might have done previously and this, in turn, has opened up greater possibilities for children's participation in research.

Research in focus

There are an increasing number of studies that focus on listening to children. Farrell et al.'s (2002) study, for instance, looks at children's perspectives of child and family services.

In considering who has an interest in the 'quality' of children's services, whose viewpoints might be important to include? We might think of these people as being 'stakeholders' in the service (Moss, 1994). Traditionally, we might have included parents, practitioners, inspectors and such like in our list. However, this would restrict our understanding of the service to a purely adult perspective. As Cook and Hess (2007) observe, this discounts the perspective of one of the 'key players'; children. Children may well have their own understandings and experiences of a particular service, which may be very illuminating.

In Farrell et al.'s (2002) study, which looked at the degree to which child and family services meet the needs of users within communities in their localities, the aim was to listen to children's perspectives of the services they used. There were 76 children aged between three and eight years in the study, from a range of settings (in Queensland, Australia), and these children were asked a range of open-ended questions about their setting. An example of a question used was 'what do you really like about coming here?' (ibid.: 30). The children were also shown a photograph of someone they were familiar with and were asked to share their views about what would help this child if new to the setting as well as what the child would need to know in order to enjoy their time in the setting.

The children's responses were audio-taped and analysed. The older children often cited that they enjoyed the opportunities to make friends and play sport and learn new subjects. The younger children in the study tended to focus on their favourite pieces of equipment or activities they enjoyed doing. In terms of things the children did not like about their setting, the children often focused on the behaviour of other children, such as being bullied or getting hurt. The children's advice to potential newcomers to their setting differed slightly according to age as the older children tended to focus on knowing the rules of the setting, whereas the younger children tended to focus upon the enjoyment to be had participating in certain activities or playing with particular pieces of equipment.

The study showed that young children are capable of expressing views about the services they receive. The researchers stress the need to think about eliciting the viewpoints of *all* members of a community – adults and children alike – when considering the quality of child and family services.

ETHICAL ISSUES WHEN INVOLVING YOUNG CHILDREN IN RESEARCH

The previous chapter was dedicated to examining the issue of ethics in research. In this section, our aim is to build on this and examine some of the particular ethical considerations that need to be taken into account when *directly* involving young children in research.

In the previous chapter we noted that an important consideration in research is whether it is of some *benefit* to the participants (Robson, 1993). In *directly* involving children in research and listening to their perspectives, we believe that there are many positive benefits, not least that the researcher gains access to the viewpoints of a key stakeholder group in early childhood research – the children themselves. As a consequence of carrying out research that involves listening to children, the researcher is adding to a body of research that views children as experts on their own lives, sees eliciting children's perspectives as possible and takes children's ideas seriously. By *participating* in research, children have the opportunity to learn a range of skills, such as those relating to speaking and listening, as well as learning about their environment and their place in it in new and exciting ways (Driskell, 2002). In addition, participatory research methods, which we discuss further in Chapter 14, allow children more *ownership* over research and this can mean that they are more motivated to participate (O'Kane, 2000). But while there are positive benefits to listening to children, we should always be mindful of Woodhead and Faulkner's (2008: 35) caution that 'respect for children's status as social actors does not diminish adult responsibilities'.

Increasingly, research with children is being governed by codes of ethics, which lay down the protective responsibility researchers have towards children who are participants in research. In this sense, research that involves children can be viewed as constituting a risky activity (Allen, 2005). These risks are not of the same kind as found in biomedical research; in the types of early childhood research we are discussing in this book, the risks are more likely to be 'social than physical' (Allen, 2005: 20). In other words, the child is unlikely to come to physical harm, but the researcher needs to consider the social and emotional harm they might inflict upon the child participant.

⟲⟳ **Reflection point**

What social and emotional harm might come to young children in a piece of research? Think about this in relation to the following hypothetical research examples:

- filming babies at lunchtime in a study aiming to look at adult–child interactions during meal times
- interviewing six children of 3–4 years as a group about what they like or dislike about coming to nursery
- carrying out research looking at children's lack of mathematical understanding in the area of conservation of number, involving children aged 5 years in various tests outside of the classroom.

If we take each hypothetical example in turn, in the first instance, the researcher would need to consider the impact of filming on the babies. S/he would need to tune in sensitively to the reactions of the babies. It is likely, for instance, that if the babies stop feeding and/or are clearly moving their faces away from the camera, they may be distressed and filming should cease immediately and the researcher may need to move further away. The filming may also make the parent or carer feeding the baby uneasy, which might also impact negatively on the meal time experience. As a consequence, it might also influence the findings of the research.

In the second example, what if the subject matter has little interest for the children? Possibly, traditional forms of group-interviewing may be inappropriate as they may involve sitting for long periods when the children would rather be playing with their friends. In other words, there may well be a power imbalance with adults deciding what to talk about as well as when and where this should happen. In addition to this, when interviewing children as a group, the researcher would need to ensure that *all* children have the opportunity to contribute to the discussion, rather than some voices dominating. The questions asked would need to be carefully thought through to ensure *all* the children are able to understand what is being asked of them, especially given that children often feel the need to 'get it right' when asked questions by an adult. This would also need thinking through in terms of whether English is the children's first language or whether any of the children have communication difficulties. Finally here, the researcher would need to consider how a child might feel if they say something that is potentially ridiculed by the rest of the group as well as how they would deal with this issue if it arises.

In the final hypothetical example, these mathematics' tests may have little meaning for the children and take the children away from their usual work and play in the classroom. The work of Donaldson (1979), although involving test situations too, emphasises the importance of tests being *meaningful* to children and demonstrates how children are able to perform at a higher level when this is the case. Hatch (1995) highlights the need to establish rapport with young children in research and make them feel comfortable. One aspect of this is the choice of place to carry out the research. Hatch argues that children are likely to be more comfortable in a familiar setting, whereas this hypothetical example sets out to put children in an unfamiliar setting, which may be unsettling and, at worst, distressing for the child. In addition to this, the research appears to be aimed at demonstrating children's lack of competence in mathematics as opposed to what they can do and could therefore be regarded as unethical. This last example, then, might also be regarded as damaging to children as a group – beyond those children involved directly in the study – because it might reinforce a view of young children as lacking or incompetent in some way (Alderson, 2000). It is far better to develop a research idea that is framed positively.

As you can see, there are many ethical implications in research with children and it is important to think this through when designing a piece of research. This can be linked to the degree of children's involvement in the research. Alderson (2005: 29–30), for instance, outlines three main levels of child involvement in research. These are as follows:

- *'Children as unknowing subjects of research'.* Here children do not know that research is being carried out and are not asked for their consent.
- *'Children as aware subjects'.* Here the design of the research is tightly within the control of the adult researcher.

- *'Children as active participants'*. Here there is flexibility over the methods used in the research. Furthermore, children themselves may become involved in planning and carrying out research projects.

Each of these levels of involvement implies a different conception of childhood, ranging from seeing the child as innocent, the child as needing controlling, or the child as confident and competent (Alderson, 2005). In a similar way, Woodhead and Faulkner (2008) ask whether children in research are viewed as objects, subjects or participants, each representing changing understandings of the competency of children as well as changing perceptions relating to the degree of sensitivity accorded children in relation to their rights and welfare.

But seeing children as competent and able to participate actively in research has ethical implications. You will recall that in the previous chapter we stressed the importance of gaining the consent of parents and other possible gatekeepers prior to research being carried out as well as gaining the consent of the children. But this may not be as straightforward as this seems. As Alderson (2005) observes, what do we do if a parent withdraws their consent for their child to take part in a piece of research but the child is keen to participate? Similarly, what do we do if a few children object to being observed if the researcher wishes to observe a whole-class situation? Children are increasingly being seen as competent enough to consent to participate in research as well as withdraw from research (Farrell, 2005) and, as the previous chapter noted, the notion of informed consent and the right to withdraw from research are key ethical concepts in any piece of research. Alderson (2005) does not offer any 'easy' answers to questions such as these, but she highlights the need to enter into dialogue with the children and adults involved to talk through the issues that have been raised by such dilemmas. David et al. (2005) maintain that rather than 'answering' ethical dilemmas such as these stated, we should recognise that such dilemmas are likely to multiply as awareness increases around the relative powerlessness of children in relation to adults.

Issues of power also need to be considered in relation to choice of method. It is important to recognise that there may be conceptual issues around interviewing children, for instance, which can be hidden in research. Westcott and Littleton (2005) argue that children may not be used to being listened to seriously. Further to this, Clark (2005) points out that all forms of communication between adults and children involve questions of power. She argues that an adult who views young children primarily as needing *protection* and as *vulnerable* may emphasise a strong role for adults and a relatively powerless role for children. Conversely, an adult who views children as capable of taking an active role in research is likely to have higher expectations of children in terms of the degree to which they are able to participate. An emphasis on children's communicative competence may, therefore, require a reappraisal of relationships between children and adults (Clark, 2005). We explore this further in Chapter 14, which looks at creative approaches to listening.

THE CHILD AS RESEARCHER

On the face of it, it would seem that young children might be incapable of being researchers; a view that has its basis in a perspective of young children as too young, too immature, and too lacking in the qualities needed to be a researcher – qualities developed with age. These might include a certain level of verbal skills or an ability to record information that can be shared.

However, Mary Kellett (2005) argues that children can be *taught* the skills that will enable them to become researchers. In early childhood literature, there are numerous examples of writers who emphasise young children's curiosity, their inbuilt desire to explore and their creativity (Athey, 2007; Bruce, 1987; Robson, 2006). In other words, if we were talking about the motivation and ability of young children to explore the world around them, we would be saying that this is present from birth.

Alderson (2000) argues that in many schools (we would extend this to all early childhood spaces), children are engaged in research on a regular basis. However, this type of research tends to remain unpublished. Examples of this might be:

- a group of 3- and 4-year-old children going out of the nursery to conduct a traffic survey following the interest a few children have shown in the transport that passes on the main road near to the setting
- a baby exploring the different textures, shapes, sounds, tastes and smells of objects in a treasure basket
- a group of 5-year-old children investigating how they can stop a lump of snow from melting (they have bought it inside excitedly on a snowy day and want to preserve it).

Alderson (2000) points out that this type of research tends to be viewed in terms of children 'practising' being a researcher as opposed to it being important, real-life research. She argues that children are often interested in research that has a practical implication and achieves an element of change. Moreover, Driskell (2002) notes this, saying that projects about the physical environment are often highly motivating for children.

 Case study

In a module that asks students to evaluate an environment such as a local post office or local woodland as a learning environment *beyond* their workplace (that is, a nursery or school), Lina looked at the playground near to her nursery. Rather than conducting the evaluation alone, she encouraged the 3–4-year-old children to take the lead in this. She found that very few of the children used the local playground and was intrigued why this was the case. She asked them what they would like to see in the playground and took the children there on a series of visits. The children drew pictures and she noted their comments next to the drawings. They also took photographs and took her on a tour of the playground telling her what they liked and disliked about it.

Primarily the children thought the playground was 'mostly for big kids' and felt that the equipment that was there was in a poor state of repair. However, Lina was surprised when some of the children stated that they liked the coloured lines on the playground surface (denoting the way space is used in different sports). She observed these children walking along the different lines and attributed their interest to other observations she had made relating to the trajectory nature of these children's schemas (see Athey, 2007, for a discussion on schemas).

Continued

Continued

Lina made a display of the children's evaluations of the playground in the nursery and was later encouraged to move the display to the local library as part of ongoing community efforts to improve the quality of play spaces for young children in the area. She found that the physical environment was a topic that children were keen to investigate and share their views about.

Key points from the chapter

- There has been a growth in interest in children's participation and projects that involve listening to young children. This is underpinned by the UN Convention on the Rights of the Child and a view of the child as a competent, rather than passive, co-constructor of knowledge.
- There are positive benefits to listening to children in research, not only for the researcher, but for children themselves.
- There are ethical issues that need to be thought through in relation to involving young children in research, not least the relative power of the adult researcher in relation to young children.
- Finally, there is a growth in interest about children as researchers. This reflects a more equitable balance of power between the child researcher and the adult researcher.

Further reading

Clark, A., Kjorholt, A.T. and Moss, P. (eds) (2005) *Beyond Listening: Children's Perspectives on Early Childhood Services*. Bristol: Policy Press. An interesting collection of chapters all concerned with listening to young children and with relevance to both early childhood research *and* practice.

Woodhead, M. and Faulkner, D. (2008) 'Subjects, objects or participants? Dilemmas of psychological research with children', in P. Christensen and A. James (eds), *Research with Children: Perspectives and Practices*. 2nd edn. Abingdon: Routledge. A chapter that looks at changing conceptualisations of children in research.

PART 2
APPROACHES TO RESEARCH

If you have read Part 1 of this book, you will already be aware that there is no 'set way' to organise research. Your underpinning assumptions, values and beliefs will be reflected in the research paradigm you hold, ultimately impacting on your methodological and ethical stance and the importance that you give to enabling children to be full participants in research.

Throughout the research process decisions are made and these are seldom clear cut. There are possibilities and limitations to any approach taken in research. This part looks at four common approaches, or strategies, used in early childhood research: surveys, ethnography, case studies and action research. We will see that each approach is the strategy of choice according to the type of research the researcher is hoping to conduct.

We start by looking at surveys. Surveys are a non-experimental research strategy that has its roots primarily in the positivist tradition, using mainly quantitative methodology. Usually, surveys are designed to enable conclusions to be generalisable to a whole population and they commonly use questionnaires or structured interviews as methods to collect data.

The other three approaches described in this section employ qualitative research methodology, and are used in situations when an *in-depth* understanding of an issue or situation is required. The findings from these approaches are usually designed to be applicable to the participants under study, that is, to small groups or 'cases', but of course they may lead to lines of enquiry which could be investigated further in larger populations.

Ethnography, having its roots in anthropology, is an approach that is designed to reveal an in-depth understanding of an individual or group of individuals paying particular attention to social relationships, culture and context. Ethnography usually involves researchers immersing themselves in a particular situation in an effort to understand the situation from the inside. In Chapter 6 we will see how ethnography offers us the opportunity to research children's worlds and their developing relationships in a *naturalistic* setting.

In Chapter 7 we look at case studies. Some of you may already be familiar with this approach as students on early childhood studies courses are frequently required to undertake a child study, which is a form of case study. Case studies differ from ethnography as the researcher may not be as deeply immersed in the situation and, on occasions, a mixture of qualitative and quantitative methods may be used.

Finally, in Chapter 8 we discuss action research, an approach which is undertaken by practitioners with an aim to *improve practice*. Action research is collaborative, in that it seeks to involve all participants in a situation and often aims to develop a *shared* understanding of measures that can be taken to improve an aspect of practice. In doing this, there is often an emphasis on a shared *implementation* of changes to practice and a group evaluation of the *effectiveness* of any changes.

When reading through this part we would ask you to keep in mind that we are looking at a range of research approaches and that, within these approaches, there will be a choice of methods that can be used to collect data. Methods, as you may recall from earlier chapters, refer to data collection techniques such as questionnaires and interviews. You will find out more about methods in Part 3 of this book.

5

SURVEYS

Chapter objectives

- To gain an understanding of what surveys are and their uses in research
- To consider how surveys are designed and conducted
- To look at how surveys have been used in the field of early childhood care and education
- To reflect upon the possibilities and limitations of surveys

The survey approach is the first of several different approaches to research described in Part 2 of this book. Surveys lie within the positivist **paradigm**, using primarily **quantitative** methods to obtain information from large groups of participants. Although widely used in the fields of marketing, politics and **demography**, surveys have been a useful research tool in studies of *early childhood*. In this chapter we will be looking at how surveys are constructed and we will investigate examples of well-known surveys involving children and their parents.

WHAT IS A SURVEY?

The word 'survey' has a number of different meanings, but common to them all is the concept of investigation or examination. You may remember what it was like being a new student in your first lecture. As you sat down, you examined or *surveyed* the other students around you, to see if you recognised anyone or just to take a close look at others starting the learning journey with you. In geography the term is used to describe the process of investigating and mapping physical features of a locality, and the term is also used in the construction industry; some of you may have paid for a survey on a house that you were thinking of buying.

In research methods, a survey is a way of obtaining information usually from a large number of people. Very often students think that a survey is just another way of describing the use of questionnaires, however, a survey is a *process*, and a questionnaire is just one of a variety of methods that may be used as part of this process. However, Hutton (1990: 8) describes surveys as a *method* of 'collecting information by asking a set of pre-formulated questions in a predetermined sequence in a structured questionnaire to a sample of individuals drawn so as to be representative of a defined **population**'.

Therefore, if a survey is designed well, the findings should be applicable to a larger population, that is, you should be able to generalise your findings. In addition to the use of structured questionnaires, Greig et al. (2007) describe how information can be collected by using rating scales or interviews. Surveys are, therefore, an example of *non-experimental research* that can make use of both **qualitative** and quantitative methods in the same research project, using a mixed **research design**. These different ways of obtaining information are described in detail in Part 3 of this book.

In a more detailed look at the characteristics of surveys, Backstrom and Hursh-César (1981) identify six main features. They consider surveys to be:

1. *Systematic.* That is they are designed according to a commonly agreed set of procedures.
2. *Impartial.* The participants are chosen carefully, so as to avoid any prejudice or preference on behalf of the researcher/research team.
3. *Representative.* The sample of participants to be surveyed is selected carefully so that the findings generated can be generalised to a wider population.
4. *Theory based.* The survey should be based upon underpinning theoretical principles that both guide the formation of the research objectives and guide the choice of **methodology** and methods.
5. *Quantitative.* Most surveys are primarily quantitative in nature, although as previously discussed qualitative methods can be used as well.
6. *Replicable.* Other people using the same methods should be able to get similar results. Of course, as we have noted elsewhere in this book, this assumes that it is possible to neutralise the effect of the researcher(s).

WHY ARE SURVEYS USED?

Coolican (2004) outlines two main purposes for surveys; descriptive and analytical.

Descriptive surveys

A descriptive survey is one that sets out to find out what people from a particular target population think and do. There are many examples of descriptive surveys in everyday life:

- *Public opinion polls.* Around election time it is hard to escape media reports of the findings of the latest public opinion polls. These polls are usually undertaken by specialised organisations that are paid by political parties, or the media, to find out people's views on which way they intend to vote. Since it is not possible to contact everyone of voting age, the pollsters ask a sample of the population for their views and hope that these views represent the population as a whole. The polls are made more reliable by choosing the sample of people to be interviewed very carefully. As far as possible the sample is constructed to represent the demographic make-up of the population, and is chosen according to characteristics such as age, gender, social class, education and ethnicity. No poll can be totally accurate, and far from being predictive of possible voting behaviour, can only reflect opinion at the time the poll was taken. However, polls have only been way off course in three elections since the Second World War (O'Grady, 2006).

- *The national census*. This is a survey of all households in the UK, held every 10 years. It is designed to give detailed information about the whole population, rather than taking a sample, asking everyone the same set of core questions. The questions are designed to help the government better plan for housing, transport, health and education. The next census is planned to be held in 2011.

Activity

Explore the census web site www.statistics.gov.uk/census/ It gives information about how a census is conducted and the findings from the latest census.

Investigate www.statistics.gov.uk/default.asp The site is part of 'National Statistics online' which publicises information from a variety of government departments. One document that is published annually is *Social Trends*, which is full of up-to-date information about all aspects of life in the UK. It is one of the sources often used when designing a survey, as it gives up-to-date demographic information: www.statistics.gov.uk/STATBASE/ Product.asp?vlnk=5748 (all websites accessed 23 March 2008).

- *Market research*. Market research is used by businesses to find out information from consumers about products and services. The information used helps producers refine their product to meet a recognised need and to target promotional material accurately to those likely to use the product. The three main ways of collecting market research information are by postal survey, telephone interview or face-to-face interview. Supermarkets and big stores also collect information from till receipts and often target promotions to individuals on the basis of this.
- *Descriptive surveys* are used in childcare and education to find out information on such topics as availability and cost of provision, achievement (results of Standard Attainment Tests, SATs), nutrition, health and attitudes of parents and practitioners on a variety of issues.

 ### Research in focus

In this research in focus section we will look at an example of a descriptive survey (Schum et al., 2002).

The parents of 126 girls and 141 boys, aged between 15 and 42 months (with no history of developmental or medical problems) were asked to fill in regular records on the progress of 'toilet training'. Findings suggested that girls demonstrated toilet training skills *earlier* than boys. The study showed that there was huge variation in the age that 'normal' children achieved bladder control (approximately 1 year) but on average, girls were dry during the day at 32.5 months and boys at 35.0 months (Schum et al., 2002).

Key questions
- Why did the researchers look at so many children? Would a similar study of 20 children be a large enough sample from which to make generalisations? Do you think the sample size used in this study was sufficient?
- Why were children with no history of developmental delay or medical problems included in the survey?

In responding to the questions posed in the 'Research in focus' feature, you may have reflected that in a quantitative study such as this, the more participants there are in a survey, the more likely it is that the results will be generalisable to a wider population. Later on in the chapter you will find a discussion about the factors that need to be considered when choosing participants for a survey. Children with no history of developmental delay or medical problems were chosen because these conditions may result in children achieving bladder control later than children without these conditions, and including these children may have affected the findings.

Analytical surveys

Ⓖ Surveys can be used to test a **hypothesis** or to answer specific research questions.

🔍 Research in focus

Hopcroft (2005) used the results of the US General Social Survey to test a hypothesis first put forward by Trivers and Willard (1973). The hypothesis is that 'In a species with a long period of parental investment after birth of young, one might expect biases in parental behaviour toward offspring of different sex, according to the parental condition: parents in better condition would be expected to show a bias toward male offspring' (Trivers and Willard, 1973: 90). Although this hypothesis is mainly applied to non-human species, Hopcroft thought that it may also apply to humans and formulated the hypothesis that 'there is an interaction between individual status and investment in offspring such that high-status individuals invest more in boys, and low-status individuals invest more in girls' (Hopcroft , 2005: 1111). Using the number of years of education of children as a measure of parental investment, Hopcroft found that sons of high-status fathers received more years of education than daughters of high-status men. For low-status fathers the opposite was found to be true, daughters receiving more years of education than sons; thus upholding her hypothesis.

Key questions
1. This piece of research was undertaken in the USA. Do you consider that Hopcroft's hypothesis can be said to be upheld for all parts of the world? How might you justify your position?
2. Do you consider number of years of education a good measure of parental investment?

In reflecting on the questions posed in the 'Research in focus' feature you may feel that the findings may not apply in cultures where traditionally the son may be expected to care for his elderly parents and dependent family members, such as in India. In such situations it is likely that in conditions of economic uncertainty it may be viewed as even more important that resources are directed towards the son's education, whereas more affluent families may be able to afford to educate their female children. The number of years of education is not the only indicator of parental investment; the degree of emotional involvement and the amount of time spent with children is also relevant.

Ⓖ Note that Hopcroft did not conduct the survey herself, she just used the **data** obtained by others. This is a common approach. Most large surveys publicise their findings so that other researchers can use the information. This is called secondary analysis.

Later in this chapter we will be investigating several well-known, large-scale surveys of children and their parents that have been conducted in the UK. It is common for a survey to throw up interesting results that prompt researchers to analyse the data in more depth. For instance, in the second report of the National Child Development Study (a survey that looked at all children born in a particular week in 1958), it was noted that children from the lowest social class had lower reading scores than children from other classes. Using information collected from the same survey it was found that overcrowded homes, and homes lacking basic amenities, led to poor reading skills in children, independent of other factors such as the social class of the child's family or area of the UK in which the family lived. The analysis therefore showed that the main influence on a child's reading level was not social class as such, but was a result of the material disadvantage that was more common for families from the lowest social classes (Coolican, 2004).

Johnson and Christensen (2008) have outlined five objectives for educational research: exploration, description, explanation, prediction and influence; surveys can be used to obtain information to fulfil all five objectives.

1. *Exploration.* This is where a researcher is trying to generate ideas about a particular issue. It is useful at the beginning of a project, helping to throw up questions that can be looked at in more depth. For instance a survey of parents' views about a particular issue may point to a common attitude or idea that needs to be looked at in more depth than a survey will allow.
2. *Description.* As noted previously, this is one of the most basic activities of research. Surveys are an ideal tool to provide descriptive data, as we saw in Schum et al.'s (2002) research, undertaken to describe the ages when children achieve bladder control.
3. *Explanation.* This is where a researcher tries to explain *why* a particular observed phenomenon occurs, as in the example of the research undertaken on survey data about reading levels reported by Coolican (2004).
4. *Prediction.* This is when the researcher attempts to forecast a particular phenomenon. The Hopcroft (2005) study is an example of this, where she formulated a prediction (hypothesis) and used survey material to confirm her prediction.
5. *Influence.* This is when researchers attempt to use research findings to make changes in practice and/or policy. An example of this is the importance attached to the results of evaluation surveys of the US Head Start Programme. This is a programme designed to support very young children and their parents in disadvantaged areas. Ongoing research, including the use of surveys, has shown the many positive benefits of the intervention and this research was one of the factors underpinning the adoption of the Sure Start initiative in the UK (Glass, 1999).

DESIGNING A SURVEY

The design stage of the survey process will determine if the results will be useful (Kasunic, 2005) and it is at this stage of the proceedings that the researcher needs to bring into play three distinct kinds of knowledge. In the first instance, it is important to have a degree of expertise in the subject matter under investigation as this will inform the aims of the research and the information to be obtained. Secondly, the researcher needs to have an understanding of how to design a reliable and valid survey and, finally, it is important to have skills to analyse the survey data.

Deming (1960) points out that there is *considerable* skill required in devising a survey. In addition, there are *considerable* limitations to the survey approach, which tend not to make it a method of choice for students undertaking a piece of *small-scale* research. Kasunic (2005: 6) outlines these limitations as follows:

- One of the characteristics of surveys is that they are designed to obtain data from a *sample* population with the expectation that the findings will be generalisable, that is, applicable to the population from which the sample is drawn. For this outcome, the survey must follow *strict* procedures in defining which participants are to be studied and how they are selected. In order to do this, it is likely that a form of probability **sampling** will be used.
- Far from being a quick and cheap option, designing a reliable, valid survey can be very *expensive* of both time and money.
- Because of the potentially large numbers of participants involved, and the need to ensure **reliability**, survey data is usually *superficial*. For example, in the Schum et al. (2002) study about toilet training outlined earlier in the chapter, the parents of over 250 children were surveyed. With this number of individuals it was not possible to conduct in-depth interviews, which may have shed light into why there is such variation in the age that children achieve bladder control.
- Surveys can be *intrusive*, asking participants to reveal aspects of themselves that they may be reluctant to reveal. If the main method to collect data is a self-administered questionnaire the response may not be truthful. However, this could also be said of other data collection methods, such as interviewing.

To overcome some of these limitations Kasunic (2005) suggests that a seven-stage process is undertaken when designing a survey.

The seven stages in designing a survey

1. Identification of the objectives

It is essential that the researcher is clear from the beginning what it is they want to find out. Without clear objectives, the survey will not be very effective. In the Schum et al. (2002) survey, discussed previously, the objective was 'to compare the ages, by gender, at which normally developing children acquire individual toilet-training skills and to describe the typical sequence by which children achieve complete toileting success' (Schum et al., 2002: 48).

It is at this stage of the process that the researcher needs to decide if the survey is to follow a set of participants over a period of time (a *longitudinal* survey) or to survey the participants at one point in time only (a *cross-sectional* survey).

- *Longitudinal surveys.* These are surveys where information is collected at more than one point in time. Johnson and Christensen (2008) describe two main types of longitudinal study. One is the *trend study* where different samples of people from a population are asked the same questions at different times. For example, in the UK there is a longitudinal study of infant feeding practices, called the

Infant Feeding Survey. Every five years, from 1985, mothers with babies aged 0–9 months have been surveyed to elicit information on infant feeding practices (Bolling et al., 2007).

The other main type of longitudinal survey is the *panel survey*, where the same groups of participants are studied at different points over time. This type of study is also known as a *prospective* study, because the researcher starts in the present and moves forward in time (Johnson and Christensen, 2008). The group of individuals studied is called a 'cohort'. Some longitudinal studies follow just one cohort, while others study successive cohorts of participants.

Longitudinal studies are very useful for looking at how individuals change over time; for instance, it is possible to see if the chances of becoming obese increase as the participants get older. However, there are disadvantages as participants may be lost from the study. These surveys are relatively expensive and time-consuming, and once started it is difficult to make modifications to the survey design, as the researcher would no longer be comparing 'like with like'.

- *Cross-sectional surveys.* In this type of survey information is collected from participants at one point in time only, and comparisons are made between different groups within the study. For example, if a researcher wanted to see if levels of obesity change with *age*, they would include participants of different ages in the study. However, as they would not be following the same individuals over time, differences between the participants may influence the results.
- Some large, prospective studies introduce a cross-sectional element, when questions are asked in one year when the cohort is surveyed, but not in other years.

2. *Identification and characterisation of the* population

The 'population' of a survey is the group to which the researcher wishes their findings to be applicable. The 'population' can be defined in terms of any variable that is relevant to the study. For example, Schum et al. (2002) wanted to find out the average age that children achieve bladder control, so their population was children who had no history of bladder problems or developmental delay, as both these variables could delay the acquisition of bladder control. This is sometimes known as the '**sampling frame**'.

Once the population of the survey has been identified then the researcher tries to understand as much as possible about the target audience. For instance in the Schum et al. (2002) study, the population was the children, but the target audience was the children's parents, as it would be a parent who would be responding to the research instruments, that is, the questionnaires. The kind of issues that may need to be considered in a planning a survey about achieving bladder control could include:

- What level of knowledge about the topic can the researcher assume?
- Do parents understand professional terminology such as 'bladder'?
- Are parents likely to use different terms than professionals, such as becoming 'dry'?
- Are there likely to be language barriers?
- What is the best way to reach parents? Personal recruitment by their family physician or media advert?
- Would it be better to post survey items to parents or can the survey be conducted by telephone or by email?
- How much time are parents likely to be able to give to the study?
- How motivated are the parents likely to be?

Understanding the target audience will help in designing information-gathering instruments that the participants can both understand and will be motivated to complete.

Activity

Yolande wants to survey the parents at her workplace (an infant school) to find out how much they know about healthy eating guidelines. Her objective is to find out the level of knowledge about healthy eating in parents of children aged 5–8 years.

1. What is the population of her survey?
2. In this case will there be any difference between her population and the target audience?
3. What characteristics of the population does she need to know to help her design her survey?

Yolande's target population are all the parents of children aged 5 to 8 in her school, and as she will be able to survey them directly there is no difference between the target population and the target audience. In a survey such as this, Yolande will need to know as much as possible about the target population so that she can design a survey that will give useful information. For example, she will need to know the parents' confidence in using English and the best way to communicate with them (for instance, if the majority of parents are at work during the day, face-to-face interviews may be difficult to arrange).

3. Design of sampling *plan*
Unless the target population is very specific, it is unlikely that the researcher can survey everyone; they have to choose a *sample*. There are two main decisions to be made:

(a) How will the participants of the survey be selected?
(b) How many participants will be needed?

If the researcher intends the results of the survey to be generalised out to the *whole* population then the sample must be chosen in such a way that every member of the population has an *equal chance* of being selected and the sample size has to be large enough for there to be a reasonable chance that all the relevant variables are accounted for. In a survey of parents, for instance, a large sample chosen at random is more likely to include mothers and fathers, of all social classes, with representatives from Black and minority ethnic groups in the proportion that they occur in the population, and parents with different levels of education. There will be a more detailed look at sampling in Chapter 15.

4. Design and writing of the questionnaire/and or designing structure of interviews
The success of a survey depends upon *what* questions are asked and *how* they are asked. Most surveys have a questionnaire at their core, to find out key information. However, some surveys also include a more qualitative measure, such as semi-structured interviews. Whatever measure is chosen, the design process must be equally as rigorous, especially if the researcher intends the results of the survey to be *generalisable*. Using more than one method to obtain information is a type of **triangulation**, whereby the strengths of one method compensate for the weaknesses of another. You will find information about how to design a questionnaire and how to conduct an interview in Part 3 of this book.

5. Pilot the test questionnaire/interview format

Before the researcher embarks on a *full-scale* survey it is always wise to test or 'pilot' the questionnaire and/or interview format with a small group of participants, who are as representative as possible of the larger sample. Many potential difficulties with the questions, layout, procedure and any technology used can be ironed out at this stage.

6. Distribution of the questionnaire/conducting the interviews

The researcher may have had to modify their questionnaire/interview format because of issues that arose at the piloting stage, but all being well s/he can move on to distributing the questionnaire and/or conducting the interviews. For questionnaires the main issues to think about are:

- controlling distribution (such as email or by post)
- deciding how long to give participants to respond
- monitoring the response rate
- deciding if and when to send out reminders to participants.

If the researchers are using interviews, they need to decide if this will be face to face or via the telephone. Often several interviewers will be used and they will have to be trained so that the same procedure is used for all participants. You will note that this links to positivist concerns about the ability of the study to be replicated and the need to neutralise the effect of the researcher.

7. Analysis of results and writing the report

When the data has been collected it then needs to be analysed. This needs to have been thought about at the design stage. If the questions have been formulated well and relate directly to the main research objectives, then analysis should be relatively straightforward. The various ways of analysing information from questionnaires and interviews will be discussed later on in this book. Finally, the report needs to be written.

THE USE OF SURVEYS IN EARLY CHILDHOOD

The use of surveys to obtain information about early childhood issues is well established and in this section we will look in more detail at some examples. You will recall that there are two main kinds of survey: *longitudinal prospective studies* that follow a cohort of children until adulthood and beyond, and *cross-sectional surveys* that tend to have a more limited focus.

Longitudinal prospective studies

There have been three main birth cohort studies in the UK. Cohort studies involve following a particular group or 'cohort' of individuals from birth, throughout their lives. This involves the use of multiple surveys undertaken at regular intervals on the same group of people. The surveys collect a huge and varied amount of information about the individuals, from the moment they are born through to adulthood. In addition, information is collected about their families. The information collected includes:

- details about the individual's birth, health and all-round development
- details about the individual's education and employment
- details about the individual's attitudes and beliefs
- demographic details about the individual's parents and their parenting style.

Because the same individuals are studied throughout their lives, it is possible to see the effect of different circumstances on their lives. For example, such a survey would be able to show if children born of wealthier parents had better outcomes in terms of health, education and employment as adults.

The three main large-scale cohort studies in the UK are:

- the 1958 National Child Development Study, which looked at 17,500 children born in a single week in 1958 (in England, Scotland and Wales)
- the 1970 British Cohort Study, which looked at 17,200 children born in one week in April 1970; (in England, Scotland, Wales and Northern Ireland)
- the Millennium Cohort Study, which looked at 18,800 children from the age of 9 months living in the UK, who were born in 2000.

Because there are now three separate cohorts being studied it is possible to see if there have been any changes across generations. For instance, it is possible to see if children's health has improved since 1958.

The organisation of these studies, together with the collating, dissemination and storage of all the information collected is now in the hands of the Centre for Longitudinal Studies (CLS), based at the Institute of Education in London. The data that is collected is made available to the wider research community and is a valuable national resource. According to the CLS (2007), the findings produced evidence for a number of government inquiries such as the Plowden Committee on Primary Education (Central Advisory Council for Education, 1967), the Warnock Report on children with special educational needs (Warnock Committee, 1978) and the Acheson report on inequalities in health (Acheson, 1998).

🔍 Research in focus

The Millennium Cohort Study included as its sample 18,800 babies born in 2000, the first survey (first sweep) being undertaken when the babies were 9 months old. As well as being designed to obtain data about children born in England, the study is particularly interested in outcomes for children born in Northern Ireland, Scotland and Wales, children from Black and minority ethnic groups and those living in disadvantaged areas. Children were drawn at random from areas in the UK chosen to represent these characteristics. As well as concentrating on particular geographic areas and upon specific groups, the study is designed so that findings can be compared with those from the earlier cohort studies. One difference is that in this study information is being gathered from the children's fathers as well as from their mothers.

The second and third sweeps were undertaken when the children were 3 and 5 years old. The fourth sweep was due when the children were 7 years of age.

So far most of the findings have come from the first sweep and show the great diversity of families that children are born into; from families where both parents, in their thirties are graduates and earning, to lone mothers in their teens with no employment and no qualifications. The survey has shown that there are great differences between the different groups in the survey, with Asian mothers being more likely to breast feed than other groups and less likely to return to employment after the birth of their baby.

Key questions
1. What are the advantages and disadvantages of having a sample of nearly 19,000 children?
2. Look at the CLS website. What is the main difference in the way in which the sample was drawn, compared to the 1970 British Cohort Study? www.cls.ioe.ac.uk/ (accessed 5 April 2008).

The advantage of having such a large sample is that findings can be generalised to a wider population with some confidence, but administering such a large survey is costly in terms of time and money. It is difficult to keep in touch with so many families and there will always be some families that cannot be contacted. The main difference in the way that the samples were drawn for the Millennium Cohort Study and the 1970 British Cohort Study is that the Millennium Cohort Study included children from Northern Ireland and particularly targeted areas of disadvantage, whereas the British Cohort Study looked at every child born in a particular week in England, Scotland and Wales in 1970.

Other examples of longitudinal prospective studies
- *The Avon longitudinal study of parents and their children (ALSPAC).* This is a longitudinal study of 14,000 children born in 1991–92 in the West of England. The study began with their parents, before the children were born, and continues to monitor the children, who are now teenagers. The study has a health focus, specifically looking at the interaction between *environmental* and *genetic* factors on children's health and development (Golding et al., 2001).
- *The Effective Provision of Pre-School Education Project (EPPE).* This is a longitudinal study of 3,000 children that was designed to look at the effectiveness of different types of pre-school education on children's development and later achievement in school. The project started in 1997 and followed the children through until 2003 when the project was extended and it is now intended to follow the children through to 2011, when they will be at the end of Key Stage 4. (Sylva et al., 2003)

Cross-sectional surveys
These studies endeavour to find out information from a sample of participants at one point in time. A good place to look at examples of this type of survey is the Sure Start website www.surestart.gov.uk/research/ (accessed 5 April 2008). Sure Start undertakes a number of annual surveys, two examples being the Parent's Survey and the Workforce Survey.

- *The Parents' Survey.* This survey was first undertaken in 2004 and was repeated in 2007. It collects information on parents' use of childcare and early years' provision over the previous year, collecting in-depth data about their use over the week preceding the survey. Parents are asked questions about the cost of childcare, their reasons for using childcare, their sources of information and attitudes about provision in their area.

- *The Workforce Survey.* This survey has been held regularly since 1998; since 2006 it has been conducted annually. The survey looks at different forms of early childhood provision and obtains information on the numbers of children attending, the numbers of staff, their qualifications, and issues to do with recruitment and retention of staff.

 Reflection point

Before concluding this chapter, reflect for a moment on what surveys *can* tell us and what they *cannot* tell us. In doing this, think back to some of the debates we introduced you to in Chapters 1 and 2. In what ways are surveys *limited* as an approach in early childhood research?

We are sure that in reflecting upon surveys as an approach to early childhood research, you can see the advantage of being able to 'speak with confidence' about large numbers of children and families. However, you may also have noted that there are other aspects of early childhood that surveys cannot illuminate. You may have thought that they would be inappropriate if the research was aiming for a detailed, holistic insight into a setting, or wishing to focus on the minutiae of early childhood practice as well as if the aim of the research was to elicit the children's perspectives directly. It is unlikely that any undergraduate student would undertake a survey as a research project as they can be a *huge* and *time-consuming* undertaking, often requiring a high level of skill in statistics. The next chapter looks at a very different approach to research, which is qualitative in nature: ethnography.

Key points from the chapter

- A survey is a way of collecting information from individuals, often in large numbers, using primarily quantitative methods such as questionnaires. Qualitative methods, such as semi-structured interviews are sometimes used if there is a mixed approach.
- Generally, the findings of surveys are designed to be *generalisable* from the participants being investigated to the whole of the population to whom the research is relevant.
- For findings to be generalisable, the sample of participants to be studied has to be *representative* of the population as a whole.
- Surveys can be *longitudinal*, following a cohort of individuals over time, or *cross-sectional*, where a group of individuals is studied at one point in time only.
- Surveys are not useful if the researcher wishes to focus on the minutiae of practice, gain detailed data on a small sample or elicit children's perspectives directly.

Further reading

De Vaus, D. (2002) *Surveys in Social Research.* 5th edn. London: Routledge. This is a 'classic' text that takes the reader through the practical steps of designing a survey and analysing the results.

Johnson, B. and Christensen, L. (2008) *Educational Research.* 3rd edn. Los Angeles, CA: Sage. Chapter 9 has a good section on sampling.

ETHNOGRAPHY

This chapter is in marked contrast to the previous chapter, which looked at surveys. Here, we will be thinking about research that falls firmly within the sphere of **qualitative** research. Ethnography, as we will see, has a long tradition in research, especially in the field of social **anthropology**. In particular, ethnography has been used in studies of chil- dren and childhoods in many sociocultural contexts and has been important in highlighting the multifaceted nature of childhood (James, 2007). In addition to this, ethnographic research has been employed in *early childhood* research illuminating a wide range of areas, such as children's play cultures (Corsaro, 1985). In terms of the *process* of doing ethnographic research, we will see that ethnographic research aims at 'immersion' or becoming a member of a setting in some way and stresses the keeping of a detailed fieldwork diary and participant observation. It is this level of fieldwork that distinguishes ethnography from case study research, which may or may not involve this. The next chapter on case studies discusses this distinction further.

WHAT DO WE MEAN BY 'ETHNOGRAPHY'?

You may recall that in Chapter 2 we observed that ethnography can be defined as a 'description of people or cultures' (Denscombe, 2003: 84). In addition, ethnography can be described as 'the study of people as they go about their everyday lives' (Buchbinder et al., 2006: 47). These descriptions of ethnography tell us that it relates to research about people going about their everyday activities, but more than this, ethnography is also associated with 'thick description' and the interpretations made of this (James, 2007). You will find out more about this key feature of ethnography as you read the chapter.

But ethnography is not as simple to define as this suggests. Pole and Morrison (2003) note that ethnography is sometimes used as a synonym for *all* qualitative approaches to research, something we highlighted in Chapter 2. In addition, they argue that ethnography is sometimes used as a noun as well as a verb. This can be seen in the way 'ethnography' is used to refer to the product of the research as well as the activity or process of carrying out the research. Despite this ambiguity, Pole and Morrison (2003) maintain that in reading a wide range of studies there are some features that studies deemed 'ethnographic' have in common:

- There is a focus on a specific location, setting or event.
- Within this specific location, setting or event, there is a focus on the *full range* of social behaviour.
- A range of methods might be employed in order to understand this social behaviour from *inside* the location, setting or event.
- **Data** analysis involves a movement from rich description to identifying concepts and theories that are *grounded in the data*, which is collected in that location, setting or event.
- There is an emphasis on capturing as much detail as possible and in so doing, not shying away from the *complexities* of the issues in the research location, setting or event. This is viewed as more important that the ability to make generalisations in ethnographic research
  (adapted slightly from Pole and Morrison, 2003: 3).

Thus, we can see that rather than aiming to test hypotheses or establish causality between variables, ethnographers focus on individuals' understandings of their social world as well as gaining an insight – at first hand – into the everyday habits, beliefs and language of the group they are studying (Edmond, 2005). There is also an emphasis on observation in a naturalistic setting in ethnographic research, with the researcher or 'ethnographer' traditionally aiming for a position where they do not 'disturb the field'. More recent approaches to ethnography recognise that it is impossible *not* to disturb the field and stress the importance of acknowledging the subjectivity of the researcher, that is, who they are in relation to the group they are studying – the notion of **reflexivity** (Angrosino, 2005; Coffey, 1999).

In tracing the history of ethnography, we can see that it evolved as a result of colonialism when the British colonialist administration wished to find out information about indigenous peoples in the countries they had colonised (Fielding, 2008). In social anthropological research, ethnography was used to study indigenous peoples and their cultural practices in a wide range of places around the world. Writers such as Margaret Mead and Claude Levi-Strauss are regarded as classic scholars in this respect and lived among diverse communities in different parts of the world in order to gain an understanding of people's lives as lived in those communities.

More recently, in the 1960s, ethnography developed a more critical edge in what is known as the Chicago School of Sociology. Sociologists within this school used ethnographic methods to help them to see the world from the perspectives of those they were studying, often with an emphasis on groups who were deemed powerless in some way, such as urban youth (Deegan, 2007). They believed that by blending into the setting in which the research was carried out and carrying out research in the 'real world', with all the 'messiness' this entails, they would be able to see the world through the eyes of those they were studying. Later on, when leaving the field, they similarly believed that they would be able to interpret and write about the setting in a detached way (Fielding, 2008).

⌇⌇ Reflection point

Pause for a moment and think about what has just been said. Imagine you are going to study a group of people in a particular context that is unfamiliar to you. This unfamiliarity might be due to economic wealth, professional activity, cultural and religious practices, trauma experienced and suchlike.

How possible is it to see the world through someone else's eyes? Also reflect on whether it is possible to represent this 'other' world in some way – as you might try to do when making field notes, analysing and writing up a piece of research. These are important questions in relation to ethnographic research and ones we will return to later in the chapter as they have been the basis of some strong criticisms of ethnography.

Crucially, ethnography involves the intensive and continuous study of a setting or small group over a period of time in order to gain detailed insights into the particular setting or group (Corsaro, 1996; Fielding, 2008). Often, this will be via a case study example, such as a school, but as noted previously, while case study research and ethnography are sometimes used synonymously, a case study does not *necessarily* involve the same level of fieldwork, particularly the length of time in the field. We will discuss what is meant by 'fieldwork' later in the chapter.

In summing up this first section it is important to highlight the emphasis on the in-depth analysis of *everyday* practices of given groups in *naturalistic* settings as key characteristics of the ethnographic approach. These practices that come to the attention of the ethnographer might be regarded as so commonplace that the community under study hardly notices them. Indeed, the notion of making the *familiar strange* is a common one in ethnographic studies (Coffey, 1999). Thus, Gallagher and Fusco (2006: 302) maintain that, 'the real power of ethnographic study, then, lies in its ability to observe and trouble such everyday practices, the ordinary and habitual moments in given cultures'.

🔍 Research in focus

The work of Shirley Brice-Heath (1983) is a good example of ethnographic research. She spent 10 years living and working among two communities in the Piedmont Carolinas in America, studying their language use. The communities were known as 'Trackton' and 'Roadville'; the former being a Black working-class community and the latter a white working-class community. Among her many findings, Brice-Heath found that ways of talking and interacting in one community that seemed 'natural' to them were culturally unfamiliar to the other community. She stresses the need to view language acquisition and conventions within a *sociocultural* context.

In terms of the research conducted, Brice-Heath engaged in 'long-term participation and observation' in the two communities (Brice-Heath, 1983: 9). She goes on to say, 'The reader should see "Ways with Words" as an unfinished story, in which the characters are real people whose lives go on beyond the decade covered in this book, and for whom we cannot, within these pages, either resolve the plot or complete the story' (ibid.: 13).

- In what ways does this differ to quantitative research?
- Can you see any limitations relating to this approach to research?

In reflecting on the differences between Brice-Heath's *qualitative* research study and **quantitative** research, you may have thought about its lack of concern for controlled measurement and researcher effect as well as the impossibility of replicating the study exactly. You may also have felt that there is a seeming lack of concern for generalisability. More pragmatically, you may have reflected that the study was highly time-consuming. However, as with all research, it is important to see that different research questions and topics lead to different methodological approaches – after all, Brice-Health's study aimed to focus on a particular naturalistic environment at a particular time in order to gain an insight into the *everyday* language use of two communities as opposed to their language use in an *experimental* situation. Her study does not purport to offer any neat and tidy 'solutions' to the complex study of language use but tells us a great deal about the importance of sociocultural context in language acquisition and in conventions used. In this sense, 'Ways with Words' provides a powerful message that has relevance beyond the two communities studied.

ETHNOGRAPHY AND EARLY CHILDHOOD RESEARCH

James (2007) documents how social anthropologists have carried out ethnographic research into the study of childhood for over a century. While she acknowledges that some of the early anthropological studies can be criticised for their questionable assumptions of the group under study, she highlights how they documented the play and social lives of children in great detail. James (2007) also observes the way that throughout the twentieth century social anthropological studies such as those carried out by Margaret Mead in New Guinea have attempted to study the process of *growing up* in particular societies. As a consequence, they detail of a range of things that relate to children's childhoods, not least children's family life, their early education, relationships between adults and children and children's social lives.

James (2007) demonstrates that although these studies did not involve the children as *participants* as might be more usual in studies carried out today, they *did* show that childhood is experienced differently according to the particular sociocultural group within which the child belongs. By studying children in particular sociocultural contexts – in their 'real' worlds – ethnographers have been able to show that children *actively* shape their own childhoods. Indeed Corsaro (1985: 286) goes as far as to argue 'child development … cannot be fully documented unless it is studied as it occurs in the life-worlds of children', highlighting the importance of researching children in naturalistic contexts. This can be contrasted with the search for universal generalisations about children and childhood through the use of highly controlled, *experimental* methods as in many studies in the field of psychology (James, 2007).

More recent ethnographic studies of children have continued to focus on socialisation and while direct participation 'in the field' continues to be a feature, studies carried out in areas such as early childhood do not necessarily involve *living and working* among a particular community in the way that Brice-Heath's (1983) study outlined earlier entailed. Corsaro (1985), for instance, has undertaken research that focuses on children's friendships and peer cultures in a *nursery*. The following 'research in focus' section outlines his study and some of its key findings.

🔍 Research in focus

Corsaro's research was carried out in a nursery school over the period of a year. He kept detailed field notes, carried out participant observations, video-taped the children's inter-actions and talked to staff. Corsaro (1985: 3) argues that to carry out his research, it was important to free himself from 'adult conceptions of children's activities, and enter the child's world as both *observer* and *participant*'.

Among the study's many findings, Corsaro found that young children are active agents in their socialisation, who begin to see themselves as 'children' – a distinct group from 'adults'. He states, 'peer culture in the nursery school was characterised by the children's persistent attempts to gain *control* of their lives through the *communal production* and *sharing* of social activities with peers' (ibid.: 272, original emphases). In their role play with peers, Corsaro argues children are reproducing their own perceptions of the adult world as opposed to directly imitating them. He also identifies themes of sharing and control as key aspects of children's experience of nursery life.

Try to get hold of Corsaro's book *Friendship and Peer Culture in the Early Years* because it is a good example of an ethnographic study. Its first chapter 'Entering the child's world' documents in detail how the research was carried out. If you cannot get this, try to find something else written by Corsaro as he has written extensively about the various ethno-graphic studies he has been engaged in. Later in the chapter, however, we will see that there are strong criticisms of Corsaro's approach.

So far in this section we have thought about the ways in which ethnography has been used in studies carried out some decades ago and the ways in which it has demonstrated that children's childhoods are differently experienced. We now wish to outline why ethnography is important in *early childhood* research.

The importance of ethnography to early childhood research

- As ethnographic studies take place over a sustained period of time, they can be particularly useful in illuminating children's development *over time* and capturing critical periods in childcare environments such as transition points (Buchbinder et al., 2006).
- As ethnographic research is carried out in *naturalistic* settings as opposed to *experimental conditions*, it is particularly appropriate for early childhood research (Aubrey et al., 2000). A key rationale for this is that a naturalistic environment is likely to show children in a more positive light than experimental situations. This is because generally children feel more comfortable in a context that is familiar to them than one that is not, such as is the case in experimental research.
- Ethnographic research provides researchers with opportunities to gain an intimate understanding of a setting owing to the possibility of developing close relationships with children (and adults) *over time*. Moreover, the *emotional* dimension to the daily work of an early childhood setting can be more readily explored in ethnographic research than in a superficial, one-off experiment (Buchbinder et al., 2006).
- Because ethnographic research emphasises the naturalistic context for its fieldwork, it illuminates

everyday practices and, consequently, enables the researcher to analyse the way everyday cultural activities are organised (Buchbinder et al., 2006). Given the number of daily activities that are of significance to early childhood practice, this might be especially important. These might include meal times, sleep times, and/or the development of peer relationships (Ben-Ari, 1997). In addition, ethnographic studies enable the researcher to document the sense *children* make of their cultural worlds.

- Owing to its emphasis on long immersion in the field, ethnography can empower children because, if carried out with sensitivity, children are able to manage the participation of the researcher. Rather than their presence being *imposed* on the children, as in observing children at a distance, participant observation allows for the researcher's engagement with the children to be *negotiated* (Edmond, 2005).
- Finally here, ethnographic research in settings enables the researcher to study early childhood practice at both micro and macro levels as early childhood settings embody a complex weaving together of government policies and sociocultural beliefs about childcare within families and institutions as well as individual practitioner's beliefs about early childhood practice (Buchinder et al., 2006).

It would seem, then, that ethnography offers a lot of possibilities for the researcher wishing to find out about children's different experiences of childhood. We will now look in more detail at some of the key features of carrying out ethnographic fieldwork. When talking about 'fieldwork' ethnographers are describing their experiences of being immersed in the setting, which is the focus for the research. In early anthropological studies the 'setting' often amounted to living among a group of indigenous people, whose culture was very different, or 'other' to the ethnographer's own. More recently, this conceptualisation of 'other' culture has been applied to groups *within* minority world countries, such as individual nurseries or urban gang cultures (Edmond, 2005).

CARRYING OUT ETHNOGRAPHIC FIELDWORK

Traditionally, and maybe in its 'purest' form, ethnographic fieldwork involves participant observation as its main research tool (Pole and Morrison, 2003). This means that the observer, that is the researcher, is part of the context they are observing and there is *direct contact* between the researcher and the people being researched. However, we should be mindful that there are various levels of involvement when carrying out observations; they might also be carried out in a way in which the researcher retains some detachment from the activity being observed (Edmond, 2005). You will find out more about observation in Part 3 of this book where we look at a range of methods that are used in research.

Generally, then, it is most likely that researchers employing an ethnographic approach will use *qualitative* research methods (James, 2007) as these are more in keeping with the spirit of naturalism that underpins ethnography. Thus, interviews may also be used in ethnographic research, but they are likely to take the form of naturalistic conversations as opposed to involving a highly structured interview schedule (Fielding, 2008). Finally, documents might be used in ethnographic research as they can tell the researcher a great deal about the values of the setting they are studying.

Fieldwork is a key aspect of ethnography. In carrying out ethnographic research, the researcher becomes a *temporary part* of the setting and this immersion in the field is viewed as enabling him or her to gain an understanding of the use of language and the cultural practices of the setting, which in turn will enable inferences to be made about the kinds of rules that govern behaviours in the particular setting under study as well as underlying patterns of behaviour (Fielding, 2008).

In becoming part of a setting, albeit on a temporary basis, the researcher using an ethnographic approach will keep detailed field notes in an attempt to try and understand the perspective(s) of the group under study. Later on in this book we devote a chapter to journaling as a research *tool*, but also highlight its importance in documenting thoughts and feelings as research progresses. This is very important in ethnographic research. Ethnographic field notes will also contain detailed observations and reflections on these, which when pieced together form a detailed picture of the setting under study. Usually field notes are written up on a daily basis to ensure things are not forgotten, even though much of the material in a fieldwork diary will not be written up in the final publication or report. Emerson et al. (2007: 353) describe field notes as a 'loose collection of possibly usable materials' and assert that in writing field notes, the researcher is *constructing* the field of their inquiry according to their ethnographic *gaze*. You may recall the reflection point near the beginning of this chapter, which encouraged you to think about whether it is possible to 'know' the 'Other'. Inevitably, *who we are* impacts on *how we see* the research setting – it directs our ethnographic gaze.

But becoming 'part of a setting' or 'entering the field' is not as easy as it might at first appear. It can involve lengthy negotiation. Clearly, in early childhood research, if you wanted to carry out an ethnographic study in an early childhood institution, for instance, you would need to do a lot of work in gaining access, working with a range of adult gate-keepers such as nursery manager, parents and staff, being clear about the kinds of things you are looking at and how you will be gathering the data. You will recall from Chapter 3 that this is an essential part of 'informed consent'. In doing this, it is important to be aware that having negotiated access with these adult gatekeepers, the researcher still needs to think carefully about negotiating access with *children* (James, 2007). After all, we should not assume that adults 'speak' for all the children in the nursery and negotiating access with very young children will often need to happen on a moment-by-moment basis (Langston et al., 2004). This too was raised as an issue in Chapter 3.

However, ethnographic studies have been carried out more covertly. An example of a covert ethnographic study is Fielding's (2008) study of the racist organisation, the National Front. In this study, he infiltrated the group covertly in order to allow him access to the group's activities and documentation. He argues that he would never have been accepted into the group if his status as a researcher had been known. In early childhood research, we would argue *very strongly* that a covert study in an early childhood related institution, for instance, is highly unethical. Even highly experienced researchers would find it difficult to justify covert ethnographic research to an ethics' committee. While we might recall watching some of the exposés of poor practice in a few nurseries that have been televised in the past, which have involved a person pretending to be an early childhood practitioner as a 'cover story' and employing the covert use of video equipment, this is journalism and *not* academic research.

Owing to ethnography's focus on ongoing participation in the field, the researcher has to consider what role they will adopt in the setting. Fielding (2008: 271) uses the phrase 'front management' to describe this process, whereas Coffey (1999: 23) refers to this as the 'negotiation or crafting of ethnographic selfhood in the process of fieldwork'. Crucially, the onus is on the *researcher* to initiate, establish and maintain a good working relationship with the setting (Coffey, 1999).

Fielding (2008) argues that this is easiest when the researcher is in tune with the values of the setting. We wish to stress the importance of this, because if the researcher's own values are at *significant odds* with the values of the research setting, there is likely to a degree of deception involved in the data collection. This is because there is a high probability that fieldwork notes will highlight this clash in values and, consequently, the researcher may not feel able to share her/his observations and reflections on these with the research setting. As you will know from Chapter 3, deception is rarely viewed as acceptable in research.

Whatever role adopted, it is important to remember that the researcher is a 'semi-participant' in the setting and needs to present a 'true self' (Edmond, 2005: 131). A concrete example of this can be seen in Debbie's research: while she is a qualified nursery nurse and teacher of more than 20 years, when she carries out research in early childhood settings she is *not* the teacher or nursery nurse of those children. However, she does draw heavily upon her professional skills in the course of participating in the everyday life of the setting and tries to support the work of the setting in ways that she can. Not to do so would mean pretending to be something she is not and would feel uncomfortable. Children are also wise to people they see as acting in inauthentic ways (Edmond, 2005).

An example of another role that might be adopted in a setting is that of 'not knowing', which can be useful as members of the group under study feel the need to explain what they do and why they do it, even if it seems obvious to them. In early childhood research, Mandell (1988) advocates the adoption of a 'least adult' role, which involves taking on the social position of a child in order to gain an insight into their perspectives. Buchbinder et al. (2006) argue that while differences between adults and children cannot be fully overcome, not least physical size, the adoption of the 'least adult' position does treat children as experts on their own lives as the adult researcher is not adopting a position of power. This is a point we return to later.

Research in focus

In a study Corsaro conducted into peer culture in a nursery in Modena, Italy, his lack of competence in speaking Italian gave him the persona of an 'incompetent adult' in the eyes of the children, who sought to educate him in the ways of their language and the cultural life of their school. He feels that this lack of knowledge enabled him to gain an insight into the relative powerlessness of children in society, not least owing to the teasing he experienced from the children and adults. Corsaro's 'incompetence', arguably, enabled him to be readily accepted by the children. In other words, he was able to 'enter their world' as he was seen as less threatening. Another example of how Corsaro negotiated access to the children's worlds was in the children's use of seemingly risqué jokes about 'poo-poo', through which they tested how he would react. As his reaction was deemed positive, he was further accepted into the children's peer culture (Corsaro and Molinari, 2008).

You might like to reflect upon the conceptualisation of 'children's worlds' as if they are somehow very different to the 'world of adults'.

In thinking about the role the researcher might adopt within a setting, we should also remember that settings change (Angrosino, 2005). If we imagine an ethnographic study being carried out in a nursery, we might envisage a huge number of things that could change within a given time span – let us say six months. These might be:

- new children starting
- children leaving for other settings and schools
- staff members coming and going
- the themes of the children's talk and play changing owing to newly co-created group interests
- new working practices introduced – maybe as a result of new policy
- changes made to the layout of the nursery environment
- an outbreak of chickenpox or other disease.

We are sure that you can imagine many other things that might change over time. Try also to envisage what might change in relation to the self of the *researcher* over time. Look at the following case study as an example of this.

 Case study

Debbie is currently engaged in an ethnographic study looking at food and eating 'events' (to use the term coined by Douglas and Nicod, 1974) in four early childhood settings. She has spent four to five months, one day a week, in each setting. When carrying out the field-work in setting three, Debbie decided to go on a weight loss programme and over the ensuing months, gradually lost 3 stones in weight. In doing this, she feels she had a differ-ent relationship to the practitioners in this setting because she did not join in with their snack-eating of cakes and biscuits bought in from home, which seemed to serve as a means of binding the group together.

Without intending to, she seemed to develop a role as someone of immense will-power, something many of the practitioners felt they personally could not sustain. This seemed to mark her out as 'other' or different in a way that had not been her experience in the prior two settings. Not only this, but her physical experience of being in the setting felt different as the small furniture in the nursery began to feel less small as her physical size diminished. It was important for Debbie to document her reflections on the impact her weight loss seemed to have on both her and the setting because she felt it impacted on the data she was gathering. Angrosino (2005) argues that an understanding of the self of the ethnogra-pher is essential in enabling the reader to interpret the written research or 'product'.

You might like to think further about the issue of physical size in relation to a study such as this, and indeed early childhood research in general – after all, a key feature that marks adults out from babies and young children is relative size. Corsaro's (1985) study, outlined earlier, discusses differences in physical size between adults and children in some detail.

What we can see from this is that it is not only the setting that is constantly changing; the self of the ethnographer in relation to the setting is also *dynamic* and ever changing (Angrosino and Perez, 2000). Similarly, Coffey (1999: 1) highlights the way that fieldwork is 'personal, emotional and identity *work*', which involves the researcher in an ongoing reflex-ive engagement of their own position in relation to the research context (original emphasis).

A final point that needs to be made about fieldwork relates to the notion of 'leaving the field'. The date when the researcher will finish data gathering should be negotiated at the *beginning* of the study, albeit that there may be some flexibility in this. Inevitably, all research comes to an end and while the ethnographer may feel they 'belong' in the setting they have been studying owing to their long-immersion in the field, s/he has to think carefully about this, knowing that the process of leaving the field is most likely to be difficult for the *ethnographer* than their *host* (Coffey, 1999). Coffey (1999) argues that it is more likely that the ethnographer remains as a 'friend' of the setting.

THE POSSIBILITIES AND LIMITATIONS OF ETHNOGRAPHIC RESEARCH

This chapter has outlined a number of benefits to employing an ethnographic approach in early childhood research. In short, these relate to the potential it offers for researching children's social worlds in the context of a naturalistic setting over time, with all the possibilities for developing relationships and observing the everyday practices of a setting it affords. For this reason, ethnographic research has been used in a wide range of studies in early childhood (Buchbinder et al., 2006).

But ethnographic research is not without criticism. The notion of 'entering the field' as used in traditional ethnographic approaches, where the researcher views the subject(s) under study as exotic or 'Other' in some way, is problematic. Coffey (1999) points to the way that ethnographers set about constructing the 'field' for their study as something alien to them, with their own position akin to being a stranger or tourist. She says, 'it suggests a distant and remote site, which the ethnographer must learn about and endure' (Coffey, 1999: 19). In doing this, the ethnographer is expected to become increasingly familiar with the values of this culture, coming to 'know' this or be enlightened, but at the same time remain coolly distant in order to achieve professional objectivity. This treatment of the setting and the participants within it as 'exotic' or 'Other' in some way has been likened to the way colonialist powers viewed the societies and cultures of the groups they colonised. Some would argue further, that ethnographic studies into children and childhood have sought to 'colonise' children's bodies in the same way that minority world countries sought to colonise majority world cultures, conceptualising children as if they are a different *species* to adults (Viruru, 2001).

Similarly, Alldred (1998) is critical of the use of ethnographic approaches in childhood research, such as Corsaro's (1996), which talk of 'entering the child's world'. This is because they seem to imply that children and adults occupy different social spheres, with the child constructed as 'Other' to the dominant *adult*-centred culture. You may recall that we asked you to reflect on this at the end of one of the 'Research in focus' sections. For Alldred (1998), such research ignores cultural meanings assigned to 'children' and 'childhood', and ignores the unequal power relationships that exist between adults and children and between researcher and research subject/participant. This masking of unequal power relationships could be applied to the notion of adopting the 'least adult' (Mandell, 1988) role discussed earlier As James (2007) asserts, a researcher is *not* a child and is able to refer to their 'adult' and thus more *powerful* role as and when they choose.

A different criticism can be levelled at ethnography in terms of objectivity. Researchers coming from a more positivistic position might criticise its potential for bias – sometimes known as 'going native' in older anthropological studies. Given the importance placed on the self of the researcher, it could be argued that ethnographic research is less reliable or valid than studies such as surveys, because different researchers are likely to obtain different results. This is why importance is placed on the keeping of detailed field notes – they can act as a crucial source of verification of what has taken place in ethnographic studies as they offer an insight into what decisions were taken and why (Fielding, 2008). Finally here, because ethnographic research is carried out over time, it generates a huge amount of material that needs to be sifted through and analysed (Edmond, 2005). This is a key strength, but can also be daunting, particularly if it is your first experience of carrying out research.

Despite these criticisms, ethnography *is* considered a useful approach to use in the study of children and childhoods (James, 2007). Indeed Buchbinder et al. (2006) believe that ethnography is *under-used* in early childhood research. When carrying out ethnographic research, it seems that an ongoing reflexive discussion about your own perspective in relation to the setting under study is vital as is a detailed description of the setting. If you are deciding what to do for a research project, we suggest that ethnography is most likely to be useful if you have a *length of time* in which to develop relationships within a setting. It is also an appropriate approach to employ if the aim is to attain *rich* and *detailed* data in relation to a setting, such as a nursery or health centre. As with any approach or method adopted in research, what is crucial is its 'fitness for purpose' (Sylva, 1999).

Key points from the chapter

- Ethnography is a qualitative approach to research that aims at providing rich and detailed data about people in particular sociocultural contexts.
- It emphasises the importance of research being carried out in a naturalistic rather than experimental setting.
- Ethnography has a long history, particularly in the tradition of social anthropology, which has demonstrated how children's experiences of childhood are different according to sociocultural context.
- In early childhood research, ethnography has been used in a wide range of studies looking at areas such as children's peer relationships and the daily routines that happen as part of nursery life.
- Fieldwork is an important part of ethnography. Immersion 'in the field' is seen as allowing the researcher a gradual understanding of the everyday lives of particular groups of people in particular contexts.
- Participant observation is usually seen as a key tool in ethnographic research. However, other tools such as unstructured interviewing are likely to be used and the keeping of detailed field notes is considered very important.
- Like any other approach to research, ethnographic studies can be criticised. The positioning of the setting and the participants within it as 'Other' in some way is seen as problematic and when applied to children, seems to ignore the many aspects of the world that adults and children share. In addition, owing to the emphasis on the self of the researcher, different researchers might obtain different results in the same setting, which might impact on its **reliability**. Therefore, in ethnographic Ⓖ

studies, it is essential to document ongoing reflections about the impact of the self of the researcher in relation to the research as this acts as verification of what has taken place in the study.

Further reading

Buchbinder, M., Longhofer, J., Barrett, T., Lawson, P. and Floersch, J. (2006) 'Ethnographic approaches to child care research', *Journal of Early Childhood Research*, 4(1): 45–63. An excellent review of a wide range of ethnographic studies in relation to childcare.

Corsaro, W. (1985) *Friendship and Peer Culture in the Early Years.* Norwood, NJ: Ablex. This book is a classic example of early childhood ethnographic research – Chapter 1 is especially useful as Corsaro discusses the research methods used in some detail.

James, A. (2007) 'Ethnography in the study of children and childhood', in P. Atkinson, A. Coffey, S. Delamont, J. Lofland and L. Lofland (eds), *Handbook of Ethnography*. London: Sage. A very useful chapter because it highlights anthropological studies into children and childhood carried out over many years that focus on a wide range of children's experiences – not just those in institutions such as schools.

7 CASE STUDIES

Chapter objectives

- To consider what is meant by a 'case study' in early childhood research
- To reflect on the historical context of the use of case studies
- To explore the relationship between case study design and purpose
- To consider some of the methods used to collect data for case studies
- To reflect on the possibilities and limitations of the case study approach

Case studies are a useful tool for early childhood researchers. This is especially the case if you are a small-scale researcher with limited resources (Blaxter et al., 1996), a description that might be applicable to many students. Case studies can be used to study an individual child, a group of children, an early years' setting, which could be a place of work, or an organisation. They are one of the most common forms of **qualitative** research and can generate rich information, allowing for an in-depth understanding of the people and/or context being studied (Stake, 2000).

WHAT IS A CASE STUDY?

Greig et al. (2007: 145) define a case study as 'an investigation of an individual, a family, a group, an institution, a community, or even a resource, programme or intervention'. In early childhood research, a 'case' could be an in-depth **child study** focusing on a particular child's development and learning or an investigation into a group of children in transition from a nursery class into reception. A researcher could undertake a case study about the setting up of a new early years' setting, or investigate one aspect of a setting's work, such as the implementation of a 'healthy eating' programme. Case studies are undertaken in a naturalistic setting and can give information on both relationships and processes (Denscombe, 2002).

It is important to note here that a case study, in itself, is not a *method* of collecting information, but is an *approach*, within which one can choose to use a variety of **data** collecting instruments. Stake (2000: 435) argues that it is a 'choice of what is to be studied' as opposed to a methodological choice, owing to its focus on a 'case' – be it one child or a local authority or a series of 'cases'. As the previous chapter noted, a case study *may* differ to ethnographic research. A case study, while detailed, could be carried out at arm's length, without the expectation of participation in the life of the setting or community under study as in ethnographic research. This said, a case study *might* be carried out this way but it does not have to be. Stake (2000), for instance, argues that case studies that are highly *qualitative* in nature will involve researchers in spending extended time 'in the field' as a participant in the life of the setting. Another difference would be that the 'case' in case study research might be one child, as opposed to a place or community as in ethnographic research.

It is up to the researcher to define the limits of the case study. For example, a case study could be conducted on a child being treated with cancer, with the aim of investigating how the child is coping with cancer treatment. The case study will probably look, not only at the child, but also at the child's relationship with his or her parents and siblings. If one of the aims of the study is to investigate the effects of the hospital experience, it may also be appropriate to observe interactions between the child and the hospital staff. The researcher has to set 'boundaries' to the case study, and for this reason case studies are sometimes referred to as 'bounded systems' (Edwards, 2001). Used in this context, the word 'system' is defined as 'a set of interrelated elements that form an organised whole' (Johnson and Christensen, 2008: 406). In a case study, therefore, the researcher is looking at the various aspects of a system and how they interrelate; in order to answer the question 'What is going on here?' (Edwards, 2001: 126).

Most case studies are *qualitative* in nature and allow the researcher to gather very detailed information with a narrow focus. Stake (2000: 438–9) maintains that it is important to demonstrate the *particularity* of the 'case', which might include:

1. The nature of the case
2. The case's historical background
3. The physical setting
4. Other contexts (e.g. economic, political, legal, and aesthetic)
5. Other cases through which this case is recognised
6. Those informants through whom the case can be known.

Although the approach can be criticised for its lack of *generalisability*, with the information obtained often seen as only being applicable to the 'case' under investigation, some qualitative researchers consider that case studies are the *bedrock* of scientific investigation (Bromley, 1986). Many scientific discoveries and advances in theory have been spurred on by case study research.

HISTORICAL BACKGROUND

The roots of using the case study approach in the study of children lie in parents' reports of their children's progress, sometimes known as 'baby biographies' (Arnold, 2003). These were written by people such as Darwin (Darwin, 1877) and Piaget (Fawcett, 1996). Psychoanalysts from the beginning of the twentieth century used child studies of individual children to advance their understanding of **psychoanalytic theory**. One famous case study was undertaken by Freud in 1909, of a 5-year-old child called Hans. Hans had a fear of horses and Freud was able to use the case study to help him develop his theory of the **Oedipus conflict** (Greig et al., 2007).

In the 1950s, a series of case studies were conducted by James and Joyce Roberson on young children who were separated from their main carers. The plight of one 2-year-old girl, who was filmed as she embarked on a brief stay in hospital without her mother, was instrumental in allowing parents to stay with their children on hospital wards (Bowlby et al., 1952). In this sense we can see that although the emphasis in a case study is on the particular 'case' under study, the information gained can still be very influential in furthering our understandings of an issue and improving practice.

Another well-known case study was of a 5-year-old child called Dibs who was undergoing **play therapy** because of his aggression, 'temper tantrums' and antisocial behaviour. The case study describes how, through play and over a period of time, he was able to communicate his underlying feelings, resulting in a positive change in behaviour (Axline, 1971).

The case study approach can also be used to look at the work of early years' settings. An example of this approach is the work by Bertram and Pascal (2001), who published a series of case studies of early years' settings, focusing on the quality of practice. The research undertaken has been influential in supporting other settings in improving their practice.

CASE STUDY DESIGN

We have already looked at several examples of case study research; from studies of single children, to studies that include a *range* of different early years settings. The type of case study chosen can vary across a number of dimensions, and there have been various attempts made to classify case study design (Blaxter et al., 1996). Knowledge of the different designs available is important as it helps the researcher choose the most appropriate design for their research and gives them the terminology to be able to describe their design to others.

Blaxter et al. (1996: 68) find Yin's 1993 classification helpful. According to this classification case studies can vary across two dimensions:

1. *Number of case studies*: whether there is one case or multiple cases.
2. *The purpose of the study*: whether the purpose of the case is exploratory, descriptive or explanatory.

In addition Coolican (2004) and Edwards (2001) suggest a third dimension:

3. *Time frame*: whether the case study is longitudinal, with the case studied over a period of time, or is conducted as a 'snap shot' at one particular point.

It is clear that the type of case study design you choose is dependent on the overall aim of your study. Edwards (2001) identifies two broad differences. In one type of case study, the aim is to find out more about the case in question, with no expectation that the information can or will be applied more widely. Edwards gives the example of the introduction of a new way of working in an early years setting. The other type of study is designed to be an example of a phenomenon that has a *wider* interest; the expectation being that the findings from an in-depth study of one case can be generalised across to similar cases/settings. An example of this would be the case studies undertaken by Bertram and Pascal (2001), outlined previously. The findings from these studies were used by other settings to improve the quality of their practice.

Stake (1995) identifies case studies as being *intrinsic, instrumental* or *collective*. We will now look at these in turn.

Intrinsic case studies

These are single case designs, where the aim of the research is to obtain a deep understanding of the case. Students on early childhood courses are sometimes asked to undertake case studies on children to help them gain an understanding of an aspect of child development. These case studies, or child studies, usually entail undertaking a series of observations on a child, together with, perhaps, details of conversations about the child with the parents and the child's key person. Child studies are not just a description of a child's development, but include reflections and analysis, often using theory to explain observed behaviour. Depending on the aim of the child study, recommendations for the care and education of the child may be included.

The intrinsic case study can be used as an evaluative tool to examine how a programme is working; for instance you may want to review how a 'walk to school programme' initiated some time before, is operating several months later. Sometimes researchers use a single case study to explore a particular phenomenon in detail. Restricting resources to a single case can mean that a very deep understanding can be obtained. Often an exploratory, in-depth study of one case can give direction to a larger research project.

🔍 Research in focus

Observing Harry (a child study written up as a book by Cath Arnold) is an in-depth case study of a child undertaken from the time he was a baby until he was 9 years of age, mostly concentrating on the period between birth and the age of 5. The information about Harry was collected, initially, by diary entries and video footage of the child by his parents and maternal grandparents. The author, Cath Arnold, is Harry's maternal grandparent. As Harry grew older he entered the nursery where Arnold was the head teacher, and observations by his key person and other adults within the setting become an important source of information.

Arnold draws on the history of baby biographies to explain the contribution that detailed observation of children, by those who are close to them, has made to our knowledge of how children learn and how we can help them. She also shares with us her experience of how child development theory can become more understandable and useful, when applied to children we are studying.

Using Harry's spontaneous actions and communications as a starting point, Arnold assesses his learning and development, using areas of the curriculum for the purpose of analysis, while recognising that Harry's learning is fully integrated. *Observing Harry* is an example of a child study that not only increases our knowledge of an individual child, but also contributes to our understanding of how to promote the interests of *other* children. For example, Arnold makes a number of suggestions, based on her study of Harry, some of which are included here:

1. It is helpful to have *open-ended* resources freely available at home and in the nursery, for example, sticky tape, string, elastic bands.
2. Children need the *freedom to explore* materials in their own way. Harry became deeply involved when he created his own problems to solve.
3. Children express their *inner fears* when using their soft toys.
4. When children are puzzled it is an opportunity for *learning*. Adults need to encourage questioning and treat questions with respect.
5. When children are *deeply* involved, they may be exploring emotional issues as well as cognitive concerns (Arnold, 2003: 148).

The instrumental case study

In an instrumental case study the 'case' is an instrument or tool used to help the researcher understand more about a general phenomenon. Johnson and Christensen (2008: 408) describe this as using the case as a 'means to an end'. For example, you may want to find out what factors contribute to the effective leadership of children's centres. An in-depth case study of a children's centre deemed successful and its leader may allow you to identify features that can then be used to assist in the professional development of other centre leaders. Used in this way case studies can be used to investigate an important issue in depth or to develop or test a theory.

Collective case study

As it implies, a collective case study, or multiple case design, is one that contains more than one case. The Bertram and Pascal (2001) series of case studies outlined previously is a good example of this. The number of in-depth cases that are studied is dependent on resources. In general, the greater the depth required about each 'case', the fewer the number of cases that are studied. Johnson and Christensen (2008) note that up to 10 case studies within one particular design is common if there are the resources available and less depth is required.

In collective case study design there is usually a focus on the *instrumental* rather than *intrinsic* value of the case, as the aim is to find out information that can be generalised out to a wider **population** that shares the characteristics of the cases. In the Bertram and Pascal (2001) series of case studies, for instance, the information was used to improve quality of early years' settings throughout England.

It would seem, then, that there are advantages to the collective case study design. These can be summarised as follows:

- Comparisons can be made *between* cases, for example, you could compare the quality of provision for children under 3 years of age provided by different children's centres.

- If the aim of your research is to test a *theory*, the findings will be more valid if you look at more than one case.
- You are more likely to be able to *generalise* your findings to a wider population by looking at more than one case.

The disadvantage of the collective case study design is that resources will be spread more thinly than in a single case study design, adversely affecting the depth and quality of the data that can be obtained. This is the 'depth versus breadth trade-off' (Johnson and Christensen, 2008: 409). In addition, Stake (2000) argues that an emphasis on making comparisons takes attention away from the particularities of a single 'case'. In other words the *comparison* rather than the *'case'* becomes the defining feature of the **research design**. After all, we should remember that in reading intrinsic and instrumental – single case study research designs – we are making connections with our existing knowledge about other 'cases' (Stake, 2000).

Activity

Using the classifications used above, how would you describe the design of these case studies outlined so far in the chapter?

1. The case study of Dibs
2. The Robertson study of the 2-year-old going to hospital
3. *Observing Harry*
4. The Bertram and Pascal study.

METHODS THAT CAN BE USED IN CASE STUDIES

In the same way that it is left to each individual researcher to decide on the 'bounds' of the 'case' or 'cases' to be studied, it is also left to the researcher to choose whatever methods are thought to be appropriate to collect the data that is required. Case studies will often make use of *qualitative* methods such as semi-structured interviews, documentary analysis and narrative observations. However, when there are many participants involved, more use is likely to be made of *quantitative* methods such as questionnaires. If the 'case' is large, a team of researchers might be used, but this inevitably raises difficulties in terms of maintaining a degree of uniformity in the data collection and analysis *across* the team (Stake, 2000). As you will recall from other chapters you have read so far in this book, the self of the researcher has an impact on research (Coffey, 1999), and it can be very difficult, if not impossible, to homogenise the behaviours and 'selves' of the researchers.

Care also needs to be taken when using a *collective* case study design to ensure that the same methods are used for each case. This helps with making a reliable comparison. For example, if using questionnaires, the *same* questionnaire needs to be used and administered in the same way for each participant.

POSSIBILITIES AND LIMITATIONS OF USING CASE STUDIES

This chapter has shown that case study research offers a number of possibilities for researchers. They can provide in-depth information and allow an insight into the special circumstances that have affected the 'case' in a way that is not possible with approaches to research such as conducting surveys. In child studies, such as *Observing Harry* (Arnold, 2003), this information can assist us in planning to meet the needs of the child concerned. Insights gained from studying one subject may cause us to rethink our position on a certain topic or area of theory.

Case studies can be used in the exploratory phase of a larger research study. The depth of information obtained can point the way to issues that can be followed up with a wider population. Collective case studies may be particularly useful when used in this way as the information from a number of studies can be pooled, often allowing common patterns and features to be identified. Moreover, case studies can be used to *confirm* or *refute* a theory. In particular, case studies are useful in challenging a theory, as all it takes is one case study that does not confirm predictions based on a particular theory, to allow for the **validity** of the theory to be questioned (Denscombe, 2002). Ⓖ

Case studies can also have ecological validity (Tobin et al., 1989); that is, the findings observed reflect what happens in 'real life', as opposed to laboratory studies, where participants may not behave in the same way as they would in their natural setting. In this sense, case study research shares many characteristics with ethnographic research and can be particularly useful in early childhood research as it might look at children in a more holistic way. In addition to this, case studies are a good approach to use when exploring sensitive areas. In an in-depth study the researcher is more likely to become aware if the participant is uncomfortable and can be proactive in protecting their well-being.

Finally, case study research is a good way of investigating the development of a child or an area of development, such as their language skills, over time. In early childhood, as we have seen in this chapter, the close focus on *one child* and their development has a long tradition in research.

While there are many possibilities for case study research in early childhood, there are limitations. Because case studies are an in-depth study of one or very few cases, the findings cannot be applied to a population as a whole; they are not *generalisable* (Gilbert, 2008a). In addition, the nature of case study research means that the findings may not be easily replicable by others. The researcher may bring bias to the proceedings by being selective in the case they decide to study, as well as in what and how they record, and in analysing the data. This is especially the case if the study is undertaken by a close family member, as in some of the 'baby biography' kinds of studies. If we are not careful, it is easy to see what we *want* to see.

Research in focus

Tobin et al. (1989) carried out a comparative, cross cultural study of three pre-schools, using a case study approach. The research is written up in a book entitled *Preschool in Three Cultures*. The three pre-schools are:

- Komatsundani, a Japanese pre-school
- Dong-feng, a Chinese pre-school
- St. Timothy's, an American pre-school.

As a background to the three case studies, Tobin et al. (1989) discuss historical changes in the way pre-school children are cared for in all three countries. They identify a move from home-based care, by family members or by people hired to care for the children in their own homes, to children being cared for and educated in group settings. At the time that the case studies were conducted '95% of four year olds in Tokyo, 80% of four year olds in Beijing and 65% of four year olds in New York' were enrolled in some sort of group care or education setting (Tobin et al., 1989: 2). Each pre-school is recognised as having its own culture and the study aims to look not only at this, but at the way the school's culture reflects the culture of the society in which it is placed. The authors emphasise that the aim is 'not to rate the preschools in the three cultures but to find out what they are meant to do and to be' (Tobin et al., 1989: 4).

The authors used a 'visual ethnographic approach' whereby a 20-minute video sequence was made of a typical day in each pre-school. This video was then showed to the children, teachers, parents and administrators of the school who were encouraged to comment on and discuss what they saw.

The videos were then shown to parents, teachers, administrators and early childhood professionals in other areas of the country in which the film was produced. This was to get an idea as to whether or not the pre-school in the case study was typical of pre-schools in that particular culture.

A third and final tier of analysis was added when the videos were shown to similar groups of individuals in the *other* countries represented in the study, thus American parents and teachers were given the opportunity to comment on the pre-schools in Japan and China.

This method gave the authors a real insight into the ideas and attitudes that influence pre-school practice. The overall conclusion they came to was that in all three countries, pre-schools promote cultural continuity rather than cultural change, working to instil the values that their parents (and wider society) want their children to have.

Key points from the chapter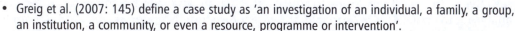

- Greig et al. (2007: 145) define a case study as 'an investigation of an individual, a family, a group, an institution, a community, or even a resource, programme or intervention'.

- Most case studies are qualitative in nature, although some employ mixed **methodology** and methods.
- The use of case studies has a long history in research with and about children – the child study is a particular type of case study used in early childhood research.

- Case study research can include only one 'case' or several.
- Case studies can be a 'snapshot' of one point in time or longitudinal.
- *Intrinsic* case studies are usually single case studies where the aim is to obtain a deep understanding of a case, the findings may be particular to the case, or may give direction to a larger research project (Stake, 2000).
- *Instrumental* case studies are used to help researchers understand more about a general phenomenon (Stake, 2000).
- A variety of methods can be used in a case study including observation, interviews and questionnaires.
- Case studies can give in-depth information about the 'case' under study, but it is difficult to generalise the findings of case study research to larger populations.

Further reading

Arnold, C. (2003) *Observing Harry. Child Development and Learning 0–5.* Maidenhead: Open University Press. This is a fascinating child study which gives real insights into the holistic development of a child.

Denscombe, M. (2007) *The Good Research Guide for Small Scale Social Research Projects.* Buckingham: Open University Press. Chapter 2 gives a good introduction to case studies.

Stake, R. (2000) 'Case studies', in N.K. Denzin and Y. Lincoln (eds), *Handbook of Qualitative Research.* 2nd edn. London: Sage. Stake is a leading authority on case study research. This chapter looks at the topic in greater depth than Denscombe.

8   ACTION RESEARCH

Chapter objectives

- To consider what is meant by action research
- To reflect upon the idea of the practitioner as researcher
- To gain an understanding of action research as a cycle
- To consider research methods that are appropriate in action research
- To consider the possibilities and limitations of this approach to research

As with the other chapters in Part 2 of this book, this chapter explores an *approach* to research rather than specific research tools such as interviews or questionnaires. Action research, as we will see, may employ a range of different research tools. Action research has gained popularity as an approach to research owing to its focus on improving practice in particular contexts and with particular people. In this way it differs to case study research, for instance, because it aims primarily to create *change* rather than produce new knowledge. Owing to its focus on improving practice, action research is often used in educational research and in research into other areas of professional practice, such as nursing.

WHAT IS ACTION RESEARCH?

Action research can be described as a 'living inquiry' owing to the way real-life experiences underpin the research (Wicks et al., 2008). Kemmis and McTaggart (2005: 564) also emphasise the way that action research focuses on *actual* rather than *abstract* practices, saying, 'It involves learning about the real, material, concrete, and particular practices of particular people in particular places'. However it should be noted that Kemmis and McTaggart qualify this by observing that inevitably, in describing and analysing the **data** gained in action research, there is a level of abstraction that occurs. Central to action research, though, is the focus on *change* (Greenwood and Levin, 2000). It is this, which makes it an attractive research approach for practitioners to employ. With this in mind, McNiff and Whitehead (2006) define action research as involving practitioners in investigating and evaluating their work with a focus on improving their own practice and the practice of others.

This is not new. From its inception in the mid-twentieth century, action research has aimed to bring about improvements to practice in some way. Kurt Lewin, who is generally attributed to developing the idea of 'action research', saw action research as a tool for bringing about democracy as *practitioners* are central to the process (Robson, 1993). However, we should not see action research as having remained static as an approach to research or as something that can be viewed in one way only. Kemmis and McTaggart (2005) argue that action research has a range of guises. They argue that recent developments in the approach are *participatory* research and *critical* action research. Participatory research emphasises community action and shared ownership and analysis of research. Critical action research shares the commitment to collective participation towards change but also focuses on injustice and disadvantage owing to social class, gender, sexuality, ethnicity, and so on. As with any approach to research, there are a range of interpretations and emphases that might come under the broad umbrella of 'action research' and we should always be mindful that different writers use the term in different ways.

Despite the multiple ways action research can be viewed and the differences in the terminology ascribed to it, *improvement* and *change* could be regarded as its key components. This will often mean that the research involves planning, acting upon, observing and reflecting upon an issue or problem that has some relevance to practice. We will look at the process of action research in more depth when we consider the action research cycle.

So, what kinds of problems, that have relevance to early childhood practice, might form the basis of a piece of action research?

- A nursery practitioner may wish to examine the way she supports (or does not support) the super-hero play of a small group of boys in her class – a group that she finds challenging at present.
- A nursery team may have observed that the transition when children leave the 0–3's room and move to the 3–5's room is not working well and want to improve this.
- A reception class team may want to develop its practice so that the children have free-flow outdoor and indoor play – something that does not happen at present.

Thus, action research is an approach to research that emerges from real-life, practical problems rather than focusing *primarily* on the development of theory or understanding of an issue. For Elliott (1991: 52), action research develops 'practical wisdom', which he defines as 'the capacity to discern the right course of action when confronted with particular, complex and problematic states of affairs'. The issue of complexity in relation to the contexts in which such professional problems arise is also expressed by Wicks et al. (2008: 17) when they argue,

> It is evident that each person's understanding and practice of action research does not stand in isolation from other aspects of their being-in-the-world; instead, action research both emerges from and contributes to a complex and panoramic view of the world in which one lives and one's own particular place within it.

Let us consider this complexity further by thinking about a concrete example such as a reception class practitioner and her team who wish to reflect on the ways that they develop close emotional attachments in their work with children and families. Let us imagine that they are working to developing a 'key person' approach (see Elfer et al., 2003, for a full discussion of what is meant by 'key person'). In this context, there is likely to be a range of factors that weave together in intricate ways:

- the present way of working in the reception class
- published material on this topic, for example, books, journal articles, and so on
- the personal and professional histories of the individual practitioners in the reception class team and wider Foundation Stage team
- the views of the children in the reception class and the rest of the school
- the ways in which the team work together
- the physical environment
- the opportunities for professional development in this area
- the generally accepted view(s) of what school should be about and how children should be supported within it at this point in history and in this geographical and cultural context
- the views of parents whose children attend the reception class
- government policy
- the views of the senior management team in the school as well as other staff members and school governors
- the funds available to support this new development
- the local authority advisory team.

The interplay between these factors, which are ever changing – and this is not an exhaustive list – is likely to be highly complex. It reflects the intricacies and realities of early childhood practice. Another way of thinking about the complexities of practice is in thinking about the types of change that action research might hope to achieve. In action research, there may be changes to the following:

- What people do
- How people interact with the world and with others
- What people mean and what they value
- The **discourses** in which people understand and interpret the world (Kemmis and McTaggart, 2005: 565).

In thinking about action research in this way, we can see that it can mean far more than trying to improve a specific area of practice. Brown and Jones (2001), for instance, point to the way action research can encourage practitioners to problematise areas of practice that have seemed 'common-sense' and encourage them to seek alternative stories as explanations of classroom events. Jones does this by reflecting in detail on her own practice as a former nursery teacher, using reflective accounts written during this period with a particular focus on gender (Brown and Jones, 2001).

Rather than aiming for simple solutions to complex problems, Jones challenges whether this is possible or even desirable, given her preference for a post-structuralist theoretical position. In other words, she does not believe in the possibility of linear progress and universal, knowable 'solutions' to complex issues, which she suggests is sometimes the lure of action research. Rather, she favours a position that embraces multiple, uncertain and shifting viewpoints, with a recognition that movements forward in one's own practice are always contingent and contextual and cannot be generalised (Brown and Jones, 2001; see also Swantz, 2008). This links back to some of the discussion had in Chapters 1 and 2.

> ⌇⌇ **Reflection point**
>
> Think about the ideas being expressed here. Is there a tension between seeing action research in terms of its possibility of improving practice (in the sense of making progress towards some predetermined, measurable goal) and the idea that certain and knowable outcomes are possible or even desirable? Think back to some of the ideas you were introduced to in Chapters 1 and 2 and reflect on some of the ideas about research that might underpin these two positions. Also consider which conceptualisation of action research might be most attractive to government institutions and why – it is a point we pick up later in the chapter.

It would seem, therefore, that despite the focus on improving practice in action research, the researcher's theoretical stance is still important. MacNaughton (2001), for instance, discusses how her action **research design** was rooted in her commitment to feminist pedagogies and the desire to improve her own practice in relation to creating greater gender equity in early childhood practice. In this sense, action research can be regarded as **praxis**. This is because theory and practice are viewed as inseparable, with theory informing practice and practice supporting the development of theory (McNiff and Whitehead, 2006). Thus, praxis supports the notion of *informed* practice because ideas are understood in terms of the way they relate to the *lived world* as opposed to purely existing in the abstract (Kincheloe, 1991).

For Freire, in particular, praxis is linked to consciousness-raising and transformation from the bottom up (Christians, 2005). Applied to an early childhood context this might mean raising the consciousness of the practitioners and children in a given setting, for instance, in relation to conceptions of 'childhood' and 'adulthood'. Through developing an understanding of their own positions and disrupting commonly held views about the relative subject positionings of 'child' and 'adult', practitioners might develop more respectful ways of working that acknowledge the rights of adults and children alike. From small beginnings – in this case an early childhood setting – Freire would argue that wider social transformation takes place (Christians, 2005).

Not only does action research focus on making changes to practice, it also focuses on the *process* of the research (MacNaughton, 2001). We will see this in more detail when we discuss the action research cycle, but first we will look at *who* carries out action research.

WHO DOES ACTION RESEARCH? THE PRACTITIONER-RESEARCHER

In order to carry out action research, researchers need to spend a considerable amount of time in a setting, such as a nursery. Therefore it is an approach that is particularly suited to those of you that are working in a setting or for those of you that are able to spend a substantial length of time in a setting, such as if you are studying part-time and have access to a setting that is willing to work with you. The reason for emphasising the importance of having a close, long-term relationship with a setting can be seen in the following bullet-pointed list that outlines some of the key features of the action research approach:

- It is a *social* process.
- It is *participatory.*
- It is *practical* and *collaborative.*
- It is *emancipatory.*
- It is *critical.*
- It is *reflexive.*
- It aims to *transform* both theory and practice (Kemmis and McTaggart, 2005: 566–8).

Action research, then, is carried out by practitioners or sometimes by researchers working closely with a group of practitioners, who, as noted previously, have a desire to change and improve their practice in some way. Thus, it is rooted in the idea that research is not the preserve of those working in academia, for example, professional researchers within universities (Greenwood and Levin, 2000). Therefore Elliott (1991: 45) believes that action research should be regarded as 'cultural innovation' because it threatens the traditional divide between professional learning and academia.

Elliott (1991) also notes that it is practitioners *themselves,* with their desire to improve their practice, that *initiate* action research. This differs to other changes that are made in professional practice.

⌇ Reflection point

Let us continue to think about the reception class team and the development of the key person approach. *Who* is likely to impact on the professional practice of these practitioners? In what way(s) might they do this?

As noted earlier, there is a range of people that might impact upon the reception class team's practice in relation to developing a key person approach. These might include the headteacher of the school or Foundation Stage coordinator; or possibly the local authority's early years' advisory team. In some areas of practice, government policy, such as the Early Years Foundation Stage (DfES, 2007) might have a direct impact. This can be seen in the requirement to have a key person in place to support young children and their families in the Foundation Stage.

The focus on the practitioner as researcher has been promoted as invigorating the practitioner's professional development. Sachs (1999) believes that this is because teachers (we would broaden this to include all early childhood practitioners) are at the centre of producing and disseminating the knowledge about practice they have gained through their research.

But we should not think of this in terms of *individual* practitioners – after all, early years practitioners rarely work in isolation. Another characteristic of action research is the *collaborative* nature of the inquiry. The democratic nature of action research is put forward by some writers as a challenge to traditional models of research, which are lead by academics in universities. Greenwood and Levin (2000: 96), for instance, employ the term 'co-generative inquiry' in relation to action research to highlight the way that knowledge is co-generated through the collaborative processes of the research and the way that the diversity of experience, knowledge and skills within an action research team are valued. Early childhood practice, like other professional work, is a social practice involving many people. Thus, in order to transform practice/praxis, change is necessarily a social and political process (Kemmis, 2008). For this reason, Kemmis (2008: 124) argues that in action research, practice needs to be understood 'not solely from the perspectives of the individuals involved, but also in terms of the collective understandings and collective efforts of those involved or affected by the practice'.

THE ACTION RESEARCH CYCLE

The process of action research is best regarded as a process that works in spirals of self-reflective cycles (Kemmis and McTaggart, 2005). Figure 8.1 shows what these action research cycles might look like.

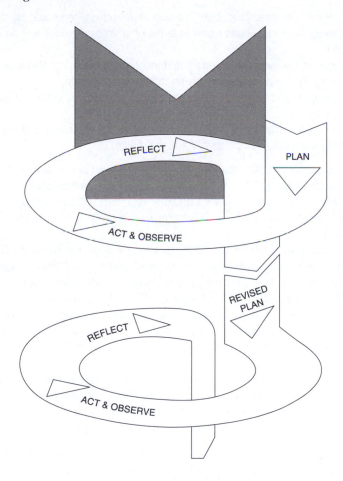

Figure 8.1 The action research spiral (Kemmis and Taggart, 2005: 564)

Movement through the action research cycle occurs as the practitioners engaged in the study reflect critically on what they are doing, the changes they have made and the changes in their understandings. MacNaughton (2001: 212) views critical reflection as the 'motor that drives the research process' – without it an action research project grinds to a halt.

Schmuck (2006: 18–19) sees action research more in terms of moving from the present situation towards a particular desired goal in a series of seven problem-solving steps:

1. *Specify the problem.* This involves a consideration of what the actual situation is like and the position the practitioner is hoping to move towards.
2. *Assess the situation with force-field analysis.* This means a consideration of forces that help to facilitate change and those that restrain change.
3. *Specify multiple solutions.* This step involves being creative in brainstorming a range of solutions to the perceived problem and considering the factors that act to restrain the change from happening at the present time.
4. *Plan for action.* Here, the researcher looks critically at the ideas generated by the brainstorming process and develops a more coherent plan in terms of what to do, who will do it, in what order, and when to do it.
5. *Anticipate obstacles.* In this step it is important to think through the things that may stand in the way of the plan working. This may involve modifying the plan in some way.
6. *Take action.* This step involves implementing the action plan, carrying out the planned changes and reflecting on them in action.
7. *Evaluate.* The final step involves reflecting on the strengths and weaknesses of the actions taken so far and then using this evaluation to identify a new problem.

The new problem then forms the starting point for the next set of seven steps of problem-solving, which Schmuck (2006) views as crucial in continuous self-improvement. Therefore we can see that Schmuck sees these seven steps as operating in a cyclical way. A common denominator in much of the literature about action research is how it operates in a series of cycles.

However, we want to suggest that the process of moving through these cycles (or Schmuck's 'problem-solving steps') is messier and more fluid than suggested thus far. Stages have a tendency to overlap and by reflecting on experience, some initial ideas are changed or modified (Kemmis and McTaggart, 2005). This also seems to reflect the nature of early childhood work as there are rarely easy answers to improving practice. In addition, given the multiple and fluid perspectives that exist in relation to different aspects of early childhood practice, it is unlikely that universal 'answers' to improving practice are possible or knowable.

Ⓖ Further to this, Kemmis and McTaggart (2005: 566–8) argue, there is a tendency to get fixated with the cyclical nature of action research, that is, its **methodology** and methods at the expense of its other features. You may recall that earlier in this chapter we highlighted the following features of action research:

- It is a *social* process.
- It is *participatory.*
- It is *practical* and *collaborative.*

- It is *emancipatory.*
- It is *critical.*
- It is *reflexive.*
- It aims to *transform* both theory and practice.

While we agree that the values and ideas that underpin action research are of central importance, we also think a brief discussion of the methods that might be employed in action research is useful here as it also further underlines the distinctiveness of action research.

METHODS USED IN ACTION RESEARCH

Action research is an *approach* to research that might employ a range of **qualitative** and **quantitative** methods depending on what the researcher wants to find out about their own particular setting/practice (MacNaughton, 2001). Indeed, Greenwood and Levin (2000: 93) argue that action research should use any methods, from a range of disciplines if necessary, in order to 'address the problem in hand'. Therefore, any of the methods discussed in Part 3 of this book might well be used. However, as noted previously, in considering action research we should not become *overly* preoccupied with the technical aspects of research methods (Kemmis and McTaggart, 2005).

Let us continue to think about the reception class team, who are beginning to adopt a key person approach to working with children and families. We will do this in order to highlight the methods the practitioners might employ as part of the action research.

- The team might use *journaling* in order to document their initial and changing thoughts about adopting this new way of working. Brown and Jones (2001) particularly emphasise writing as a research tool in action research and we will think about this further in Chapter 12.
- They might send a *questionnaire* to parents in the initial and maybe later part of a cycle to elicit their views on this aspect of practice.
- The practitioner leading the action research might facilitate a focus group *interview* or even interview the practitioners in the team individually in order to elicit their initial and subsequent feelings about the key person approach. It is likely that any changes to practice will be monitored by the team and then discussed in team meetings, which might also be recorded in some way.
- The team might analyse and review any *documents* they have in this area.
- The team might carry out timed *observations* to gain an understanding of the number of adults a child has contact with in a given period, such as a day or week in order to gain a picture of the initial situation prior to adopting a key person approach (assuming they think this should be kept to a minimum). They might also use observation to monitor whether the number of adults a child is expected to interact with decreases once the key person approach is adopted. Another way of using observation might be to carry out some detailed, narrative observations of registration and story times at the initial planning, sometimes called 'reconnaissance' phase of the action research cycle (let us imagine that these classroom events happen as a group of 30 children with one teacher at present, with other members of the team, such as a nursery nurse, engaged in setting-up tasks). The team might instigate a change to practice that involves going into smaller key groups for registration and story times and could monitor the impact of this new practice through observation.

Reflection point

Given what has been said so far in this chapter, how does action research differ from a practitioner's usual professional practice? Is it not usual for a practitioner or group of practitioners to try to improve their practice when they perceive something is not working as well as they would like or if they have to implement something new?

The question raised in this reflection point is one we will consider in the next section as it is a criticism sometimes levelled at action research.

THE POSSIBILITIES AND LIMITATIONS OF ACTION RESEARCH

Much could be said about the possibilities and limitations of action research – indeed it would be a chapter in itself. We will, however, confine ourselves to a brief discussion of what we feel are the key issues.

Action research is conducted by practitioners in areas that relate directly to their own practice. It therefore offers a challenge to the idea that research is the preserve of traditional academia. It is also context specific (Greenwood and Levin, 2000). This, as has been suggested, is the strength of action research, but it is also a limitation – not least because the findings cannot be generalised. However, further to this, Campbell et al. (2004) point out, as we have done, that issues relating to professional practice are complex and there are rarely easy solutions, if indeed 'solutions' are possible or even desirable (Brown and Jones, 2001). Possibly, there is a danger that practitioners might naively think that action research can solve all the problems that manifest themselves in their professional work (Campbell et al., 2004).

In addition to this, it might be easy to confuse action research with what practitioners do anyway – reflecting upon and improving their practice. Like the previous reflection point noted, this is something that could be levelled at action research. We believe, therefore, that it is important to reflect upon some of the underpinning premises behind any project undertaken. A distinction between action research and what practitioners do routinely in their practice, for instance, can be seen in the idea of praxis. This is because an understanding and application of theory to practice and practice to theory is important to action research but is not necessarily a *routine* part of every practitioner's daily work. Our hope, though, is that those of you who work with young children and are studying on early childhood related courses apply your professional work to the ideas you are introduced to in your studies and equally, your studies to your practice.

We should also be cautious about emphasising the claim that action research is empowering to practitioners, owing to the way they themselves identify and initiate change. Campbell et al. (2004) discuss practitioner research and professional development in education, with a focus on teachers. They argue that the growth in evidence-based practice, with teachers conducting school-based research, has had a tendency to focus on raising *standards* rather than *empowering* the teachers themselves. Moreover, they draw upon Elliott's work to argue that the promotion and funding of such research has served to legitimise the government's agenda – one of driving up educational standards. In an earlier reflection point, for example, we asked you to consider how action research might be conceptualised and which conceptualisation might be most attractive to governments.

Another issue relates to the democratic and collaborative nature of action research inquiry, discussed earlier (Greenwood and Levin, 2000). While we believe this is a positive feature of action research, it can also be problematic. On a very practical level, it can be difficult to stimulate interest in a research topic in a team, especially if the research is perceived as an add-on to their ordinary work. One's position within an organisation may be important here. A nursery manager, for example, may be able to use her or his higher position to engender support for a particular action research project but on ethical grounds would need to reflect on issues of power in relation to the research, for example, whether the nursery team would feel able to say 'no' to participating in the project or feel able to withdraw from it part of the way through. Further to this, there is an assumption within the notion of collaborative inquiry that the person leading the research is able to facilitate a group to work together effectively. Inevitably, managing group dynamics can be difficult, especially if the practitioner-researcher is inexperienced in this.

There are also advantages and disadvantages to being an 'insider', that is, a person who works in the setting where the research is carried out. On the positive side, it can be easier to gain access to a setting or a group of children – whatever the sample is for the research. The ongoing relationship a practitioner has with his or her colleagues may engender support that would be impossible for an 'outsider' to muster. An 'insider' is also more likely to be in tune with the issues that are pertinent to the particular context where they are planning to carry out the research when compared to an 'outsider'.

However, being an 'insider' can also be difficult. Examples of these difficulties are as follows: it may be easier for colleagues to ask for interviews and suchlike to be postponed as they may feel comfortable enough with the practitioner to say 'no' when compared to 'outside' researchers. This point links to power issues in research. In addition, when carrying out research as an 'insider', it is important to set boundaries around what you will and will not document. It would be very easy to document the comments of colleagues in unguarded moments in the staffroom, if pertinent to the study, but the practitioner-researcher would have to consider the ethics of doing this – after all, in a one-off interview situation, the interviewee is clear about the boundaries of the interview in terms of the time and space in which it takes place. This is less clear in action research, especially when one is an 'insider'.

Finally, action research may not necessarily change the world, but it does not claim to do this and it would be a huge claim for *any* research! But as Kemmis and McTaggart (2005) note, it does have the potential to improve things for 'particular people in particular places and in many other places where their stories have traveled' (p. 600). Thus, there may well be a gradual shift in practice as other practitioners become familiar with the research. This can be seen in the following example of Penny Holland's (2003) research.

 Research in focus

Penny Holland's (2003) research into young children's war, weapon and superhero play did not result in an *immediate* change in early childhood practice beyond that of herself and the practitioners engaged in the research. Indeed she rejects strongly what she describes as 'a neatly packaged alternative strategy to zero tolerance of this area of play' (ibid.: 95). Over time, her work has been disseminated to a worldwide audience through her writings, workshop sessions with practitioners, conference papers and interviews with the media. Gradually, many practitioners are coming to know her work and are beginning to ask similar questions of their *own* practice, but owing to their different subjectivities and different contexts may come to different understandings and alternative ways of developing their practice. Thus, the uncritical acceptance of an unwritten rule that 'you can't play with guns here' is beginning to be questioned widely as her story has travelled.

Key points from the chapter

- Action research is concerned with changing and improving *practice* in some way.
- It is initiated and carried out by practitioners working in a setting, sometimes with the help of a facilitator such as a professional researcher.
- It is particularly appropriate for those of you that are working in a setting or have the opportunity to spend a considerable length of time in a setting that is willing to work with you on an action research project.
- Action research is often regarded as democratic and emancipatory owing to its focus on collaborative working and the focus on the *practitioner* as researcher as opposed to a more traditional research model where a researcher *outside* of professional practice initiates, carries out, analyses and evaluates a piece of research.
- Action research operates in a series of cycles, each involving reflections on practice.
- A variety of methods or combinations of methods may be used in action research depending on the focus of the project being undertaken.
- Despite the cyclical nature of action research, some advocates of the approach argue that the primary focus of action research is not its methodology but its capacity to transform practice.
- While action research does not try to affect change on a grand scale – it is particular to people and contexts – it has the capacity to make changes on a wider scale as people tell the stories of their research and share their reflections on practice.

Further reading

Brown, T. and Jones, L. (2001) *Action Research and Postmodernism: Congruence and Critique.* Buckingham: Open University Press. This is a challenging read if you are new to research methods but we recommend it as highly thought-provoking with some interesting early childhood exemplars of action research in practice from Liz Jones' own research in a nursery classroom.

McNiff, J. and Whitehead, J. (2006) *All You Need to Know About Action Research.* London: Sage. Primarily concerned with action research in schools, this book is a very useful overview of action research with some practical examples of action research in action.

PART 3
METHODS

In Part 2 we learned that there are a variety of strategies or approaches that can be used to structure research; we discussed surveys, ethnography, case studies and action research. This part of the book looks at the data gathering instruments or methods that might be employed in research.

Although some research studies will only use one method to collect data, it is common for more than one method to be used. Sometimes this is a pragmatic decision; for example, if you wanted to investigate the understanding of parents and practitioners about role play, it may be practical to interview all the staff but impractical to interview *all* the parents, so a questionnaire may be used. Using more than one method can also be used to enhance the validity of a study by looking at a topic from a variety of different perspectives (a form of triangulation).

You may recall from Chapter 2 that there is some debate as to whether one should mix methods that 'belong' to different methodologies, in the same research study. For instance, highly structured questionnaires lie within quantitative methodology, underpinned by the positivist paradigm, whereas informal interviews lie within qualitative methodology and the interpretivist or post-structuralist paradigms; some researchers would consider that combining methods in this way is inadvisable (Denzin and Lincoln, 2005).

In this part we begin by looking at three methods with which you may already be quite familiar: observations, interviews and questionnaires. We look at theoretical and practical issues to do with these methods as well and give examples of how these methods have been applied in early childhood research. In Chapters 12 and 13 we look at using documents and other visual texts, and journaling as a research tool. Using documents as a method of obtaining data has a long tradition, especially in disciplines such as history, but are also useful in early childhood research. In the chapter on journaling we introduce you to the idea that 'you' as the researcher, are a legitimate source of information. For example, reflections recorded immediately after conducting an interview can add powerful contextual information and insights. In ethnographic studies, the interactions between the researcher and the individual, or group being studied, may reveal additional and salient levels of understanding.

Finally, in Chapter 14 we look at creative ways of involving children in research. These include ways of giving children 'voice', by giving them cameras, looking at their drawings, listening to their narratives and stories and sharing in their play. This chapter is the practical application of one of the principles outlined in Part 1 – listening to children – although we recognise that interviewing and observation, in particular, continue to be important methods in early childhood research.

9 OBSERVATION

Chapter objectives

- To consider how observations have been used as a classic method in early childhood research
- To discuss the different types of observational methods available and their uses in research
- To look at the possibilities and limitations of using observations in early childhood research

One of the characteristics of early childhood care and education is the emphasis that is placed on the role of child observation as a tool to help practitioners understand the children they care for, so they can provide appropriate experiences that will promote the children's learning and development. When used in this way, observations can supply information about a particular child or group of children, which can be used for planning and assessment. You may have used observations of children as part of a course, to help you learn more about child development.

In early childhood *research*, observations are used as a way of gathering primary **data** as part of both **qualitative** and **quantitative** methodologies. The decision about which observational method to choose will depend upon the research question that is being investigated and the use to which the findings will be put. In this chapter we will look at a variety of observational methods that are available and their possibilities and limitations.

HISTORICAL OVERVIEW

Human survival depends upon individuals being able to observe the world around them accurately. At its most basic level, accurate observational skills help us to avoid dangers and keep us safe. As social beings, much of our learning depends on us observing what others are doing; the actions and reactions of people around us. As Rolfe (2001: 224) comments, 'Observation is something we do'.

Children became a focus of *systematic* observation in the eighteenth century when Rousseau suggested that children's behaviour was worthy of study in an attempt to promote their 'natural development' (Fawcett, 1996: 10). Of course people were observing children prior to this, as parents commonly made anecdotal records of what their children were doing and how they were developing. Following Rousseau's lead, there was a succession of publications by educationalists, such as Pestalozzi, who recorded their children's early development, leading to what may be considered one of the most important forerunners of **child study**: the observations undertaken by Charles Darwin of his son (Darwin, 1877).

 Reflection point

Charles Darwin's work can be viewed online: http://darwin-online.org.uk/content/frame-set?itemID=F1779&viewtype=text&pageseq=1 (accessed 24 August 2008).

Read 'A biographical sketch of an infant'. What similarities can you find between this observational study and observations about children you may have read or conducted yourself?

The child study came to be seen as a legitimate tool for the study of child psychology and Fawcett (1996) describes how, at the beginning of the twentieth century, universities in the USA opened up child study centres where parents were encouraged to bring their children so that they could be observed under 'controlled' laboratory conditions. Some psychologists, however, expressed concern that behaviour observed under controlled laboratory conditions may not be a true reflection of how children behave in their natural environment. As a response to this there was a move to undertake observations of children in their normal, everyday settings. Fawcett describes this as the 'Ecological approach' as it takes account of 'the child's real habitat: the location, other people present, and the expectations and rules under which the child is operating' (Fawcett, 1996: 13).

In Europe, psychoanalysts such as Freud, psychologists such as Piaget and educationalists such as Susan Isaacs all used observations on children to further their knowledge (Fawcett, 1996). Observations and measurements of children continue to inform the work of developmental psychologists. Without systematic child observation:

- Piaget (Wadsworth, 1996) and Bruner (2006) would not have been able to formulate their theories on cognitive development
- Bowlby (1969) and Ainsworth (Ainsworth et al., 1978) would not have been able to recognise the importance of human attachment
- Athey (1990) would not have developed her ideas about children's schemas.

Child observations have also contributed to the compilation of schedules of development or developmental norms (descriptions of sequential steps, or milestones, that most children pass through as they mature). Perhaps one of the most well known of these schedules of development was devised by Mary Sheridan. Originally published in the 1960s, the most recent version was published in 2008 (Sheridan et al., 2008). The developmental norm approach has been the subject of much criticism for advocating a 'one size fits all' approach to child development and because it can fail to take into account the wide variety of factors that might impact upon the development of children around the world, including culture and economic disadvantage. These variations can mean that using checklists or a milestone approach may be unhelpful as 'the unique individuality of every growing person can easily be devalued by over concentration on measurement and the achievement of norms' (Fawcett,1996: 17).

WHEN IS IT APPROPRIATE TO USE OBSERVATION IN RESEARCH?

Before we investigate when it is appropriate to use observations in research we need to look a little closer into what we mean by the term 'observation'. When we observe something we use all of our senses, as this is the way that we take in information about the world around us.

〰 Reflection point

It is lunch time at a nursery. Joe is sitting with his key children around the table, interacting with the children as they eat their pasta and sauce. Fumi, a girl aged 18 months, is eating with obvious enthusiasm and, at the same time, is experimenting with the food on her plate. She is laughing and tries to feed him with her spoon.
   What senses might Joe be using to take in and process (perceive) this information?

You may reflect that Joe is using his eyes and ears, his sense of touch, taste and smell. In fact Joe is using all his senses.

We use the same processes whether we are interviewing, administering a questionnaire or making a direct observation, and Rolfe (2001: 226) suggests that 'if we define observation broadly as one person's perception' then we could say that all research is based on observation. However, in this chapter, we will be focusing on *direct observation* of participants' behaviour, be they children, parents, early years practitioners or other individuals relevant to a piece of research.

Coolican (2004) makes the distinction between observation being used as a method of data collection *within* the overall **research design**, or *as* the overall research design. When observations are used as the overall design of a piece of research, the study is often known as an 'observational study' to make it clear to the reader that they are not looking at experimental research. You will find information on research design in Chapter 15.

- An example of observations being used as a method of data collection is the structured observations focusing on the 'quality' of pre-school settings as part of the EPPE project (Sylva et al., 2003). Within this longitudinal study there were a variety of methods of data collection used, including structured observations.
- Another example of observations being used as the overall research design is the work conducted by Plowman and Stephen (2003) where in-depth observations of pre-school children's use of information and communications technology (ICT) were conducted in seven pre-school settings.

Rolfe (2001) considers that observations are useful when researchers want to understand or explain everyday behaviours, or examine the effect of something on everyday behaviour. Often, with very young children and babies, it may be the only way of obtaining information because they may lack the communication skills needed to give an interview or fill in a questionnaire.

TYPES OF OBSERVATION

Observations can vary across a number of dimensions. Already in this chapter we have made the distinction between observations undertaken within a *laboratory* and those undertaken in a *naturalistic* environment. We will now look at a few of these types of observation.

Laboratory or naturalistic?

- *Laboratory observations.* These are carried out in a controlled environment that has been set up by the researcher in an effort to make the situation as similar as possible for all participants. When studying children, a laboratory may be a room set up like a nursery, with a one-way mirror on one wall, through which a researcher can observe what is going on in the room, but with the participants unable to see the researcher. The advantage of laboratory observations is that all participants are observed in conditions that are, as near as possible, the same, reducing the effect of confounding variables. This is the 'scientific' or experimental approach and you can read more about this in Chapter 1. The disadvantage is that researchers may not be seeing 'normal' behaviour, as the participant is not in their everyday environment (Hayes, 2001).
- *Naturalistic observations.* These are undertaken in the everyday setting of the participant, which in young children's case might be their home or nursery setting. These are the type of observations that most practitioners are familiar with and are not without limitations.

〰 Reflection point

In a naturalistic observation it is *impossible* to ensure that all the participants are observed under the same conditions. If a child is being observed in their own home, or in a nursery, what sort of variables might have an effect on the child's behaviour? Does this matter?

The kinds of variables that might have an effect on the child's behaviour could include the physical environment, the people with whom the child is interacting and the presence or not of the observer. In experimental research this would be considered problematic, because it is difficult to control variables in a naturalistic situation. However, as you may recall from Chapter 2, it could also be argued that researchers should try to observe children in a naturalistic environment in recognition that children grow and develop in complex social worlds – not worlds that can be easily controlled. Thus, researchers should try to observe children in the context of their everyday lives (Dunn, 2005).

Quantitative or qualitative?

Observations can either be quantitative in nature or qualitative. We have looked at this classification several times already in this book as it is one of the main methodological distinctions in planning research.

- *Quantitative observations*, sometimes known as structured observations, are designed to give standardised, numerical data, in an effort to reduce the number of variables and improve **reliability** of the findings. Johnson and Christensen (2008: 211) suggest that the following variables could be standardised in quantitative observations: who is observed, what is observed, when observations are to take place, where the observations are to be carried out, and how the observations are to be done. Very often, in large studies involving several observers, training is given before hand to increase the reliability of the observations.

- *Qualitative observations* are often undertaken for exploratory purposes and exactly what will be observed is not specified beforehand. Qualitative observations are usually undertaken in naturalistic situations, with *what* the researcher records being guided by the overall aim of the research and interesting things that they see at the time. In the Froebel Blockplay Research Project, for instance, many observations of children playing with blocks were carried out over time (Gura, 1992).

Participant or non participant observation?

Another dimension to the type of observation being used is the degree to which the researcher/observer is *part* of the actual observation. Consider the scenario outlined previously when Joe was observing Fumi as she ate her lunch. Joe, while observing, was also fully participating in the exchange. You may recall that participant observation is a key component of ethnographic research and is discussed in Chapter 6. Although the degree to which an observer is a participant or not lies on a continuum, for convenience sake, Johnson and Christensen (2008) have identified four conditions.

- *Complete participation* is where the observer is a full member of the group being studied. If the researcher is a complete participant it is not usual to inform the group about the research aim, as this may alter the group's behaviour towards the researcher. This aspect of *complete* participation is considered unethical as it involves deception and the participants have not been given the right 'not to participate'. In Chapter 6 we discussed this in relation to Fielding's (2008) covert study of the National Front. Students should *not* be engaging in research that involves deception.
- *Participant as observer* is when the researcher spends a considerable amount of time with a group and attempts to become a full member of the group, but explains to the group from the beginning that they are conducting research. This is similar to practitioner research in early years settings. The staff team will be fully aware that the researcher is undertaking observations (and for what purpose) and may give insightful comments on what has been recorded or even help with data collection. If observing children, it is important to gain the written permission of parents too.
- *Observer as participant* is when the researcher spends only a limited amount of time with the group s/he is observing, seeking permission from the participants to join in only with the activities that they wish to observe. This is similar to a student on a course attending a session for a limited amount of time a week. The advantage of this is that it is easier to remain objective, but a complete understanding of what is happening may be difficult to attain because the observer remains an outsider (Johnson and Christensen, 2008).
- *The complete observer* does not involve themselves with the group being observed at all. S/he remains anonymous and endeavours not to be noticed by the participants. An example of this may be a researcher observing children playing in a public place, where Johnson and Christensen (2008) consider that the participants do not need to be informed that they are being observed. The advantage of this type of observation is that the participants' behaviour is likely to be completely natural, but the information obtained will lack the insiders' point of view.

 Reflection point

You may wish to reflect upon the advisability of observing children in this covert way. Although your intentions may be innocent, your behaviour may be misinterpreted by others. Is it ethical to carry out research without informed consent? Could you call the people being observed 'participants' in this type of study?

Narrative methods

Narrative observations are those which endeavour to write down in everyday language (or otherwise record) what the participant says or does. Narrative methods are qualitative in nature, although it may be possible to reduce the information obtained to allow a quantitative analysis if this is thought appropriate.

We will be describing three main methods: naturalistic observations, target child observations and diary entries. There is no real agreement about what each method is called and you will find different sources will use different terms to describe similar methods. Rolfe (2001) suggests that to avoid confusion it is best to focus on what the method *involves*, rather than its *name*.

Naturalistic observations
Naturalistic observations are also known as narrative observations, descriptive narratives, running records and written observations. Although this is a reasonably straightforward method, and often the one that students of early years' care and education are introduced to first, it is by no means an easy skill to acquire. This method involves observers writing down exactly what they see and hear as it happens. Observers usually use a notebook to record what they see, often using abbreviations to speed up the process, writing up the observation neatly as soon as is practical, while what has been seen is still fresh in the memory.

There are several points to remember when writing a naturalistic observation:

- The present tense is used.
- Only behaviour is recorded, the observation will be analysed at a later date, so you would not write 'F was upset when he came into the nursery' because that is an interpretation of his behaviour.
- Using initials instead of using participants' names can be confusing. You can use pseudonyms instead. As long as the real names of the setting and the participants are not used you will be able to maintain confidentiality. If you work with young children and you are carrying out observations as part of your *professional* work, you would retain the child's real name so that the information can contribute to the child's record. It is good practice in research to share your observations with participants.

The main advantage of this method is that behaviour can be recorded as it happens and little advance preparation is needed. The disadvantage is that decisions have to be made about exactly what to record; if there is a lot going on something might be missed.

Moreover, the data that is produced is *unstructured* and will require careful analysis later on and, although it will give you information about that particular event, it is hard to *compare* observations.

Excerpt from a naturalistic observation

Date: 25-08-08   **Time observation starts**: 07.55

Time observation finishes: 08.05

Child's initial: F (or pseudonym)   **Gender**: M

Age: 1:3   **D.O.B**: 25-05-07

Main language of child: English

Context: Children's centre in inner city London, toddler room. F is being brought into the centre by his mother M. He has been attending for 2 weeks. F's key person has seen the family arrive and is waiting for them.

Number and age of other children: 2 children 1:6 and 2:1

Number of adults: 2 F's key person K and 1 other.

M pushes open the door and ushers F into the room. He has tears on his face and holds onto M's legs, burying his head in her skirt.

M: 'What's all this about? You enjoyed yourself yesterday. Don't cry. Look, here is K.' M picks F up, he buries his head in her shoulder.

K approaches F, she touches his shoulder gently.

K: 'Hi F. Don't you want to play with me today? M why don't you help F take off his coat? Shall we see if F remembers where his peg is?'

M puts F on the ground and F lets her take the coat off.

M: 'Can you show me your peg F?'

F points to where the pegs are, he walks towards them and M finds his peg.

M: leaves the room. F looks at her going and begins to cry loudly. He goes towards the shut door. He tries to open it, but can't. He sits on the floor, banging his feet on the door. He is still crying loudly.

Target child method

This method was developed during the 1970s as part of the Oxford Pre-School Project (Sylva et al., 1980) and was used as a research tool in the EPPE project (Sylva et al., 2003) where it was originally used to discover the situations which promoted children's concentration. Green (2007) comments that the method is also useful for noting socialisation and language use. The method involves the use of a pre-prepared template on which to record the observation, which makes use of pre-decided abbreviations. This is particularly useful if more than one observer is involved in data collection. The following is a list of commonly used codes, but any code can be used as long as it is decided before hand and every observer uses the same codes.

- Activity codes:
  - TC = target child (the child's name or initials are not used)
  - C = child
  - A = adult
- Language codes:
  - To record language (what the child is saying), you would simply write: TC>C, if the target child is speaking to another child, or TC>A, if they are speaking to an adult.

- Task codes:
  - LMM = large muscle movement
  - LSC = large-scale construction
  - SSC = small-scale construction
  - MAN = manipulation
  - SM = structured materials
  - PS = problem solving
  - SVT = scale-version toys
  - IG = informal games
  - SINP = social interaction, non-play
  - DB= distress behaviour
  - This is just an example of what can be an extensive list.

- Social codes:
  - SOL = the target child is playing on their own (solitary)
  - PAIR = the child is with one other person, child or adult
  - SG = the target child is within a small group (three to five children)
  - LG = the target child is within a large group (six or more children)
  - PAIR/P = the target child is playing parallel to one other child
  - SG/P = the target child is playing parallel to a small group
  - LG/P = the target child is playing parallel to a large group
  - If there is an adult interacting with an activity, there would be a circle drawn around the social code.

Excerpt from a target child observation			
Details of the child and the setting (Note: these details will be similar to the ones recorded for the naturalistic observation described previously)			
Activity record	**Language record**	**Task code**	**Social code**
TC takes cup in right hand. Pushes it under the sand and brings it up filled with sand. Holds funnel in left hand. Pours sand from cup into funnel.	TC>C Look it's falling	MAN	PAIR
C adds water to the sand. TC stirs it around. C puts the damp sand in to the cup. TC takes cup and tries to pour the sand into the funnel.	C>TC it won't go	MAN PS	PAIR

Once observers have memorised the codes, this method is a time efficient way of observing children's behaviour. It is useful for identifying children who are not socialising with other children or who rarely communicate.

The clinical interview

Jarvis et al. (2004) describe how this method of observation, involving a mixture of observation and interview, was developed by Piaget, as a way of trying to understand young children's thinking and reasoning. Piaget would watch children playing or trying to complete a task and then ask them questions about what they were doing and why they were doing it. In clinical interviewing there are no set questions because the questions depend on what the child is doing and later questions depend on the answers to the earlier ones. The disadvantage of this method is that children are not all asked the same questions so the findings are not generalisable. In addition, there is a danger that the children's intentions can be misinterpreted. For example, Jarvis et al. (2004) describe how clinical interviews were used to suggest that children believe in *animism*: a belief that inanimate objects are alive and can understand the children. Jarvis et al. point out that if a child hits a teddy and calls it 'naughty', it may not mean that the child believes the toy is alive, the child may just be engaged in imaginative play.

The diary method

Diaries contain records of significant events that have been observed over a period of time and may contain both observational material together with personal reflection and analysis. There are no hard and fast guidelines as to what should be recorded in a diary, as the observers decide for themselves what is worthy of inclusion. Coolican (2004) considers that diaries can be a rich source of information as they can document change, however they can become highly subjective, making any comparison with other diary studies very difficult. Chapters 6 (ethnography), 12 (documents) and 13 (journaling as a research tool) in this book provide further information about the use of diaries and field notes in research.

Structured methods

In narrative observations, children's behaviour is recorded in some detail, often with no prior decision as to *exactly* what should be observed. *Structured* observational methods narrow down the focus of the observation and are often guided by a very *precise* aim. Most structured observations are quantitative in nature and can generate numerical data. We will be looking at three different types of structured observation in this section: the time sample, the event sample and the checklist.

Time samples

Time samples involve observing a participant (adult or child), group of participants, or an area of the nursery at regular intervals during the day. Before observing, it is important to be clear about:

• the *aim* of the observation

- *who* or *what* is being observed
- exactly *what* will be recorded
- how *often* the recordings will be made
- the *length* of each recording.

Before starting to observe, a grid should be drawn up. For example, it may be that the aim is to investigate what proportion of the day staff members are interacting with children as opposed to being involved in other activities. The recording grid may look like this:

Extract from a time sample recording adult–child interaction Total number of staff in room: 5			
Time	No interaction	Interacting with 1 child	Interacting with more than 1 child
09.00	3	1	1
09.15	3	0	2
09.30	1	2	2
09.45	0	3	2
10.00	4	0	1
11.45	4	0	1
Total			

Time samples need to be repeated at different times of the day and different days of the week, as just one observation will not help you reveal if there is any consistent pattern. Rolfe (2001) notes that enough time samples need to be made to enable the researcher to make some generalisations about the behaviour of individuals or groups.

Time samples can be used to look at individual children, such as observing a child every 5 minutes to see what the child is doing. This can be very time-consuming, and the researcher is unlikely to be able to do much else, unless some sort of timer is used as a reminder when to look up and find the child. The advantage of time samples in research is that they are repeatable and it is possible to 'measure' the success of an intervention by undertaking 'before' and 'after' observations (as long as it is remembered to keep variables such as the time of day and day of the week constant). The disadvantage of time samples is that examples of the behaviour under observation could be missed because they fall in between two time points. In addition, the information recorded may lack detail.

Event samples

Event samples are similar to time samples, except that instead of **sampling** at regular times, a particular event is chosen, whenever it occurs (Rolfe, 2001). This type of observation is very useful for looking at aspects of children's behaviour, for example, the researcher may wish to find out what is provoking a child's frequent 'temper tantrums', or why a particular area of the nursery appears to provoke conflict among the children.

When investigating instances of challenging behaviour it is useful to know the ABC of the event (Mukherji, 2001):

- *Antecedent*: what was going on immediately beforehand that may have provoked the event?
- *Behaviour*: what the child/children did, possibly as a response to what was going on beforehand.
- *Consequences*: what followed on immediately after the event?

The following is an example of an event sample used to investigate a child's 'temper tantrums'.

Excerpt from an event sample			
Time	Record of event	What was happening immediately before-hand	What was the outcome of the event
09.15	F looks around and sees that his mother is leaving the room. He runs after her, holding on to her skirt. He yells and screams. He kicks her legs with his feet. 'Don't go' he cries.	F was playing in the sand tray. His mother, who was watching, quietly moves towards the door.	F's mother picks him up, cuddles him and says 'Don't worry, I will stay a bit longer'. F stops crying.
09.43	F is lying on his front on the floor, crying loudly. He is beating the floor with his fists. An adult goes towards him. He lashes out at her with his arm.	F was playing with the farm animals with another child, H. He grabbed a toy from H's hand, saying that he wants it. H asks an adult for help. The adult had explained to F that he should give the toy back to H.	H gives the toy to F. 'Here, you have it'. F stops crying. The adult finds another toy for H.

If this event sample was undertaken throughout a day it may be possible to detect that F's 'temper tantrums' occur in situations when he cannot get his own way. He may have learned that such behaviour may get him what he wants. The disadvantages of event samples are that observers need to be alert to what is going on around them, so that they are aware of the events as they occur. It is also necessary to be clear beforehand about exactly what constitutes an 'event' (Mukherji, 2001). In addition, if there is more than one observer, then training in recognising salient events will be necessary.

Checklists

Checklists are commonly used in recording aspects of child development and are commonly based on schedules of development such as Sheridan et al. (2008). The use of checklists to record children's development in early years' settings used to be very popular, and many local authorities provided settings with developmental booklets that could be used. However, the use of these checklists has fallen out of favour in recent years as it is recognised that a checklist approach contains very little information and should really be thought of as *summaries* of observations (Fawcett, 1996: 62). Checklists are still used as a guide for health professionals, and parents are invited to fill in checklists about their children's development in their personal child health record (NHS, 2006).

Excerpt from a checklist to assess vision in babies aged 2 months		
Behaviour	Yes	No
Baby opens his/her eyes and looks at parent		
Baby follows the movement of the parent's head by following with his/her eyes or by moving his/her head.		
Do the baby's eyes look normal?		

It is possible to make up checklists for practically any aspect of development, or work procedures. You may be familiar with checklists that are used by staff to record when a task has been completed. Data from checklists tend to be quantitative in nature and easy to analyse numerically.

RECORDING INFORMATION

Data-gathering devices

Most of the techniques we have looked at lend themselves to paper and pen methods of recording, although, a checklist could be entered electronically. Some researchers like to use digital camcorders to record events. The advantage of this is that you have permanently captured an event and can review it over and over again as Tobin et al. (1989) did in their study of pre-schools in three cultures. Unfortunately, unless recording under laboratory/studio conditions, it is often difficult to hear what is going on because of interference from the noise in an early years setting. The human ear is very good at screening out background noise, allowing you to concentrate on the event you are observing, but camcorders record everything, making analysis difficult at times.

The same applies to electronic sound recorders, such as Dictaphones, as trying to decipher what has been heard can be difficult. The other drawback of these methods is that participants may behave *differently* with recording devices around. Researchers tend to introduce these devices some time before using them in their research, to give participants a chance to get used to them and for their behaviour to return to 'normal'.

It is important to consider the additional ethical responsibilities that digital recording of observations presents. In recording observations in this way, it is imperative that participants have agreed to this method of recording and know how the recording will be used, that is, *who* will see it and *how long* the recording will be kept.

Research in focus

In the Bristol study of language development (Wells and Wells, 1984), radio microphones were used to record the language of 128 children. Half the children were approximately 15 months of age and half were approximately 39 months old. The children were recorded on several occasions in their own homes over a period of two and a half years. The children were fitted with radio microphones, which sent information to pre-programmed recording devices left in their homes. This enabled recordings to be made without the researchers being present. On each occasion that they were studied, eighteen 90-second samples of their speech were recorded. On the evening of the day that recordings were taken, researchers played the recordings to the children's parents, who were interviewed to obtain information about what was happening at the time of the recording, so the excerpts of language could be placed in context. Later, the recordings were transcribed. The study revealed common patterns of language development, with different rates of development.

- Using the information in this chapter describe what type of observation was used?
- What are the possibilities and limitations of recording language in this way?

In the 'Research in focus' feature the observations were a type of naturalistic, non-participant time sample. The main limitation is that the observer was not present and the parent had to be asked to supply contextual information. In addition not *all* speech is recorded in this method, which may have been illuminating. Nowadays it is likely that the observation would use visual recording as well.

Recording contextual information

When undertaking observations, it is important to have all the relevant details about the participants and the setting as there is nothing worse than realising, when it is too late, that a vital detail has not been recorded. The details that you need to record will vary according to the aim of your research study, but should include information that may have an influence on what you have observed. The following list *might* be pertinent to include:

- details of the child/children observed, such as age, date of birth, gender, ethnicity, language spoken, length of time at setting
- date, time and length of observation
- method of observation used
- details of the setting, for example, a playground, child's home, or playgroup
- details of the area in which the setting is located (rural/affluent suburb/multicultural inner city and suchlike)
- immediate context, for example, in the garden
- what was happening immediately before the observation
- details of the adults involved (numbers/roles and so on).

Clearly, if researchers are undertaking a *series* of observations in the same setting, or on the same child, many of these details only have to be recorded once. It is important to remember that permission should be sought from *all* involved and that you should maintain *confidentiality*. In addition, due consideration must be taken of data protection. Please see Chapter 3 where these details are looked at in some detail.

Observer bias

In this chapter we have looked at a variety of techniques, ranging from naturalistic observations where observers attempt to write down everything that they see, to the checklist approach where all that is required is a tick in a box if a particular event/aspect of development is seen. Observers are different. They have all had different life experiences (Reinharz, 1997) and these differences affect what they focus on when they are observing. For example, if you asked two observers to write a naturalistic observation of children playing outside, one person may have focused on the children's gross motor skills and their confidence in using the play equipment, while the other observer may have focused on how the children cooperated together. Physical characteristics of the observers, such as whether they are tired, too hot or cold, hungry or unwell may also contribute to their attention span and their ability to make accurate recordings. These considerations are important as they affect the *reliability* of observations. The use of some of the more structured forms of observing and the prior training of observers may overcome these effects to some extent.

In addition to the differences in what observers may record, different observers may *interpret* what they see in very different ways (Coffey, 1999).

⌁ Reflection point

Anil is 3 years old and has just started nursery. He lives with his parents who are of Indian descent, but who were born and brought up in the UK, and his grandmother, who came to the UK as a young woman. Anil communicates well in both Bengali and English. It has been observed that Anil is reluctant to feed himself and is still unable to put his coat on independently.

One observer is very worried about his development, fearing that he is lacking in independence skills. Another observer considers that his behaviour is completely normal. Why are there such different interpretations?

Factors such as culture, class, religion, level of education and past life experiences all contribute to the way we interpret what we see. We bring to the observation process our opinions and prejudices (Coffey, 1999). To increase objectivity, the researcher should aim to avoid including 'evaluations, judgements, impressions and personal speculations' when recording observations (Nicholson and Shipstead, 1998: 13, in Rolfe 2001).

Key points from the chapter

- There has been a long history of using child observations to further our understanding of child development and education.
- Observations can be undertaken in a laboratory or in naturalistic surroundings.
- Observers can be placed somewhere along a continuum, with complete participation in the situation being observed at one end, and complete non-participation at the other.
- Observations can be used to generate both qualitative and quantitative data.
- There is a variety of different methods of observation that can be used, from unstructured narrative types of observation to more structured methods.
- The self of the researcher impacts on what they see and how they analyse observations. Raising awareness of this, training and the use of more structured observations may help to overcome elements of bias.

Further reading

Dunn, J. (2005) 'Naturalistic observations of children and their families', in S. Green and D. Hogan (eds), *Researching Children's Experience: Methods and Approaches.* London: Sage. In this chapter, Dunn draws on her considerable experience of using observations as a way to study children's lives.

Fawcett, M. (1996) *Learning Through Child Observation.* London: Jessica Kingsley. This is a good basic text on child observation: theory and practice.

Rolfe, S. (2001) 'Direct observation', in G. MacNaughton, S. Rolfe and I. Siraj-Blatchford (eds), *Doing Early Childhood Research. International Perspectives on Theory and Practice.* Buckingham: Open University Press. In this chapter, Rolfe describes the decisions she made when planning a research study involving child observation, and gives an excellent overview of the topic.

10   INTERVIEWS

Chapter objectives

- To consider the use of interviews as a method in early childhood research
- To outline the different types of interview and the research paradigms that underpin them
- To reflect on key issues, which need to be considered when designing and conducting interviews with adults as well as children
- To consider ways of recording interviews
- To reflect on the possibilities and limitations of using interviews in early childhood research

It has been said that we live in an 'interview society' (Silverman, 1993). It is difficult to open a magazine or newspaper, or turn on the television without being made aware of how many interviews are conducted, not only to find out about current events and the world of celebrities, but also in more 'scientific' research. Interviews are a highly versatile research tool; they can be used in **quantitative** or **qualitative** research involving adults and children, as individuals or in groups. All of the approaches discussed in Part 2 of this book could involve the use of interviews as a way of obtaining **data**.

In this chapter we will outline the various types of interview that are available as tools for researchers to use and we will discuss some of the decisions that have to be made to ensure that interviews are reliable, valid and ethical.

WHAT IS AN INTERVIEW?

Fundamentally an interview is a method where one person asks questions of an individual or group of people with the expectation of getting answers to a particular question or an elaboration of their views on a particular topic.

 **Reflection point**

It is the first day of a course. You, and everyone else in your class, are new to the university and to each other. In a break from lectures you sit with another student in the student cafeteria. You tentatively start talking to her, revealing that you had felt anxious before you entered the classroom and asking her if she felt the same way. You find yourself asking questions to find out her name and how far she has travelled to get to university, while sharing these details about yourself. Gradually you begin to get to know each other.

In the developing conversation you both ask questions of each other, but one would not describe this as an interview; it is a conversation. What is the difference between an interview and a conversation?

Johnson and Christensen (2008: 203) define an interview as 'a data collection method in which an interviewer asks an interviewee questions'. In a conversation we frequently ask questions of each other, it is one of the ways we form and maintain relationships, and at first glance it is possible to conceive of these sorts of conversations as interviews. However, Densombe (2003) notes some important differences:

- There is consent to take part in an interview – the interviewee should know the purpose of the interview, how it will be recorded, how the data will be stored and what the information will be usedfor. This relates to the issue of 'informed consent' discussed in Chapter 3 and is clearly different from the informality of ordinary conversation.
- In addition, the words of the interviewee are likely to be analysed and written about in a way unlike usual conversation. The interviewee is 'on the record'.
- A conversation will often happen by chance and at the whim of the participants. Interviewing, on the other hand, needs more planning and even in unstructured interviewing (a term we will discuss later), there is an 'agenda' on the part of the interviewer.
- In an interview, the interviewer usually has some grasp of the subject under discussion, maybe through carrying out a thorough review of literature related to the topic, and the interviewee has lived experience of the issue being researched, which the researcher hopes to tap into (they may, of course, also share this experience). This is different to a conversation (Roberts-Holmes, 2005). We are sure you have had conversations where some or all of the participants have little knowledge or experience in relation to the topic under discussion but are happy to air their opinions.

In Chapter 11 we discuss another method of data collection, questionnaires. One of the fundamental differences between a questionnaire and an interview is that interviews are always *interpersonal* in some way, that is, there is always personal contact between the researcher (interviewer) and the participant (the interviewee). The interpersonal contact may not always be face to face as interviews can be conducted by telephone or video link. The extent to which the interview relationship develops is dependent on the research **paradigm** within which the research is located. As we will see, for positivist researchers, it is important to neutralise the effect of the interviewer whereas interpretivist researchers tend to value and analyse the effect of the researcher on the interviewee's responses (Fielding and Thomas, 2008).

WHEN TO USE INTERVIEWS

When discussing research proposals with students, it is our experience that often the first choice of data collection instrument is a questionnaire. This is because using a questionnaire seems to be viewed as less time-consuming when compared with interviewing. The perception is often that all that has to be done is to write out a list of questions, distribute the questionnaire and wait for the completed questionnaires to return. Chapter 11 will argue that it is nowhere near as straightforward as this, but it is true that a student could potentially obtain the views of many more people using a questionnaire than interviewing. However, it is important to stress that the information obtained from using questionnaires is likely to be more superficial than that obtained through an interview. Interviews are used when 'in-depth' information from participants is needed. Depending upon the type of interview used, the interviewer can clarify what the interviewee is trying to say, and can investigate areas of interest as they emerge, probing and teasing out strands of thought. This is a key advantage of interviewing as a research method (Robson, 1993). In all of the approaches described in Part 2 of this book (surveys, ethnography, case studies and action research) interviewing can be included as a way of collecting data.

TYPES OF INTERVIEW

Interviews can vary according to a number of dimensions:

- The underlying research **methodology**. Is the interview designed to produce quantitative or qualitative data?
- The degree of flexibility of the interview.
- The number of interviewees being interviewed at one time.
- Whether or not the interview is conducted face to face or via telephone or video.

We will look at each of these in turn.

Quantitative or qualitative?

In Chapters 1 and 2, the main approaches to research methodology were discussed. You may recall that positivism usually leads to a choice of quantitative methodology and is primarily concerned with obtaining data that can be converted into numbers. On the other hand, interpretism and post structuralism, although different, tend to lead to a choice of qualitative methodology and are primarily concerned with finding out participants' thoughts, ideas and opinions in more detail. Interview design reflects this state of affairs. This is because:

- interviews can be *highly structured* and aimed at collecting information that is easily converted into numbers
- interviews can be completely *unstructured* with no intention that the results should be subjected to numerical analysis. This is often the case in biographical or life-history interviewing
- interviews can be *semi-structured* including elements of both the quantitative and qualitative approaches, but primarily focusing on the former.

The degree of flexibility of the interview

Interviews are frequently classified according to the degree of flexibility that the interviewer has to probe and ask additional questions and the degree of flexibility that the participant has to say what they want, in the way that they want (Cannold, 2001; Fontana and Frey, 2000; Johnson and Christensen, 2008; Kumar, 2005).

Structured interviews

This kind of interviewing is linked to the positivist research paradigm. Structured interviews, sometimes known as *standardised* interviews (Fielding and Thomas, 2008), consist of mostly 'closed' questions where only a limited number of responses can be given. You will find that Chapter 11 contains a discussion on the difference between open and closed questions. The researcher is given an interview schedule, a written list of questions that have to be asked in the same way and in a specific order, which looks very similar to a questionnaire. This type of interview is used in large studies such as surveys, where it is seen as important to control variability, so that the results of the study can be generalised to the wider **population**.

Often a team of interviewers may be used in this type of interviewing, but inevitably the way an interviewer behaves (what they do and say) is a major source of variance. Therefore, interviewers will be trained to administer the interview in exactly the same way – using exactly the same words and question order (Fontana and Frey, 2000). This written 'script' is known as the interview *protocol* (Johnson and Christensen, 2008) or *schedule* (Fielding and Thomas, 2008). However, it is questionable, if not impossible, to completely control for the effect that different interviewers will have on the interview situation (Fielding and Thomas, 2008; Robson, 1993).

Activity

If you are an early childhood studies' student you may be able to try out this activity in your university or college. Choose a topic that everyone will be able to say something about, such as what people remember about playing as a child, and write a series of questions about this. Then ask a few students in turn if they would be willing to answer your questions – try to choose students who have different backgrounds to yourself or students you do not know well. You will need to have worked out exactly how you will introduce yourself and the interview topic before you conduct the interview, so that you say the same thing to everyone.

As you are interviewing the participants, take note of how you react, feel and behave towards them, and how they react to you. Reflect upon how the characteristics of the participants may have had an effect on the interview proceedings.

The characteristics of both the interviewer and the participant are likely to have an effect on the interview process (Fontana and Frey, 2000). The interaction between two students of roughly the same age, gender, sexuality and ethnicity may well be different than when these characteristics are not shared between the interviewer and interviewee. Not only do we tend to act differently depending on characteristics such as age, ethnicity and gender (Fielding and Thomas, 2008), but power relations between the interviewer and the participant can also have an effect. You might like to consider this in relation to an adult interviewing a child and a nursery manager interviewing a parent whose child has just started nursery.

Patton (1987) refers to structured interviews as 'closed quantitative interviews' because the questions are fixed and the responses that the participant can give are limited. The data collected are easy to convert to numerical data for statistical analysis because the responses are often pre-coded. Here is a typical excerpt from a structured interview.

Q1 How many children do you have?
1. none
2. one
3. two
4. three
5. more than three

Q2 Do your children attend any of the following schools?
1. Sheldon primary school
2. Wexfield middle school
3. Armitage infant school
4. Seacole primary school
5. Middleworth infant school

As you can see, with structured interviewing the response categories are fixed and the information obtained is likely to be limited in nature. In addition, the interviewee is given little room to elaborate their responses to the questions or statements. On this basis, we would argue that this type of interviewing is of little benefit when interviewing young children as there is no room for them to talk about the things of interest to them, in the way that is meaningful to them.

Westcott and Littleton (2005) argue that structured interviewing of children is underpinned by a view of the child as powerless and passive in the research process. This is because this kind of research, located within the positivist paradigm, focuses primarily on trying to *reveal* children's understandings as opposed to *creating* understandings *with* children. We should remember that when conducting any of the interview types discussed in this chapter, children may not be used to being listened to. Moreover, their lack of experience in being interviewed, especially if carried out in a formal way designed for older, more experienced children and adults, may be a barrier to their participation rather than their lack of age and maturity (Westcott and Littleton, 2005).

Semi-structured interviews

Semi-structured interviews or 'structured conversations' (Cannold, 2001: 179) contain a mixture of both open and closed questions but are primarily used in qualitative research. For example, an interview may start off by asking the participant details such as the number of children they have, and then continue to ask questions on a particular topic where the participant can respond freely. An example of an open question might be 'how did you feel when you started back to work after your maternity leave was over?' Although open questions are mostly used, the same questions are asked of everyone, so some degree of standardisation is achieved. However, unlike structured interviewing, there is greater flexibility to probe for detail in relation to a particular response given. Furthermore, the interviewer can adapt the questioning to suit the needs of the interviewee, such as their level of understanding (Fielding and Thomas, 2008). This type of interviewing may be appropriate for some children, particularly the oldest children in the 0–8 years age range. However, when interviewing young children, we believe that unstructured and focus group interviewing offer the most potential.

It should be noted that writing questions for structured and semi-structured interviews requires *careful* consideration. The next chapter that looks at questionnaires gives detailed guidance about avoiding common pitfalls in question design that applies equally to interviews.

Unstructured interviews

Unstructured interviews are also qualitative in nature and are designed to provide in-depth information about participants' beliefs, thoughts and feelings. Kumar (2005:124) refers to these interviews as '*in-depth*' interviews and Fielding and Thomas (2008: 247) refer to them as '*non-standardised* interviews'. The main difference between structured interviews and unstructured interviews is that the aim of structured interviews is to explain behaviour within categories that have been decided beforehand (*deductive*), whereas unstructured interviews are seen as trying to understand complex behaviour, without deciding beforehand what categories of response may emerge (*inductive*) (Fontana and Frey, 2000).

In unstructured interviewing, the topics to be investigated are not decided in full detail beforehand. Thus, it is often an approach to interviewing that is used in biographical or life-history interviewing. The interview proceeds more like a conversation or a discussion with questions being asked as themes and topics emerge *naturally* and the participant is free to respond as well as lead the discussion as s/he wants. Thus, control during the interview does not lie *permanently* with the interviewer (Fontana and Frey, 2000). For this reason we believe that unstructured interviewing is the most appropriate tool when interviewing young children because it allows children to set the pace and the direction of the interview on a range of topics that have meaning for them.

We can see, then, that an unstructured interview is a research tool that is characterised by its flexibility and sharing of power between interviewer and interviewee. This can also be seen in the way that the interviewer may add their own opinions on the topic under discussion in a way that would be unthinkable in structured interviewing (Fielding and Thomas, 2008). Although this means that it is difficult to compare responses between individuals, what is lost by not being able to generalise the results, is gained by the richness of the information obtained. Unstructured interviews are fundamentally different from other types of interviewing that seek a degree of standardisation, since the aim is to establish 'human to human contact with the desire to understand rather than to explain' (Fontana and Frey, 2000: 654).

Increasingly, new trends in interviewing see the interview as a 'negotiated text' (Fontana and Frey, 2000: 663) as there is growing recognition that researchers are not 'invisible, neutral entities; rather, they are part of the interactions they seek to study and influence those interactions'. Thus, there is acknowledgement that the direction in which the interview takes place is influenced not only by the interviewer but also by the interviewee. This relates to the idea that 'reality is an ongoing interpretive accomplishment' (Holstein and Gubrium, 1995: 16). We hope you can see that it is a perspective that is far removed from the positivist position outlined in Chapter 1.

Looking at the types of interview we have discussed so far, it is possible to identify that there is significant difference in the amount of interpersonal rapport between interviewer and interviewee according to the type of interview used. In the structured interview it is important that the interviewer remains as objective as possible and adheres very closely to the 'script'. In the less formal, unstructured interview, where the aim is to obtain an 'in-depth' understanding, there needs to be an interpersonal exchange between the interviewer and the participant. This method relies on the interviewer contributing something of themselves, which would be considered undesirable in structured interviewing (Fontana and Frey, 2000).

 Research in focus

Degotardi et al.'s (2008) study was designed to find out what parents believe is in their children's minds, in an effort to devise a way of categorising these beliefs. The research was undertaken with 25 mothers whose children were 12 months old at the start of the study. Each mother was visited at home three times, when her child was 12, 18 and 24 months old. Semi-structured interviews were used which were designed to elicit descriptions of the infants. The researchers decided not to ask direct questions about what the parents thought the children were thinking as they did not want to prompt parents into commenting on ideas that they had not previously considered. The interview schedule was used as a guide, rather than rigidly adhered to, the aim being to allow parents to speak freely in as natural a way as possible. The interviews were taped and transcribed later for analysis. The following is the interview schedule

Mothers' beliefs interview questions
Can you begin by describing (infant's name) to me as he/she is now?
Can you describe his/her temperament and disposition?
Tell me about his/her general development
What are his/her routines?
What are his/her likes and dislikes?
How does he/she spend his/her awake time?
What are his/her favorite toys?
What is his/her favorite game or activity that he/she plays with you?
How much does he/she involve you in his/her activities? (Degotardi et al., 2008: 262)

Using the information that you have been given so far in this chapter, try and answer the following questions.

- These interviews were all conducted by the same researcher. What issues need to be taken into consideration if there had been different interviewers at different times and for different parents?

- The questions did not directly relate to what the researchers were trying to find out, to avoid prompting parents. Is this misleading parents? How can this difficulty be overcome? Chapter 3 looks at ethics and you may find it helpful to read this chapter before responding to this question.
- What makes this a semi-structured interview rather than a structured interview? Would similar results have been obtained with a structured interview or a questionnaire?
- All the participants spoke English as their first language. What factors need to be considered if the participants' first language was not English?
- The article does not tell us many details about the interviewer, except that she was the first author (Sheila Degotardi). How might characteristics of the interviewer such as gender, age and ethnicity affect the outcomes of research such as this?

Interviewing more than one participant at once

So far we have looked at interviews that involve just one interviewer and one participant. There, are, however, situations where it is desirable to interview several participants together. Group interviews, commonly called focus groups, are where an interviewer, sometimes called a moderator or facilitator, leads a discussion with a small group of people (Johnson and Christensen 2008). It is a very common method used in market research.

Stewart and Shamdasani (1998) and Fontana and Frey (2000) identify many uses of focus groups, including:

- finding out background information about a topic
- generating ideas that can be tested using more systematic, quantitative methods
- evaluating a new process or product
- generating impressions of a product, organisation, and so on
- interpreting results obtained from other research methods
- pre-testing questionnaires, tests or interviews for use in further research
- as a method of **triangulation**, aimed at increasing the **reliability** of a research study.

Characteristically a focus group consists of between six and twelve participants, who are likely to be selected because they are relatively similar to each other. Johnson and Christensen (2008), for instance, consider that homogenous groups are more likely to promote discussion than groups which are dissimilar to each other. However, one of the disadvantages of holding a focus group with comparable individuals is that their views are likely to be similar. In order to get around this problem it is usual to hold a series of focus groups, containing participants selected according to different criteria. For example, Penny, one of the authors of this book, was involved in finding out what students in a further education college felt about the quality of student support. In order to get a range of opinions, she selected groups composed of:

- students under the age of 18 studying A levels
- students under the age of 18 on vocational courses
- adult students studying vocational courses
- adult students studying part-time.

Before the focus group is held the researcher needs to have decided on the format the interview will take. As with individual interviews discussed previously, there are decisions to be made about the degree of flexibility the moderator will have in conducting the interview but, usually, focus group interviews are semi-structured in nature. In order to conduct the focus group interview, the group moderator needs a high level of interpersonal skills because s/he has to be able to promote discussion between individuals who may not know each other. It is the role of the moderator to make sure that everyone has a chance to give their views and that the conversation is not dominated by one or two individuals. In addition, unless a completely flexible approach is to be taken, the groups must be brought back to the topic under discussion if they start to wander too far from the research agenda.

Focus group interviewing is considered to be particularly appropriate in research with young children. Lancaster and Broadbent (2003) see the main strengths of focus group interviewing with children as follows:

- Focus group interviews are especially useful when children (of around 5–6 years) know and like each other.
- *Interaction* between children is encouraged.
- Focus groups help to build *confidence* and can be *empowering.*
- Children are able to raise issues that *they* would like to discuss.
- Children are recognised as *experts* in their own setting.
- An insight is gained into children's *shared* understandings of everyday life.
- New ideas and meanings are generated through the interaction of different members of the group.
- It is more akin to the kind of conversations children are used to having than the question-answer style of interviewing.
- Children are familiar with taking part in shared discussions at 5–6 years of age (and older) through story-times or circle-times
  (based on Lancaster and Broadbent, 2003: 46).

However, we should not see focus group interviewing with children as devoid of problems. Lancaster and Broadbent (2003) seem to echo Robson's (1993) concerns when they argue that children can be influenced by individuals within a group and it can be difficult to identify individual children's perspectives. Furthermore, as in any group situation, some individuals' voices may dominate. Possibly, then, focus group interviewing with children is best employed by researchers who are used to working with children in groups. Those of you who are practitioners may be particularly well placed to do this as you are likely to be used to managing a group at story times, for instance, and ensuring that all children have the opportunity to have their say.

Research in focus

Mayall's (2008) research into the extent to which children promote, maintain and restore their health at home and at school involved spending time with children in their homes and school. One of the groups in the study were a group of 5–6-year-old children, the other group consisted of children aged from 9 to 10 years. Mayall spent two days a week for two terms in the school so the children would come to accept her as a familiar figure. Mayall's rationale for this was that it would enable the children to talk to her with confidence and would lessen the possibility of disrupting their usual behaviours in their classroom. You may recall in the chapter on ethnography that becoming a familiar part of the group is considered important.

As well as interviewing key adults for the study, that is, parents and school staff, Mayall engaged with the children undertaking their usual activities and began to hold discussions with the children in pairs or threes, drawing pictures and encouraging the children to talk about them. She calls these interviews 'research conversations'. Mayall states, 'I aimed to engage with them in conversations, where an opening gambit could lead wherever children wished' (ibid.: 112).

To increase individual children's confidence she asked the children to choose a friend and talked to the children in pairs, something she believes the children found both supportive and enabling. The children stayed in the classroom for the interviews rather than being taken away from their usual environment, because their teacher and the researcher (Mayall) believed it would be a more familiar and comfortable context for them. As the children grew in confidence, they began to talk between themselves about points made rather than the conversation developing in the mode of adult question – child answer.

In the home interviews, Mayall gradually involved the children's parents as lead interviewers in the study, briefing them beforehand about the research purposes and topics. Children were encouraged to discuss their school day with their parents, with Mayall present and providing occasional prompts. As these interviews took place in the home the children were surrounded by familiar objects and were able to leave the room if they wanted to. Having parents interview their own children was helpful because their shared history of people, places and events of significance to the children enabled a greater understanding to be gained about the issues raised.

In both the home and school, 'research conversations' enabled children to take some control over the research agenda, such as controlling the topics to be explored as well as the pace and direction of the conversations. Mayall sees a key advantage in interviewing children together as it enables them to share their experiences of being a child and learn about different experiences of childhoods. This is similar to the argument that interviewing women as a group allows them to collectivise their experiences (Mies, 1993). Finally, Mayall highlights the high degree of social skills the children demonstrated in listening to each other's viewpoints, replying and adding to the discussion, as well as helping to facilitate discussion with children who find it difficult to communicate for one reason or another.

This 'Research in focus' section has raised a number of important issues in relation to interviewing that are pertinent to interviewing adults *and* children. These relate to:

- where and when to conduct an interview
- establishing rapport in an interview
- how the interview 'works' in practice.

We will look at these areas later in the chapter when we think about carrying out and recording interviews, but before we do this we wish to note the development of remote forms of interviewing that have been made possible with developments in technology.

Remote methods of interviewing

So far in this chapter we have described face-to-face interviews; however, telephone interviewing is increasingly used as a method of collecting information both for market research and surveys. For example, the National Child Development Study 2004/5 follow-up used a 30-minute computer-aided telephone interview (Centre for Longitudinal Studies, 2007).

In computer-aided telephone interviews, interviewers located in a call centre, read out a structured questionaire from a computer screen and enter the participants' responses directly onto the computer. Generally these sorts of interviews tend to be short, less than 30 minutes, and do not require participants to give personal information as it has been suggested that interviewees are reluctant to do this over the telephone (Carr and Worth, 2001). More recently, telephone interviews have been used for smaller-scale qualitative studies, especially where contact has already been made with the participants. Research has found that telephone interviewing produces data that are comparable in quality to face-to-face methods (Carr and Worth, 2001).

One criticism of telephone interviews is that the sample cannot be selected at random, because it relies on the participant having a telephone at home. Recently, then, there has been an increase in the number of studies using mobile phones and email as ways of reaching more people. McCoyd and Kerson (2006), for instance, suggest that email interviewing, if it occurs in 'real time', compares favourably with telephone interviewing. Email interviewing should not be confused with sending a structured questionnaire by email; using email to conduct an interview in real time involves a degree of personal interaction between the interviewer and the interviewee which is absent if email is used as a means of sending out a questionnaire instead of using the postal service.

CARRYING OUT AND RECORDING INTERVIEWS

When carrying out an interview, it is important to think about the time and location in which the interview will take place. Interviewees should feel comfortable in their surroundings and interviewers should always be mindful that they have been good enough to give up their time for the interview and try to make the experience a pleasant one. Robson (1993: 232) argues that the interviewer should aim to:

- listen more than speak

- put questions in a straightforward, clear and non-threatening way
- eliminate cues which lead interviewees to respond in a particular way (but see earlier note on unstructured interviewing)
- enjoy it (or at least give the appearance of enjoyment)
- take a full record of the interview.

Robson (1993) argues that usually, an interview will follow a similar pattern, although for unstructured interviewing this may well vary from interview to interview:

Introduction

Here, the researcher will introduce her/himself, explain again the purposes of the interview and restate assurances in relation to confidentiality. S/he will also check that the interviewee is comfortable and is happy with the method of recording the interview.

'Warm up'

The first few questions should aim at putting the interviewee at ease. Often interviewers using any type of interviewing method will ask some non-threatening questions that do not require long answers at the beginning of an interview.

Main body of interview

This is the part of the interview when the interviewer will ask the key questions in their study. Depending on the interview type, the question order might be varied and the interviewer might probe for further information if the interviewee says something interesting that could be explored further. An example might be as follows: in a study looking at how nurseries celebrate individual children's birthdays, a practitioner might be asked 'do you do anything in the nursery when it is a child's birthday?' Let us say the practitioner responds with 'we don't let children bring in cakes from home as it goes against our new healthy eating policy'. As an interviewer, you might like to probe for her views on the nursery's position; probe what the policy contains and who contributed to its development; or probe how parents and children have reacted to this policy.

Closing comments

This is another important phase in the interview. This is the point when the interviewee is thanked and recording stops. Sometimes, interviewees continue to talk about issues raised during the interview so it is important that the interviewer *asks for permission* to make notes if they wish to use this material. In addition, any promises that are made at this point, such as having the opportunity to see the interview transcript or finished research project should be adhered to and the interviewer should clarify how the interviewee can be reached in order to do this.

> ### 〰 Reflection point
>
> We have looked at Robson's thinking about the pattern an interview should take, with its warm-up and in-depth questions later on. How do you feel about it? Fontana and Frey (2000: 658), for instance, draw on Oakley's (1981) work and argue that the friendly manner of the interviewer is a 'ruse to gain the trust and confidence of the respondent without reciprocating those feelings in any way' – we noted this in Chapter 3. In structured interviewing, the researcher is expected to ask the questions in exactly the same way to each interviewee. Is this good research practice, owing to its emphasis on objectivity and minimising researcher effect, or is it unethical in its lack of reciprocity and lessening of the importance of relationships? These questions are much debated in research and link back to the discussions in the earliest chapters of this book about paradigms and principles.

The method of recording an interview depends upon the type of interview used. Where interview questions are closed, it is possible to record pre-coded responses onto a written questionnaire, or into a computer. For example, we have discussed the use of computer-aided telephone (usually 'structured') interviews where the findings are entered directly onto a computer, ready for data analysis. More flexible interviews make direct recording of responses very difficult. Interviewers could try to make rough written notes, but this distracts from the interview process. For this reason it is recommended that the interviewer records the interview electronically and writes up a transcript of the interview later (Fielding and Thomas, 2008). This is because note-taking is not only slow, but can be questionable in terms of **validity**. Fielding and Thomas (2008) argue that by offering to give interviewees a copy of the full transcription of their interview, tape-recording might seem more palatable. It is also useful in terms of gauging the reliability and validity of the responses, acting as a further check on the data. Recording interviews systematically is important, as the record acts as 'the best index of the interviewer's effect on the respondent's testimony' (Fielding and Thomas, 2008: 256).

Recording can be via an audio-recording device or by using a camcorder. The advantage of using a camcorder is that you not only record the words spoken but also aspects of non-verbal communication. The disadvantage of more obtrusive methods of recording an interview is that the participant is likely to find it difficult to act naturally. When using equipment like this the researcher needs to be completely at ease with the technology, and should have had a trial run before conducting their first 'real' interview. Choosing the right place for an interview is essential if using electronic methods, such as a camcorder, as too much noise or lack of light will all have a negative effect. The positioning of the device in relation to the participant and the interviewer is also important.

Whatever means of recording the interview you choose, the participant should be told beforehand the method that will be used and s/he should be given the opportunity to decline to be interviewed or to have the interview recorded in a different way. This is all part of 'informed consent', a term we discussed in Chapter 3. Finally here, before recording starts, decisions need to have been made about how confidentiality will be maintained and how the recordings, whether they are written or on tape, will be kept secure.

Key points from the chapter

- Interviews are a common way of finding out information. They are used in the media, politics and consumer research, as well as in scientific research.
- Interviews can be used both in quantitative and qualitative research studies.
- Interviews always involve a degree of personal interaction (not always face to face) between the interviewer and the interviewee.
- Quantitative interviews are very structured and may resemble questionnaires. To reduce variance interviewers are trained to deliver the interview in exactly the same way.
- Qualitative interviews are less structured and are used to obtain 'in-depth' information from participants with the aim of understanding as much as possible about the research situation, theme or topic.
- Interviews with less structure may be especially useful when interviewing children as they are able to take some control over the pace and direction of the interview and talk about topics of meaning to them.
- Focus group interviewing is also a useful strategy with children because they may be familiar with taking part in group discussions such as during story times and many are able to share their experiences with other children.
- Thought should be given to how interviews are carried out. Recordings of interviews can be made directly onto computers, on paper or recorded using electronic means.

Further reading

Fielding, N. and Thomas, H. (2008) 'Qualitative interviewing', in N. Gilbert (ed.), *Researching Social Life*. 3rd edn. London: Sage. This chapter looks at the practicalities of conducting focused interviews 'in the field' and takes the approach that interviews can be likened to a 'guided conversation'.

Mayall, B. (2008) 'Conversations with children: working with generational issues', in P. Christensen and A. James (eds), *Research with Children: Perspectives and Practices*. 2nd edn. Abingdon: Routledge. This chapter looks at some of the key issues that relate to interviewing children and draws upon the author's own research.

11 QUESTIONNAIRES

Chapter objectives

- To reflect on the use of questionnaires as a research tool
- To consider the different ways that questionnaires can be designed
- To gain an understanding of the different ways of administering a questionnaire

In Chapter 5 we looked at surveys and noted that questionnaires are a common way of obtaining information from participants. Questionnaires are a versatile and cost effective research tool (Walliman, 2001) and are used for collecting primarily **quantitative** data. At first glance, designing a questionnaire may appear a relatively simple task. However, producing a questionnaire that will provide the information wanted from a group of respondents has to be undertaken *carefully* if the questionnaire is to be *valid* and the findings *reliable*.

Anderson (1998: 170) warns that 'the questionnaire has become one of the most used and abused means of collecting information'. Therefore, in this chapter we will look, in some detail, at how to design and administer a questionnaire, pointing out some of the possible pitfalls that may render a questionnaire invalid or unreliable.

WHAT IS A QUESTIONNAIRE?

Very few of us will have escaped completing a questionnaire, so it is likely that you already have a good idea about what constitutes a questionnaire. In its simplest form, a questionnaire is a piece of paper on which is printed a number of questions or statements, with space for someone to respond. It is a 'written list of questions, the answers to which are recorded by respondents' (Kumar, 2005: 126). Nowadays many questionnaires are not paper based, but come to us via the Internet or via our email, but the principle is the same.

WHY ARE QUESTIONNAIRES USED IN RESEARCH?

In Chapter 5, we saw various examples of the uses of questionnaires in surveys. For instance Schum et al. (2002) used questionnaires to ask parents of over 250 infants about the progress of 'toilet training' and questionnaires filled in by parents was one data collection instrument in the Avon Longitudinal Study of Parents and their Children (Golding et al., 2001).

〰️ **Reflection point**

Think about the occasions that you have been asked to fill in a questionnaire. What sort of information was the questionnaire designed to collect? How was it given to you: by post, by hand, by email or Internet?

Sometimes we are more motivated than others to fill in questionnaires. What factors influence how enthusiastically you respond to them?

We find that we are motivated to fill in questionnaires if they are seen to be relevant in some way, that is, to do with work, or a cause we are interested in. We also tend to complete questionnaires if they are conducted by colleagues, friends or students (when we have time) as we have a personal and/or professional commitment to them.

Johnson and Christensen (2008) have identified that typically questionnaires are designed to find out information on the following aspects of individuals lives:

- *Demographics and background information*, such as age, gender, social class and numbers of years of education.
- *Knowledge about a particular topic*, such as asking early years' practitioners about their understanding of what constitutes healthy eating for toddlers.
- *Attitudes, beliefs, opinions and values*, such as parental attitudes towards having their children immunised or the value of working in partnership with their children's early years' settings.
- *Experiences*, such as the experience of a parent taking their child to an early years' setting for the first time, or asking early years' practitioners about their experiences of implementing a new policy.
- *Behaviour*, such as the number of times parents read to their children, or whether or not parents smoke in front of their children.

It is clear that the design of the questionnaire very much depends upon its intended use. For example, asking someone for his or her age will require a different type of question than a question designed to elicit an attitude. It is therefore essential that, before attempting to design a questionnaire, there is clarity about what it is you want to find out. There is nothing more disheartening than carrying out a questionnaire only to find out later that an important piece of information is missing because a relevant question was not asked. For this reason, large-scale surveys allow considerable time for consultation with all interested stakeholders, to ensure that the appropriate questions are included.

Reflection point

Mary is undertaking her undergraduate research project and is looking at healthy eating in early years' settings. Her research question is, *To what extent does early years practitioners' knowledge of the healthy eating guidelines for toddlers correspond with the advice given by the Food Standards Agency?*

The areas included on her questionnaire are as follows:

Name:
Age:
Male/Female (please state):
Please outline what you consider a healthy diet for children.
Please describe the meals that are provided in your setting.
Please supply a typical menu for a week.

The questionnaires were sent out to a variety of different settings and when they were returned she realised that she had not got all the information she wanted. What further information do you think would have been useful?

The main omission was that Mary did not ask the settings to specify what type of setting they were, or the age of the children involved. In addition, she wanted to find out what practitioners knew about *healthy diets for toddlers*, and this questionnaire would not elicit this information specifically. There was nowhere for respondents to indicate their role within the setting, or their qualifications. This may have been important as, afterwards, Mary wondered if members of staff with early years professional status knew more or less than the practitioners who possessed level 3 vocational qualifications. In addition, she had asked questions that were not really relevant. For instance, did Mary really need to know the name of the participant?

We strongly recommend that students show questionnaires to their research supervisors and any gatekeepers to the research, such as head teachers, before sending them out. Piloting a questionnaire with someone (or a few people) who shares characteristics with the intended group can also help to iron out difficulties, as we will see later in this chapter.

TYPES OF QUESTION USED IN QUESTIONNAIRE DESIGN

When designing questions to be included in a questionnaire, one of the main decisions is whether to use open questions, closed questions or a mixture of both. This will relate to the underpinning **paradigm** and **methodology** within which the research is located. Chapters 1 and 2 look at this in some detail and we also raised the issue of open and closed questions in the previous chapter, which looked at interviewing.

Open or closed questions?

Open questions are ones that encourage the respondent to answer the question in any way they want, using the language that they want. Closed questions are ones where the respondent has to choose from a number of answers that the researcher has chosen beforehand (Kumar, 2005).

Very often the same question can be written in both open and closed versions. For example, if you wanted to find out the qualifications of a respondent, the question could be asked directly as an *open question*:

What qualifications in early years care and education do you have?

Or in a more *structured* way:

What qualifications in early years care and education do you have? (please tick one box)

[ ] NVQ level 2 or equivalent
[ ] NVQ level 3 or equivalent
[ ] NVQ level 4 or equivalent
[ ] NNEB
[ ] Foundation Degree in Early Childhood Studies
[ ] Early Childhood Studies Degree
[ ] PGCE Early Years

In looking at these examples, we can see that the more structured approach does not allow respondents to contribute qualifications outside the categories put forward by the researcher. Sometimes, a questionnaire will have a category 'Other (please state)' at the end of a list like this to enable respondents to contribute another category (Simmons, 2008). Given the number of qualifications that exist in early childhood, the list could potentially be very long.

Open questions are often used when a researcher is trying to find out respondents' views in some depth. In the previous reflection point, Mary wanted to know the level of knowledge that practitioners had about healthy eating guidelines for toddlers. She could have chosen closed true/false questions, but this would have supplied the practitioners with prompts as to facts that were important. For example, a question such as: '*A two year old child can be given skimmed milk to drink. True/False?*' could be correctly answered by guesswork. By stating '*Please outline a healthy diet for toddlers*' – an open statement – the respondent's knowledge of healthy eating is more likely to be revealed. However, Simmons (2008) notes that if a question requires a lot of thought from respondents, they may not make the time to write their response in full.

Using open questions can often produce 'rich' information about ideas, attitudes and values that would not have been provided by using a closed question. Open questions give primarily **qualitative** data, however, if there are a number of similar responses, then the number of times a particular issue is mentioned can be counted, thus converting qualitative data into *quantitative* data. Chapter 17 looks at data analysis in more detail.

Closed questions, on the other hand, give responses that are easy to count and convert into numbers, thus they tend to elicit *quantitative* data. Because there is the same choice of responses (owing to pre-coding), the resulting data can be compared and analysed reasonably easily (Simmons, 2008). This allows for hypotheses to be tested and the influence of specific variables to be examined. In reality, many questionnaires contain a mixture of both open and closed questions and fall somewhere on a continuum with qualitative at one end of the continuum and quantitative at the other.

In addition to open ended questions Blaxter et al. (1996: 16) list six different types of question:

1. Quantity or information.
2. Categories.
3. Lists or multiple choice.
4. Scales.
5. Ranking.
6. Complex grids or tables.

We will look at each of these in turn:

Quantity or information

This is a simple, direct question such as:

> *How many years have you worked in childcare and education?* _____

Categories

As it suggests, this type of question invites participants to decide which category they belong to, for example:

> *What is the highest level of education you have achieved?*
>
> GCSE or equivalent ☐ A level or equivalent ☐ Degree or equivalent ☐

Lists or multiple choice

A list or multiple choice is similar to the category type of question, except that there are more possibilities. Respondents may be asked to check the categories that are relevant to them and usually more than one response is permitted. There are disadvantages with presenting people with a list of categories, because there is a tendency for individuals to tick the first items on the list (Johnson and Christensen, 2008). One way of getting over this tendency is by using a rating scale.

Here is an example of a list or multiple choice:

> *How do you keep up to date with current initiatives in childcare and education?* Please tick as many as apply.
>
> Information from your manager [ ]
>
> Reading a journal such as *Nursery World* [ ]
>
> Receiving regular email newsletters from organisations [ ]
>
> Going on short professional development courses [ ]
>
> Attending college or university to study for an award [ ]

Scales

Unlike the types of question looked at previously, scales do not pose a question; rather, they give a statement to which there are a number of responses to choose from set out along a continuum. For example:

> *Please indicate the extent to which you agree with the following statement.*
>
> *I am happy with the opening hours of the library.*
>
> | 1 | 2 | 3 | 4 | 5 |
> |---|---|---|---|---|
> | Strongly disagree | Disagree | Neither agree or disagree | Agree | Strongly agree |

In numerical scales only the end points are given descriptors, for instance:

> *How satisfied are you with the quality of food on offer in the university canteen?*
>
> | 1 | 2 | 3 | 4 | 5 |
> |---|---|---|---|---|
> | Very dissatisfied | | | | Very satisfied |

Whatever type of scale used, there are some important points to remember:

- The descriptors must agree with the statement. For example, if you want the respondents to rate things according to the degree that they agreed with a statement, it would not be appropriate to use an evaluative scale such as 'Excellent, Good, Fair and Poor'.
- Make sure that the scale items are placed exactly the same distance apart.
- Ensure that there is no bias towards one end of the response continuum.

◞◟ **Reflection point**

Consider this item in a rating scale. Why do you think it may render results invalid?

Indicate the extent to which you agree to this statement.

Children should be formally introduced to phonics by the age of 3.

1	2	3	4	5
Very strongly disagree	Strongly disagree	Disagree	Neither agree nor disagree	Agree

---

You may have identified that there are three descriptors that are about disagreement and only one that allows the respondent to say that they agree with the statement. In situations such as this, it is reasonable to assume a degree of bias on the part of the researcher.

Other factors that need to be considered in the use of scales are to avoid using too many points on the scale, usually no more than five. Respondents should be able to discriminate easily between, for example, 'strongly disapprove' and 'disapprove'. The more points used, the harder it is for respondents to choose where to make their response, and the more inaccurate the results will be.

In addition, there is no real agreement as to whether an odd or an even number of descriptors should be employed. It could be argued that respondents should be allowed the option to be neutral about a particular topic, whereas leaving out a middle point forces a response in one direction or the other.

Ranking

Questions that use ranking are generally used when the researcher wishes the respondents to indicate the *importance* they place upon a particular issue or concept. Respondents might be asked to rank using either open or closed questions; an open question often being used in a preliminary study to reveal items that can be used in a subsequent study using closed questions. The following are examples of both the open and closed approach.

An open question:
'What do you consider to be the three most important things early years settings can do to help a new toddler settle in? Please write them in rank order with the most important thing first and the least important last.'

A closed question:
'Below is a list of suggestions about what can be done to help a toddler settle into an early years setting. Please rank them in order of importance, using the numbers 1 to 5, where 1 is the most important suggestion and 5 is the least important.

[ ] Make sure the setting is warm and welcoming for the child and parent(s).

[ ] Visit the child and family at home so that you can begin get to know them and they can get to know you.

[ ] Have a flexible settling in policy that encourages a parent to gradually introduce the child to the nursery over a period of time.

[ ] Operate an effective key person policy to enable the child to build a close relationship with a member of staff.

[ ] Give the family a booklet all about the setting and how they can prepare the child beforehand.

Now carry out the following activity:

For each of the issues below, devise an open and a closed question. When using closed questions try to use a range of question types, that is, scales, lists and ranking.

- The importance of a play-based curriculum
- Parental views on the MMR vaccination
- Creating a quality environment for babies in early years' settings.

Complex grids or tables

These are used when the researcher wishes to explore respondents' views about an issue in some depth while retaining control over the range of possible responses. For example, a grid could be used for exploring how students studying for a Foundation Degree in Early Childhood Studies perceive the level of support they have had from a range of people.

Please indicate how supportive the following people have been while you have been studying for your foundation degree. Please tick the relevant boxes.

	Very supportive	Quite supportive	Neither supportive or unsupportive	Quite unsupportive	Very unsupportive
Your line manager					
Your work colleagues					
The college staff					
Your friends					
Your family					

Another type of grid is the *semantic differential*. This was first used in the 1950s by Osgood and this is sometimes called an Osgood Semantic Differential (Heise, 1970). In this grid, the respondent is asked to rank an idea or concept on a number of scales that use opposite adjectives at each end of the continuum. It is a useful way of finding out information about complex ideas and attitudes. In the following example a semantic differential is used to explore attitudes held by early years' practitioners about parents. As suggested previously, the items that make up the scale could have been obtained by asking open questions to a group of practitioners in an exploratory study.

Please rate the parent group who use your setting on the following scales. Place a tick on one of the lines between each pair of words to indicate your feelings.

Helpful	———— ———— ———— ———— ———— ———— ————	Unhelpful
Supportive	———— ———— ———— ———— ———— ———— ————	Unsupportive
Punctual	———— ———— ———— ———— ———— ———— ————	Unpunctual
Authoritative	———— ———— ———— ———— ———— ———— ————	Permissive
Friendly	———— ———— ———— ———— ———— ———— ————	Unfriendly

PUTTING A QUESTIONNAIRE TOGETHER

So far in this chapter, we have investigated various ways that questions can be formulated and we have emphasised how important it is that the questions match the aims of the research. This is vital in order that the questions used elicit the information wanted. In this section, we will give some thought as to how to present a questionnaire in order that it will give reliable results. The following points are developed from suggestions by Johnson and Christensen (2008).

Know the characteristics of the potential respondents

One of the first considerations is who the respondents are likely to be. A good understanding of their characteristics is important as it may affect how the questionnaire is constructed.

 Reflection point

What factors might you need to take into account when devising a questionnaire for the following two groups?

1. A questionnaire about the Early Years Foundation Stage targeting early years professionals
2. A questionnaire about parental involvement within an early years setting, targeting Bangladeshi families in an inner city area

In the above examples, you may have considered that early years professionals have more knowledge of the curriculum than parents and that a questionnaire directed towards the professionals can contain 'technical terms' that they use every day. For parents, such terms may be unknown to them and would need explaining. A questionnaire about parental involvement intended specifically for Bangladeshi families may not be understood if it is written in English. A straightforward translation may also cause difficulties because some families may be unfamiliar with written Bengali. In this case, it may be appropriate to ask a translator to read the questionnaire out to the parents. When producing a questionnaire, the researcher should use language that is familiar to respondents and pay due regard to their expected reading age; a questionnaire that is too complex will mean that a respondent is unable to complete it, whereas one that is too simple may lead respondents not to take it seriously and to give superficial responses.

Be clear and precise

If items in a questionnaire are long-winded or unclear, respondents may not give the information wanted. It is a good idea to get someone unconnected with the research but who shares some of the characteristics of the respondent group to read through the questions to see if they can understand what is being asked. In addition, it is important to avoid questions that are ambiguous or imprecise (Blaxter et al., 1996).

Never ask biased questions

A biased question is one that is written in a way that increases the likelihood of a particular response. One way of influencing how people respond is by including words that may elicit a strong negative reaction in individuals. The use of highly emotive words can be so powerful that individuals may make a negative response to a questionnaire item when a more emotionally *neutral* word would produce a different result. Using a phrase such as 'drug *addict*' may produce a different response than using 'drug *user*', for instance.

The use of *leading* questions is another way that a questionnaire can become biased, as they suggest a certain response.

〜〜 **Reflection point**

Can you identify the bias in these questions?

1. Please tick the appropriate response.
   The new Early Years Foundation Stage Curriculum is ... :
   A great improvement on the old curriculum   [ ]
   A slight improvement on the old curriculum   [ ]
   Not an improvement on the old curriculum   [ ]

2. Some people suggest that fast food is leading to both tooth decay and an increase in obesity in children. Do you agree?
   Yes   No

The main difficulty with question 1 is that the respondent is not given the opportunity to say that they think the new curriculum is worse than the old one. In addition the use of the words 'old' and 'new' introduce an emotive element, as 'new' generally conjures up positive images, whereas 'old' *may* conjure up more negative thoughts. In question 2, it is likely that the response will be always 'yes' because some people do suggest that fast food leads to these ill effects. Can you think of ways that this question could have been better expressed?

Avoid the use of double-barrelled questions

Double-barrelled questions are those where two or more issues are combined into one question. In question 2 in the previous reflection point feature, respondents were asked to consider the effects of fast food on both dental health *and* body weight. It may be that respondents would agree with one association, but not the other.

Avoid double negatives

Consider the following sentence: 'I do not want children not to have a healthy diet.' The sentence contains a double negative and could be better written: 'I *want* children to have a healthy diet.' Occasionally when writing a questionnaire it is possible to find oneself in a 'double negative' situation that may lead to respondents making mistakes.

Avoid overlapping categories when using numbers

Overlapping categories are confusing because a respondent could put their response in more than one category. For example, if asked to tick a box to indicate age, it would be confusing if the options were written like this:

   0–10, 10–20, 20–30, 30–40, 40+.

The categories should be written 0–9, 10–19, 20–29 and so on, in order that the respondent can only fit into one category.

Be aware that respondents may get into patterns of responding

Not all respondents will respond to a questionnaire with focus and concentration. Lack of concentration may result in them responding according to a pattern. We both have considerable experience of reading module evaluation forms where students are given a five-point scale to rate various aspects of a module. There is a strong tendency for students to tick the same response for all items, even though they are asked to evaluate such disparate items as the suitability of the rooms in which teaching was held and the quality of tutor support. In a similar way, some respondents will have a tendency to either agree or disagree with items, regardless of the content of the item. One way to counteract this is to use a variety of types of question in one questionnaire and to keep the number of items to be rated in a similar way to a minimum.

Be aware that respondents may give a socially acceptable response

In questions about behaviour and attitudes, respondents may feel embarrassed to respond truthfully. For example, if you wanted to find out how many hours of television parents allow their children to watch a day, you are likely to get an underestimation, because many parents now know that too much television is viewed as detrimental to children's development. If the parent knows who is administering the questionnaire, and that person is a person in authority, then the tendency is strengthened. This is important to consider if sending out a questionnaire to people with whom you are familiar (Anderson, 1998).

Decide on how you will *introduce* your questionnaire

Questionnaires are either introduced by means of a covering letter, or the details are contained on the questionnaire schedule itself, by means of an introduction. Denscombe (2007) recommends that the following information is included:

- *Who is responsible for the questionnaire*. Is there a sponsor or organisation involved? If the questionnaire is for a student research project then this needs to be explained. Full contact details of the researcher/organisation should also be given (Cohen et al., 2007).
- *The purpose of the questionnaire*. The reason why the questions are being asked needs to be explained.
- *The return address and date*.
- *How confidentiality will be maintained*. This should include an explanation that respondents' identities will not be revealed and that there will be due consideration paid to the secure storage of data.
- *The voluntary nature of the questionnaire*. Everyone who is asked to respond has the right to say 'no'.
- *Thanks*. Respondents will have chosen to give up valuable time to help fill in the questionnaire and a *sincere* statement of thanks should be included either at the beginning of the questionnaire or at the end.

Decide on how to present your items

- There is some evidence that the response rate improves if the items that respondents consider to be important are placed at the *beginning* of a questionnaire (Robertson and Sundstrom, 1990). Bell (1993) argues that personal data, such as income, should be put towards the *end* of a questionnaire.
- Start with positive, non-threatening items first (Bell, 2005) that can be answered easily (Simmons, 2008).
- Limit the number of questions that direct respondents to another question depending on how they answer a previous question (Johnson and Christensen, 2008). An example of this type of question is: '*Do you use the Internet? If yes go to question 3, if no, go to question 6*'.

- Include clear instructions and indicate where a new topic starts by using an introductory sentence. Examples can be included to help respondents see exactly what you mean (Denscombe, 2007).
- Give the questionnaire a title, number *each* question and include page numbers.
- Consider ending your questionnaire with an *open* question asking respondents if they have any other comments they want to contribute.
- Finish with a couple of straightforward questions to allow the respondent to 'cool off' (Siraj-Blatchford and Siraj-Blatchford, 2001a).
- Finally, thank the respondents for completing the questionnaire.
- Check that the questionnaire looks *professional*. Is it laid out well? It should not be overcrowded and the text should be easily read. Using the typeface 'Arial' and a font size of at least 12 will make text clear. Bell (2005) suggests that the font and style of the typeface for instructions should be different from that of the main questionnaire. It is also vital that the questionnaire is proofread carefully for errors in spelling, grammar and punctuation.

Pilot the questionnaire

It is unwise to send out a questionnaire without testing it out on a few people first; initially family and friends might be helpful, and once any obvious modifications have been made it can be piloted with people that are representative of the group you want to study. Respondents in a pilot group could be asked to 'think aloud' and verbalise and record their thoughts as they are filling in the questionnaire. Anderson (1998) suggests using a focus group approach, where six to twelve volunteers are gathered together to fill in the questionnaire and are encouraged to write comments in the margins. Afterwards the researcher could conduct a discussion about how the questionnaire worked.

Feedback from the pilot phase helps to identify if the questionnaire is too long or confusing, for instance. The researcher can ask for comments on presentation and any proofreading errors may be identified. Looking at the responses will also indicate whether the questionnaire has elicited the information expected – a key factor for **validity**. If not, the questions may need amending.

The response rate

Decisions made about putting together a questionnaire and how to distribute it can have a profound effect on the number of questionnaires that are completed and returned. The proportion of questionnaires returned is commonly known as the *response rate*, and is calculated as the percentage of completed questionnaires returned compared with the number sent out; calculated as the $\frac{\text{Number returned}}{\text{Number sent out}} \times 100$.

Cohen et al. (2007) suggest that the response rate can be increased by ensuring the questionnaire is attractive and easy to use, it is clear how to return it (and it does not require the respondent to spend money on postage), and if follow-ups and reminders are sent. Sometimes researchers use an identification code on questionnaires so they can identify who has returned them. This helps to identify if a specific group have chosen not to return the questionnaire. For example, if you wanted to find out information about school–parent links, it would be important to know that parents whose first language was not English failed to respond. Clearly, non-response does need to be thought about, because this can impact on the validity of the findings but being able to identify respondents will impact on their anonymity.

ADMINISTERING A QUESTIONNAIRE

There are a variety of ways to administer a questionnaire, which all have advantages and disadvantages. The aim in choosing a method should be to maximise the *response rate*. As noted previously, before sending out a questionnaire a covering letter should be written introducing the researcher and the aims of the study and providing details about how to return the questionnaire. Let us now think about some different ways of administering a questionnaire in turn:

Handing out questionnaires directly

This is a very common way of distributing questionnaires, especially if carrying out a piece of small-scale research such as in the workplace. It has the advantage that the respondents are known to the researcher and they may be predisposed to help. It also has the advantage that the research can be explained in person and the procedure for returning the questionnaires explained (Walliman, 2001). The disadvantage is that there is an increased risk of respondents telling you what they think you want to know. In addition, the respondent may be too embarrassed to respond to questions on sensitive issues. An added disadvantage of the personal approach is that it can be especially annoying if questionnaires are not returned; it is easy to personalise this and be disappointed that someone you *thought* would help, has let you down. It is best to remember that people lead busy lives, and if, after a couple of prompts, the questionnaire has not be returned, nothing more should be said.

Using the post

This is a common way of sending out a questionnaire. The advantages of using the post are that it is a relatively effective use of time and it is a good way of reaching a large number of respondents. However, it is not always that easy to get an accurate database of addresses of potential respondents owing to data protection issues. In addition, sending out questionnaires by post can be expensive and the response rate is often low (Bell, 2005).

Using others to distribute your questionnaire

Sometimes it is possible enlist the help of *other* people in distributing questionnaires. This is known as *collective administration* (Kumar, 2005: 129). This can improve the response rate, although it does *not* negate the need to obtain direct permission for your questionnaires to be distributed if they are going to be distributed via these 'helpers' in settings such as in a range of nurseries. In this instance, permission would still need to be sought from the nursery managers.

Sending out a questionnaire electronically

Email can be an effective way of reaching a large number of people, particularly if they are all members of a network and it is easy to send a group email. The disadvantage is that the method is limited to those individuals for whom there is an email contact. Placing the questionnaire on an Internet website is another way of reaching potential respondents, but access needs to be gained to a site whose users fit the profile of the sample you wish to reach. Crucially, both email and Internet distribution will automatically exclude individuals with no access to this technology and complete anonymity may be difficult to achieve.

Telephone and face to face

It is possible to administer a questionnaire over the telephone, or by asking the questions face to face. It is a common method used by market researchers and has the main advantage of getting an instant reply, thus increasing the response rate. The main disadvantage of this method is that you may well meet with a refusal because people do not have the time to talk. In addition, Cohen et al. (2007) point out that sometimes, the person taking a phone call is not the most suitable one to answer the questionnaire. Telephone and face-to-face administration of questionnaires is also both costly and time-consuming.

POSSIBILITIES AND LIMITATIONS OF QUESTIONNAIRES

Questionnaires are a popular way of collecting information as they can be administered to a large number of people and can glean a lot of information, albeit not in any great depth. Topics involving feelings and attitudes, for instance, are better explored using qualitative methods. Questionnaires are usually cost-effective of time, as opposed to interviews, because they are generally not administered face to face. However, as a student, they can incur high photocopying costs.

The main disadvantage is that the design process is *not* straightforward, and that without care and attention to the suggestions contained within this chapter, questionnaires can be rendered unreliable and invalid. Bell (2005) goes so far as to suggest that questionnaires can be fiendishly difficult to design. Finally, as a method to use directly with *young* children, they are unlikely to be useful.

Key points from the chapter

- Questionnaires are a common way of obtaining information but they are difficult to design.
- There are a variety of ways questions can be asked including questions designed to find out information about quantities and numbers, categories, lists, multiple choice, scales, ranking and complex grids and tables. Questions can also be open or closed.
- When putting a questionnaire together it is important to think about the characteristics of the respondents so that the questions are accessible to them. Questions need to be clearly written, unbiased and designed to reduce response bias. Ethical considerations also need to be taken into account.

- Questionnaires should be piloted so that any potential problems are picked up before the final questionnaire is sent out.
- Questionnaires can be sent out by post, via the Internet or email, delivered by a third person, or by the researcher, or read to respondents over the phone or face to face.

Further reading

Bell, J. (2005) *Doing Your Research Project: A Guide for First-Time Researchers in Education, Health and Social Science*. 4th edn. Buckingham: Open University Press. Chapter 8 contains a useful, basic guide to questionnaires.

Johnson, B. and Christensen, L. (2008) *Educational Research*. 3rd edn. Los Angeles, CA: Sage. Chapter 7 contains a clear and comprehensive explanation of how to construct a questionnaire in a little more depth than Bell.

12 USING DOCUMENTS AND OTHER VISUAL 'TEXTS'

Chapter objectives

- To consider what is meant by 'documents' in research
- To reflect on why we might use documents in research
- To consider how access to different types of documents might be gained
- To gain an understanding of how we might evaluate different documents in terms of their usefulness in research
- To look at the possibilities and limitations of using documents and other visual 'texts' in research

So far, in this part of the book, we have looked at observation, interviewing and questionnaires. Each of these involves direct engagement with people – even a self-completion questionnaire is designed with a specific audience in mind. Documents, by way of contrast, may be centuries old and may not have been written or designed with an audience in mind, such as in the case of personal diaries. In this chapter, then, we are thinking about analysing documents as a *research tool* as opposed to using written documents as background reading for a literature review. We will also be reflecting on the term 'document' in its widest sense, including the use of other visual 'texts' in research.

WHAT IS A 'DOCUMENT'?

Activity

At the beginning of this chapter it is important to begin to consider what we might mean by a 'document'. Make a list of things you consider to be documents before moving on to look at this section.

When you do move on to read this section, compare your own list to the examples considered below. Do some of the items included challenge your own definition of 'documents'?

We might expect to list journals and books as important documents. Indeed they are an important starting point for researchers in helping them to find out about studies that have been carried out in their area before. The Internet also provides an enormous amount of information, some of it more credible than others. We will reflect upon the usefulness of a range of sources of information in Chapter 16 when we consider reviewing the literature.

However in terms of actual *methods* that a researcher might employ, alongside the inclusion of questionnaires, interviews and observations, we could also include documentary research as a research *tool*. Indeed Macdonald and Tipton (1993) argue that documentary research has a long history and is valuable as a research tool in its own right as well as in conjunction with other methods as part of the researcher's attempt at triangulating their study.

Denscombe (2003) summarises the types of documents that might be used as:

- newspapers and magazines
- records
- letters and memos
- diaries
- government publications and official statistics.

Let us look at each of these in turn.

Newspapers and magazines

Newspapers and magazines are useful to researchers because they are up-to-date documents. While some might be considered more reliable than others as sources of information, all are useful in gaining an insight into how a story is reported and the kinds of language used in the reporting of particular stories.

Records

Denscombe (2003) notes how the bureaucratisation of industrial societies has produced a range of documents. These might include records of transactions, minutes of meetings, decision-making of committees and suchlike. This type of documentation often serves to enhance public accountability, for example, the minutes of a parents' committee meeting in a nursery will be publicly available so all parents whose children attend the nursery, those who attended the meeting and those who did not, can see what was said and not said, agreed or not agreed. For a researcher, these types of documents may be useful for a range of purposes, such as tracking the development of a new policy or possibly by using **discourse** analysis – something we return to in Chapter 17 – to investigate the way language is used to promote the power of particular individuals or groups, for example. As these types of document are usually publicly available, they are often easy to access by researchers.

Ⓖ

Letters and memos

Private correspondence such as letters can be interesting but differs in many ways to the kinds of publicly available documents such as minutes of meetings. Letters are written to specific people and will often contain detail about people's personal opinions on an issue as opposed to giving an impartial account of something that has happened as, some would argue, might be contained in the minutes of a meeting. Their value lies in the way they allow us to enter the private world of the writer and gain their perceptions of an issue or event and the way they share this with another person. However, in terms of research, as letters are private documents, they can be difficult to access unless the person is well known and their letters form part of an archive. In early childhood, there are archives of writings by people such as Margaret McMillan as their work was so influential on the development of early childhood provision.

Sometimes, private correspondence is made available to a more public audience owing to a sense of duty to add further information about a particular person's life and work or to shed light on an important event and make this information available to the public. Examples of this might be the letters that were exhibited in the Imperial War Museum in London that highlight the experience of child evacuees in the Second World War, or the notes exhibited in the Thomas Coram Foundling Museum in London, which were written by mothers and pinned to their babies when they left them at the foundling hospital in the knowledge they would not see them again.

Diaries

Ⓖ Diaries can be a rich source of **data** to researchers. Denscombe (2003) notes the way that they might contain detail about factual data, for example, a log of things that have happened, significant incidents and personal interpretations. Like letters, diaries should be seen as subjective accounts of things that have happened, affected by the identity of the diarist. However, this is also their strength.

Sometimes, researchers ask people to keep a diary as part of the research. Bell (1998: 73) refers to this type of diary as a 'solicited diary' as it is produced at the request of the researcher. An example might be asking a parent to keep a diary of books read with his or her child or food eaten over a given period. This can be very useful in allowing the researchers some insight into the research participants' world when they are not together, as in an interview. Inevitably, though, it is a research tool that involves a lot of commitment from the participants, who complete much of the data collection themselves away
Ⓖ from the researcher. This can impact on their **reliability**.

Government publications and official statistics

These types of documents are sometimes seen as having greater authority or credibility than documents such as letters or diaries, because they are produced by, or on behalf of,
Ⓖ the state by expert professionals (Denscombe, 2003). The kind of statistical, that is, **quantitative**, data produced in such documents is often seen as 'hard facts' and objective. However, we should always be wary that there may be vested interests in producing the statistics and be mindful that statistics may well mask other information. You may recall, in Chapter 2, that we argued that the real-life social world that we live in is a complex place and the positivist approach of reducing this to numerical data can be problematic.

If we think of a practical example such as bed-turnover in hospitals, official statistics might show a decrease in time that patients stay in hospital after their operations and an increase in patients treated. However, possibly those patients are being discharged from hospital before being fully recovered and are being re-admitted to hospital at a later date. The statistical evidence might mask the way the same patients are being re-admitted and seem positive in demonstrating a high bed-turnover. We have to remember that statistics, like other sources of data, can be open to alternative interpretations.

So far in this section you may have found that the list you made of items you consider to be documents is similar to those discussed. We will now move on to think more broadly about the term 'document'.

As well as text-based documents there are other documents available to researchers that are based on visual images. Just as the number-based information contained in official statistics and the word-based information contained in diaries, letters and suchlike are considered as documents, visual images can also be considered as 'documents' (Denscombe, 2003). In this sense they can be viewed as different forms of 'text'. Hodder (2000: 703) calls written texts and artefacts 'mute evidence' as, unlike an interview, they may well exist long after their creator or user is available for comment. They are therefore invaluable in historical research – one might, for instance, look at the development of children's toys here. Toy museums, for example, are likely to exhibit toys that were produced and played with many years ago, even beyond living memory. These toys can still, however, tell us something about children and childhoods in the era(s) they were designed and used.

Researchers, who base their research on the use of visual images, see images as containing information in the same way as numbers and words do. They are often concerned with the way images serve to represent different attitudes, ideas and values. In other words, their focus will often be on the meanings and symbolism that appear to be behind an image (Denscombe, 2003). This type of research would be regarded as falling within the umbrella of **qualitative** research. However, as you will see in Chapter 17, there are also ways of analysing documents in a more quantitative or number-based way such as in content analysis (Jupp and Norris, 1993).

Activity

Look at the cover design of this book. It has an image of a 'slinky' on it. Make some notes about what this suggests to you.

In looking at the front cover of this book, you may have thought of similar things to our friends, family and colleagues when they looked at the design prior to publication. Here are some examples of their comments:

- 'It seems to represent the learning curve the students might take when reading the book.'
- 'It makes you think research is fun.'
- 'It seems to represent the shifting nature of research.'

We included this example to encourage you to think about documents in their widest sense. But more broadly, what can be described as an image-based document? We might include the following as examples of image-based documentary data (Denscombe, 2003: 223):

- photographs
- films and videos
- archive film footage
- drawings
- the built environment and places
- clothing and fashion items
- cultural artifacts
- body language/signs
- advertisements
- graffiti.

In addition to the above, Macdonald and Tipton (1993: 188) encourage us to think about documents in terms of whether they were meant for public or private record. They add,

> But in addition to the purposeful record, there are those things which may be overtly intended to provoke amusement or admiration or pride or aesthetic enjoyment – songs, buildings, statues, novels – but which nonetheless tell us something about the values, interests and purposes of those who commissioned or produced them.

Before we move on to think about how we might use this vast array of documents, you might like to reflect on the degree to which you considered the above as examples of documents when you started to read this chapter.

〰️ **Reflection point**

Think about a document that is personal to you – it might be a photograph that you keep in a bag or on display at home. Consider the following in relation to it:

- Why is the photograph important to you? Does it remind you of people or a place or an event that is special in some way?
- Why do you keep it in the way that you do? Is it in your bag so you have a constant reminder of the people/place/event with you at all times? (This is often the case with family photographs.) If on display, does the type of frame used or positioning of the photograph tell people something about the value you place on the photograph?

These questions are intended to encourage you to begin to think about how you might 'read' a photograph as you might another sort of text. You will learn more about why and how documents might be used in research as you read on in this chapter.

WHY MIGHT WE USE DOCUMENTS IN RESEARCH?

Some documents, such as letters and diaries can give the researcher an insight into how an issue or event was perceived by individuals or groups at a particular point in history (Barbour, 2008). Another important use of documents – here we are talking about artefacts – is that some areas of experience do not involve language. Many of the research tools used in research are dependent on the use of language, notably questionnaires and interviews. Hodder (2000) draws on research that has looked at how slaves working on plantations in the American South expressed their feelings about and made sense of their oppression through the food and pots they used. Thus, a group whose perspective is often silent has a 'voice' through the study of their artefacts. We should remember, though, that inevitably in this instance, the *interpretation* was done by the researcher years later, and was not done by the those living in slavery themselves. This is an important point to bear in mind and can also be applied to the following example.

We might also think about the artefacts pinned to babies left at the foundling hospital again, as we did earlier in this chapter when we considered the notes left. These artefacts included items such as buttons and could be 'read' as symbolising the love, care and hope these mothers had for their babies when they left them to the care of others in the hospital owing to the dire financial and personal circumstances they found themselves in. It is likely that many of these women could not read and write, given their poverty and the lack of education available to them at that time, making letter-writing impossible. Thus, the items pinned to the babies' clothing still have the power to 'give voice' to the intense emotions these particular mothers may have experienced centuries after they left their children at the hospital. However as Hodder (2000) reminds us, it is important to consider that in using documents, both written texts and artefacts, researchers are not only looking at the context in which the document was produced. They, themselves, are looking at the document within the lens of their own particular context.

Hodder (2000) also argues that we should view artefacts as important components of social relations. Uniforms, for instance, are often developed with a view that they create a common identity among those that wear them – be they adults or children. Thus, if carrying out a study looking at the ethos of a particular school, while one might interview staff, children and parents about this – to name but one strategy – one could also examine the 'mute' material such as the clothing the children and staff are expected to wear. This would add another dimension to the study.

There are other advantages that can be put forward in relation to using documents. Unlike interview data, for instance, looking at documents (in the widest sense of the term) enables the researcher to look at 'material traces' of human life. This can be important because what people *say* they do may well be different to what people *actually* do (Hodder, 2000).

Research in focus

An interesting approach to using artefacts was used in research carried out by Bunting and Freeman (1999). Their research aimed to look at what children eat at school during break times. Rather than interviewing parents or children about this, the research team asked the children to place any empty food packaging and leftover foods (writing down their name if there was no wrapping) into a labelled plastic bag and at the end of the allotted time, they analysed its contents. By doing this, the researchers were able to gain an account of what was consumed without relying on the memory or perceptions of those who had produced the snack (the parents), those who had consumed it (the children), or indeed those who had supervised the break time.

They found that girls were more likely to eat fruit when compared with boys and that children from economically disadvantaged backgrounds were more likely to eat sweets during break times. They concluded that gender and poverty are associated with children's snack choices and recommended that efforts should be made to increase the availability and affordability of healthy foods.

HOW MIGHT WE EVALUATE DOCUMENTARY SOURCES?

Macdonald and Tipton (1993) argue that there is a range of problems a researcher might come across when carrying out documentary research. They group these under four main headings: authenticity, credibility, representativeness and meaning. We will now look at each of these in turn.

Authenticity

Authenticity is clearly important in research that uses documents. It is important that if using diaries or letters, for instance, the researcher knows that they are the work of the person who is accredited with writing them.

Credibility

In considering the credibility of a particular document, the researcher needs to think about whether the document is free from distortion and error (Macdonald and Tipton, 1993). Of course this is affected by a range of factors:

- who produced the document
- who it was produced for (it may never have been intended for public gaze)
- when it was produced
- in what context it was produced.

But this is not as clear-cut as it seems. After all, what source counts as more credible than another?

We are sure that in thinking about the issues raised in this reflection point you might have reflected that the government statistics offer some general, quantitative information but give no indication of the thoughts and feelings associated with being a particular parent of a particular child with SEN in a particular context. As you know from the first two chapters of this book, numerical data such as government statistics do not aim at this.

The diary, however, would allow access to such a partial account, but it is unlikely to have been kept in a systematic way; the mother may have written in the diary only on days when she was exasperated at something that had happened rather than logging her reflections every day whether or not they were negative. Also, crucially, the mother's diary is one account among *many* possible accounts of this same situation. Other family members – not least the child with SEN – his or her siblings and staff in the setting the child attends will also have their own perceptions of inclusive practice in this particular instance. In addition, the diary is a document that is unlikely to have been written with an audience in mind and is highly context specific. After all, we could not generalise this person's account in order to 'speak' for *all* parents of children with SEN.

Representativeness

Representativeness is a key issue in any piece of research. Just as in carrying out interviews or questionnaires, when the researcher needs to think about how their sample represents the **population** as a whole, in documentary research the researcher needs to consider whether the document is representative of the entirety of documents that exist from which the sample was drawn. Sometimes a full archive of documents may exist, but there may well be missing documents. Some may have been destroyed or may be missing. In addition, relevant documents may be held in a range of places.

We might think about the range of information held about key early childhood pioneers here. The Froebel archive at Roehampton University would be a key source of information about Froebel, but does not contain *all* the documents that exist about him. Researching documents is akin to being a detective (Macdonald and Tipton, 1993) as the researcher needs to 'sniff out' new leads on information and be able to identify anything that might be suspect.

Meaning

Macdonald (2008) argues that there are two levels of meaning when looking at a document; its surface and its deeper meaning. To a certain extent, surface and deeper meaning are not so distant from each other. After all, when in conversation with someone we understand the message the speaker wishes to convey, that is, the deeper meaning alongside the grammar. We do not usually separate these out, but it is useful to encourage us to think about the way we 'read' different forms of text (Macdonald, 2008).

Deeper meaning is arrived at through analysis and interpretation. You will learn more about this in Chapter 17, which looks at analysing and presenting data. We will show that for post-structuralists such as Foucault, a 'text' might be a visual image, an object, an event, or process (Woolfitt, 2008). An example of such a 'text' might be a card that is sent to parents to celebrate the birth of their new baby. We might look at the card and, owing to our knowledge of the cultural practices of a particular group of people at a given point in history, might recognise the object as a 'new baby card' and recognise the practice of sending cards. We could look at other more superficial aspects of the card such as whether it says 'boy' or 'girl' on the card. However there are deeper meanings that could be elicited. What colours are used in the image – what are they meant to signify? What is the baby doing in the picture – is s/he active or passive? Does the baby seem to be expressing emotion – if so, what? Is the baby alone or with someone else in the picture? What does the image say about children and childhood in a particular culture, such as the way new babies are welcomed into a family or community or issues of gender in relation to childhood? Who benefits from the perpetuation of the discourses that inform the text, that is, the card? In undertaking such an analysis, it is important to be aware that any interpretations will always be through our own sociocultural and historical lens.

Holland's (2004) book, for instance, is a fascinating look at the way childhood and children are portrayed in popular visual imagery. She argues that we need to look at lots of visual material in order to draw inferences from it. We would not say that *all* new baby cards depict girls as passive and dressed in pink clothing on the basis of one card for example.

This chapter has moved a long way from the idea that documents are letters, diaries, minutes and other forms of written text. We have ended here with the idea that almost anything can be read as a 'text'. This view is open to criticism, not least because it is far easier to 'read' these many forms of 'text' (used in the widest sense of the word) than actually achieving real and lasting *change*. After all, in the real world of human interaction, some ideas dominate and repression is *real* (Bordo, 2003; hooks, 1990). Thus, we might 'read' new-baby cards for their portrayals of gender, but achieving real movement towards gender *equity* is far more difficult to achieve. However, a reading of such 'texts' is useful in encouraging us to look again at some of the taken-for-granted assumptions we might hold about the world around us.

Key points from the chapter 🔑

- There are many different types of 'document'. These might include written texts such as diaries and newspapers as well as artefacts such as toys, clothing and photographs.
- Documentary analysis can be employed as *part* of a research project but can also be used as the primary research tool.

- Care needs to be taken to ensure that if documents are used in research, they are authentic and credible. However, the issue of credibility does not preclude the use of partial sources, such as personal diaries. Different types of document allow the researcher different insights and it is important to acknowledge this when writing up the research.
- Documents can be analysed for their surface and deeper meanings – a point we pick up in more detail in Chapter 17.

Further reading

Hodder, I. (2000) 'The interpretation of documents and materials culture', in N.K. Denzin and Y.S. Lincoln (eds), *Handbook of Qualitative Research*. 2nd edn. London: Sage. A more challenging read than the others noted here, but an excellent chapter looking at the use of documents and visual texts – in their widest sense – in research.

Holland, P. (2004) *Picturing Childhood: The Myth of the Child in Popular Imagery*. London: Tauris. This book is a fascinating look at how popular cultural images of children and childhood can be analysed and interpreted.

Macdonald, K. (2008) 'Using documents', in N. Gilbert (ed.), *Researching Social Life*. 3rd edn. London: Sage. A useful introductory read about using documents in research in a general research methods' text.

JOURNALING AS A RESEARCH TOOL

Chapter objectives

- To consider how an examination of oneself can be legitimate in research
- To develop an understanding of how journaling can be employed as a primary mode of data collection
- To outline some of the tools that can be used to enhance reflection in journal writing
- To gain an understanding of the possibilities and limitations of journaling as a research tool

Rather than thinking about research as something carried out with *other* people, in this chapter we think about how the *self* can be a legitimate subject for research. As you will see, this is an area of research that has been a feature of **qualitative** feminist research in particular. But it has also been employed by professionals, who are interested in examining aspects of their practice and responses to these with a view to gaining greater insight into their work. Therefore, there is a link to the action research chapter, which was also concerned with an examination of one's own professional practice.

In this chapter, we will be introducing you to the use of journaling in research and will consider how it can be employed as a research tool. A key concept that we return to in this chapter is '**reflexivity**'. It is a term we looked at in Chapter 2. In writing this chapter, we debated whether to include it in Part 2 of this book as it is strongly linked to Chapter 8 on action research and can be regarded as an *approach* to research. In addition, owing to its usefulness in the research *process*, we might have included this chapter in Part 4 of the book. We eventually decided that it should be included here as its focus is primarily on using journaling as a research *tool*.

THE SELF AS A LEGITIMATE SUBJECT FOR STUDY

For some of you reading this book, looking at *oneself* as legitimate research may seem strange because traditional models of research have tended to emphasise the need to neutralise the self of the researcher. You may recall this from Chapter 1. Indeed control, restraint and even the silencing of the researcher's own voice is often pursued in order to attain 'respectability' as a researcher in a particular academic discipline (Charmaz and Mitchell, 1997). Furthermore, in the academic world, the 'proper' subject for research has traditionally been seen as someone *other* than the researcher him/herself (Mykhalovsky, 1997).

This is changing. Increasingly, the self of the researcher is being seen as important in research. Wasserfall (1997) argues that this, in part, has been due to the increasing recognition that the self of the researcher is a key *instrument* in research. The personal history, biases and suchlike of the researcher are seen as inevitably impacting in some way(s) on the research, from initial design to writing up. In addition, there is acknowledgement that the self of the researcher is in constant flux, impacting upon the research and changing as a result of it (Coffey, 1999; Reinharz, 1997). You may recall, from Chapter 2, that this is known as reflexivity.

The corollary of this is that there has been a growth in research that puts personal writing at the centre of its analyses (DeVault, 1997). Sometimes this is known as autoethnography. As the term suggests, it is a combination of the words 'autobiography' and 'ethnography', and refers to research that places the self of the researcher firmly within the narrative of the research. Etherington (2004) views it as both a method and the resulting text. Autoethnographers sometimes present their writing in texts that could be regarded as more 'experimental' than those described elsewhere in this book, such as through the use of poetry or dance. While we would not want to dismiss the use of such presentations of people's research owing to their possibilities for *creative expression*, we think this might be difficult for a novice researcher to justify and achieve within early childhood studies as a field at the present time.

What follows in this chapter is a discussion of some of the uses that can be made of journaling in a research project. Journaling can be employed as a tool to help the researcher reflect upon his or her research as and when issues arise, but may not be the main **data**-gathering instrument. It can also be used as the primary research tool in itself. **Ⓖ** It is this final usage of journaling that we will be concentrating upon.

WHAT DO WE MEAN BY A 'JOURNAL'?

A journal is a private document that is used by the writer to document their thoughts and feelings about any number of issues that seem important to them (Etherington, 2004). In other words it can be viewed as a 'vehicle for reflection' (Moon, 2006: 1). Moon (2006) refers to journals as 'learning journals' but recognises that they are variously referred to as 'diaries' or 'logs'. For Moon, 'learning journal' is a useful term to employ because it gives a sense of the journal reflecting the writer's ongoing processes of reflection and learning. However, for the purposes of this chapter we will use the terms 'journal' and 'journaling'.

The writer of a journal will use whatever they are most comfortable with or whatever is available to them for the purpose. Thus, it might be a pad of paper, an attractively bound book, a Dictaphone or tape-recorder if writing is difficult, or it may be kept on a universal serial bus (USB) stick. At some point, it may be useful to develop an index or means of accessing the information contained in the journal in order to ease access to specific entries as well as help with the reflection process (Clough and Nutbrown, 2002; Moon, 2006).

Entries into a journal may include small notes about something or extended discussions about an issue or situation. There may be entries made every day or only occasionally. These entries might be in the form of notes, stories, diagrams, poetry and so on (Etherington, 2004; Bolton, 2001). In addition, journaling may include a revisiting of past entries with additional journal entries made in relation to these. We discuss the importance of this later in the chapter. Bolton (2001: 160) exhorts her readers to 'experiment!' Therefore, a journal is a personal document that is kept in an idiosyncratic way (Clough and Nutbrown, 2002). Moon (2006: 27) encapsulates this idea by employing a driving metaphor, saying, 'the writer is at the wheel and is steering'. Bolton (2001: 155) similarly describes a journal as an 'organic tool' that aids the reflective process as opposed to its being a 'created product.'

It is likely that the writer of a journal would not want their journal to be open to scrutiny in its entirety but may choose specific entries to share with others. However, when using journaling as a *research tool* as opposed to purely for personal use, some of its contents inevitably become part of an assessment process. This might be at a university where the researcher is studying or through a peer-review process when writing a paper based on the research for a journal.

WHY USE JOURNALING AS A RESEARCH TOOL?

Journaling is used in a variety of different spheres. It is increasingly being suggested as a tool for professional development. This can be seen in the growth in the idea of the 'reflective practitioner' (Bolton, 2001; Moon, 2006; Schon, 1983). Many writers encourage researchers to keep a reflective journal throughout their research (Clough and Nutbrown, 2002; Roberts-Holmes, 2005). Other writers emphasise writing as a *primary* research tool or data-gathering instrument (Brown and Jones, 2001; Richardson and Adams St Pierre, 2005). Researchers are variously encouraged to document their thoughts and feelings in a journal and use these writings to:

- act as an aide-memoire for points to think about further or to note things to explore later or that have been useful in some way
- help with sorting out an initial focus for the research
- document any thoughts and feelings during the research. This might involve the researcher in reflecting on their impact on the research and the impact the research is having (and has had) on them
- form the main basis of the data.

We will think about each of these points in turn.

Journaling as an aide-memoire

This is probably the least interesting use of journaling, but it is nonetheless useful. While this use of journaling cannot make claims to being a data-gathering instrument or research tool as such, a journal is beneficial to researchers as a central point for jotting down things s/he would like to look up, such as a reference and suchlike. You may have experienced losing notes made on scraps of paper or Post-it notes and therefore value the idea of having a location such as a journal to keep such information. Thus, there is a very practical reason for keeping a journal (Etherington, 2004).

Journaling to help find an initial focus for research

Journaling may be useful at the initial stage of carrying out a research project as it can help to develop an idea for the research. Tripp (1993) discusses how journaling what he describes as 'critical incidents' can be useful in providing starting points for research. The term 'critical incident' refers to how one interprets a given event and is highly individual. In this sense, the practitioner-researcher *creates* an incident as 'critical'. Critical incidents may seem like commonplace events that occur in one's practice, but on deeper reflection they trouble the writer who journals about them in some way.

In looking at one's journal, the researcher may be able to identify areas that they would like to explore further in their research. Possibly a similar issue keeps coming up in their journal. An example might be a practitioner reflecting that s/he keeps writing about the way sleep times are organised in his/her early childhood setting. However, it should be noted that Tripp (1993) maintains that what moves an event from the 'typical' to the 'critical' is the detailed analysis one undertakes of it. We will find out more about analysing critical incidents later in the chapter.

Journaling to document thoughts and feelings during the research process

Journaling can be a useful tool in encouraging the researcher to document the *process* of their research. It can encourage the writing down of personal feelings alongside the keeping of field notes and observations for instance. This, in turn can encourage greater empathy with participant(s) in the study as well as attunement with oneself (Etherington, 2004; Moon, 2006). This material might be drawn upon at the writing up stage of the research in order to account for any decisions made in relation to research methods, for instance. De Vault (1997) argues that this documenting of the research story is usually done in order to establish the authority of the researcher, that is, 'why they did what they did' in the research process. In carrying out a piece of early childhood research at a college or university, you are usually expected to justify any decisions that were taken in relation to **methodology**, methods and suchlike.   Ⓖ

Research in focus

Miller (1998) carried out research looking at the event of childbirth and the process of becoming a mother. She interviewed a group of mothers at three points on their journey into motherhood, during and after pregnancy. Her personal story is interwoven with the stories of the women she documents. An example of this is the way she shares her own feelings in her writings about the research. An example of this is as follows: 'I had experienced feelings of elation and desperation, but the overriding feeling was that no one had said it would be like this: the lived experience of becoming a mother did not resonate with the 'public' account of what it would be like' (ibid.: 59). This is a departure from the idea that research should only report on what *participants* in the research are saying.

Miller notes how her own autobiography in relation to motherhood was central to her decision to undertake research into becoming a mother. She notes, 'as a researcher the private and the personal in my autobiography led to my desire to privilege women's personal narratives … the researcher's autobiography can be discerned as a continuous and dynamic thread running throughout all stages of the research process in qualitative research' (ibid.: 60). She argues that the idea of research being 'ordered' and 'rational' did not fit easily with the messiness of everyday personal experiences and stresses the need to document personal feelings during research.

Journaling as the main tool in data gathering

While journaling is a useful tool in documenting the researcher's feelings and thoughts during the research process, it is also a useful tool in itself, as a *prime* method of data gathering. It is to this that the chapter now turns.

Brown and Jones (2001) see writing as central to action research as opposed to the use of other methods such as questionnaires. Through writing, they argue that the writer (practitioner-researcher) is commentating and responding to changes they have made to their practice as well as reflecting on what any future actions might be. They maintain that the practitioner-researcher *evolves* in the context of their *ever-evolving* place of work. As you can see, this is a far cry from the positivist concern with developing a universally agreed understanding of an issue that is relevant for all time and in all contexts.

We can also see this rejection of positivism in Richardson and Adams St Pierre's (2005: 961) discussion of writing. They claim that 'language does not "reflect" social realities but rather produces meaning and creates social reality'. In addition, they argue that 'language constructs one's subjectivity in ways that are historically and locally specific' (ibid.).

 Reflection point

There are some complex ideas being expressed here about writing and language, not least that its meaning is not fixed in a way that can be understood by everyone in the same way for all time in different contexts. It is a viewpoint that is strongly allied to the post-structuralist position on language. Let us think about this in relation to a concrete example:

smacking young children. There are many discourses that exist around this, with some occupying a more powerful position for particular individuals owing to a range of factors such as their childhood experiences, experience of parenting, work with young children in some capacity, locally accepted practice at that point in history and so on. Here are some you may have come across:

- 'A smack never did me any harm when I was a child.'
- 'It's OK to smack *young* children – it's all they understand.'
- 'Professionals should not smack young children but it is alright in the context of a loving home environment.'
- 'It is children's right to be protected from harm just like we would protect adults from harm.'
- 'It's the right of every parent to care for their children in their own way – it is not the job of professionals to tell families what to do in the privacy of their own homes.'

(You should note that these are but a few of the many discourses that are taken up (or rejected) in relation to smacking – we are sure you could add to these.)

Reflect on the different ideas being expressed here about what it is to be a child and a parent and the role of the state in supporting children and families. You might also like to reflect on the issue of smacking in relation to different aspects of your life, that is, some early years' practitioners would be horrified at the idea of smacking children in their professional work but believe it is acceptable to smack their *own* children. You may also like to deepen your reflection on this issue, if you feel able to, by journaling your thoughts and reflecting on why you hold the position(s) that you do. Try also to journal some competing positions to disrupt your initial thoughts on this issue in order to offer an alternative story. Journaling, as we shall see, can be a very useful tool in doing this.

A key advantage of journaling is that it enables the researcher to re-enter the same story and reinterpret that story in the light of new understandings and experiences. This might be an ongoing process as you might look at a piece of writing many times and interpret it differently each time. You may, for example, look at your journaling about the issue of smacking on another occasion and think differently about what you had written previously. The new insights and interpretations could also be noted in the journal in order to deepen your understanding of this complex issue. As Richardson and Adams St Pierre (2005: 962) note, writing enables us to know ourselves and 'explore new ways of knowing', acknowledging that we are all constantly in a process of creating ourselves. Moon (2006) also emphasises the way that a journal reflects the changing ideas and ongoing learning of the writer. In essence, inevitably, we change!

It would seem, then, that the use of journaling in research acknowledges the complexity of issues in our case, in relation to early childhood. In Chapter 8 we noted this in relation to early childhood practice. In writing, the 'up close and personal' nature of the inquiry is rarely easy and the use of journaling also welcomes data into the research that may not always be written about. Adams St Pierre (in Richardson and Adams St Pierre, 2005: 970) variously refers to this as 'dream data, sensual data, emotional data, response data and memory data' and discusses how she uses writing to think by writing her 'way into particular spaces'. She highlights the importance of this because she maintains that other data collection methods such as interviewing, on their own, do not document *everything* that is important in a research project. The next section looks at some tools that might enable the writer to write their 'way into particular spaces' and deepen their reflection on the issues with which they are concerned.

TOOLS TO HELP DEVELOP REFLECTIVE JOURNAL WRITING

So far in this chapter we have discussed a range of ways that journaling might be used in research. In this section, the aim is to provide an introduction to some of the many creative ideas that have been developed to encourage deeper reflection in journal writing. A couple of these are outlined in the following activity section.

Activity

Richardson and Adams St Pierre (2005) offer a range of interesting ideas for creating what they term 'analytical writing practices'. We think some of these could be useful in early childhood research. You should note here that we are relating these tasks to those of you that *work* with young children and families, but the tasks could easily be amended to other contexts.

Activity 1
Consider a particular setting, for example, a children's centre. Think about the range of subject positionings you have or have had in that centre. As an example, this might include being a parent of a child in the centre, taking the lead in running parenting classes, organising fundraising events in the evenings in the centre, and studying for an early childhood qualification. Thus, one might (*now or in the past*) be a team leader, a parent, a fund-raiser, a student. We could also add being a Black woman or a lone parent or 'green' activist (whatever subject positionings you might apply to yourself). Write about the children's centre from these different perspectives and consider what you 'know' from these various subject positions. Richardson and Adams St Pierre (2005: 975) then recommend that you let these different points of view enter into dialogue with each other and reflect on what you learn through these dialogues. But more than this, they ask the writer to consider what this tells them about social inequities in the particular context chosen – in this instance, a children's centre.

Activity 2
Another analytical writing practice suggested by Richardson and Adams St Pierre (2005: 975) is one which consists of writing about something that has happened to you from your own perspective – we are suggesting that it might be something that relates to your work with young children and families. Then interview another participant in this story – it might be someone from a different professional group or another person in your team for instance, depending on the story chosen to write about. As the writer, you need to try to see yourself as part of the *participant's* story in the same way as they are part of *your own* story. Now think about how you could rewrite the story from the participant's point of view and the *challenges* this raises.

The analytical writing practices outlined in the activity box may certainly prove challenging, but could offer valuable opportunities to interrogate practice and recognise alternative avenues for interpretation. This might be especially important in the area of multi-agency working, which is recognised as being complex owing to variations in the way different agencies and professionals understand and put into practice issues relating to – in our case – working with children and families (Anning et al., 2006).

Moon (2006) devotes a chapter to activities designed to enhance journal writing. In one section she encourages the writer to work on self-improvement and problem-solving through journaling. Through writing about solving a problem, the writer also learns about the *process* of problem-solving. This might be a useful strategy to employ as part of an action research project where improving practice is central as its aim. She also suggests strategies such as using a SWOT analysis of an event, project or situation. By this, she means reviewing this event, project or situation in terms of its strengths (S), then weaknesses (W), then thinking through the opportunities (O) and threats (T) to making possible changes.

Earlier in the chapter we looked at how 'critical incidents' might be useful in deciding on a focus for a research project. Tripp (1993: 44–54) outlines a range of ways that they might be used. Here are some of them:

The 'why?' challenge

This, as the title suggests, involves subjecting the incident deemed 'critical' to ongoing 'why?' questions. This can help the writer to progressively challenge their beliefs relating to a particular incident.

Dilemma identification

Tripp (1993) maintains that many critical incidents involve a dilemma or a series of dilemmas. An examination of these can be helpful in enabling the practitioner to deal more effectively with it next time but, importantly, it helps her/him to see that the source of these dilemmas is not always of their own making. In early childhood, an example might be that a practitioner writes about a critical incident when s/he was torn between meeting the needs of an individual child, who wanted her or him to read a particular story near to home time. The practitioner felt unable to do this because of perceived competing demands of ensuring the nursery room was tidied up and the children got ready for home time.

Personal theory analysis

This can help deepen the analysis of the dilemma identification because here, the writer reflects on their personal theories and the way they influence their professional judgements. Any decisions made in relation to dilemmas have their basis in a range of often unstated values and these can be opened up to scrutiny through reflective writing. If we take the example outlined in the previous section – a practitioner torn between meeting the needs of an individual child and the need to get a task done in a particular time frame – this might involve reflecting on fundamental questions about the individual v. group and children v. tasks to be done.

THE POSSIBILITIES AND LIMITATIONS OF USING JOURNALING AS A RESEARCH TOOL

So far in this chapter, we have thought about how a journal might be used as an *aid* to the research and as an actual *method* in itself. We have also explored some of the tools that might be useful in encouraging the writer to develop a greater degree of reflection in their journaling. This final section summarises some of what we see are the possibilities and limitations of using journaling as a research tool.

First, the action of writing enables the writer to slow down their thoughts and in so doing it may seem as if the world slows down long enough to take stock (Brown and Jones, 2001). This can be very useful, but the time this takes up can also be its downfall (Moon, 2006). After all, if something takes time it can be easy to think of excuses for not doing it. But we should remember that any methods that are employed in research *will* take time. The use of any data gathering instrument will involve time and effort, not least in developing the understanding and skills needed to be able to use it effectively. This leads to our second point.

We should be mindful that keeping a journal in itself does not necessarily mean that the entries will be *reflective*. It may well be that early attempts at writing are descriptive and the writer may need to practise journaling in order to improve the level of reflection it might engender (Moon, 2006). The use of a range of different tools to enhance the reflection is recommended in this chapter as this enables writers to go beyond merely *outlining* an event, situation or project to a position that *asks questions of it* and crucially, asks questions of them *personally*.

Thirdly, the use of journaling as a research tool could be regarded as narcissistic or overly self-indulgent. DeVault (1997: 225), for instance, expresses a concern that 'the recent emphasis on the personal may signal a retreat from the attempt to interpret a wider social world'. However the corollary of this is that voices that are sometimes excluded or on the margins might be given a central platform. Examples of groups of people whose experience has often been marginalised might include lone parents, Black women, or travellers. But while journaling seems a highly promising avenue for research, we should recognise that this might reinforce journaling as a tool for those marked out as 'others' (DeVault, 1997). DeVault goes on to argue that it is important that personal writing is located within a larger picture – the situations that produced and continue to produce the story. Sometimes people talk about this as 'situating oneself' (Letherby, 2003: 143). Letherby (2003) is positive about writing about oneself in research, drawing upon Okley's work to make a distinction between 'self adoration' and 'self-awareness and a critical scrutiny of the self' (p. 143). We believe this is an important distinction to emphasise as a justification for using journaling as a research tool.

Therefore, on a positive note, journaling is attributed to developing greater self-awareness in researchers in relation to their thoughts and feelings, biases, responses and behaviours (Etherington, 2004). However Etherington also acknowledges that in autoethnographic approaches to research, which put the self firmly at the centre, there is an inevitable *telling of the stories of others*. If we think about a concrete example here, in journaling about one's experience of working in an early years' setting, a practitioner is likely to be telling a story about the children, families and colleagues with whom s/he works. Thus, there are ethical implications associated with doing this in terms of consent and anonymity.

A consideration of ethics also needs to be thought through in terms of the researcher. In becoming the *subject* for the research, there is no anonymity for the researcher. In this sense, opening oneself up to scrutiny in research could be regarded as emotionally dangerous (Letherby, 2003). Letherby (2003) notes this in relation to her own work, stating that this has an impact upon the decisions she takes as to what to include and exclude in her published work. This might impact on any research findings. However, this charge could also be levelled at other methods such as interviewing and questionnaires. Research participants will pick and choose the aspects of their lives they want to share with a researcher. In doing this, they will inevitably leave some things out.

We hope you can see that there are many ideas about using journaling as a research tool. As with any other method, journaling is a tool that has possibilities as well as limitations for the researcher. We believe that journaling is useful for *all* researchers in order to document their feelings and thoughts in relation to a range of issues to do with their research. In terms of being a *central* mode of data collection, it may be particularly useful in action research studies in relation to early childhood where the researcher is also a practitioner.

Key points from the chapter 🔑

- The self of the researcher is now considered to be a legitimate subject for research.
- Journaling during the research process can help the researcher to reflect on thoughts and feelings related to the research as and when they arise.
- Journaling itself can also be seen as a research tool. This is especially the case in research that is linked to professional practice, such as in action research.
- A key use of a journal is the way it can enable the researcher to re-enter stories and reinterpret them in the light of their new experiences and understandings – in the recognition that ideas are in constant flux. In this way, journaling can act in a way to disrupt 'common-sense' or present thinking about a given topic or situation and encourage the writer to consider alternative or competing stories.

Further reading

Etherington, K. (2004) *Becoming a Reflexive Researcher: Using Ourselves in Research*. London: Jessica Kingsley. An interesting book on the subject from an author with a counselling and psychotherapy background.

Moon, J. (2006) *Learning Journals: A Handbook for Reflective Practice and Professional Development*. 2nd edn. Abingdon: Routledge. A useful introduction to using a journal – not necessarily only for research purposes.

Richardson, L. and Adams St Pierre, E. (2005) 'Writing: a method of inquiry', in N. Denzin and Y. Lincoln (eds). *The Sage Handbook of Qualitative Research*. 3rd edn. London: Sage. A far more challenging read than the other texts mentioned here but a chapter that is highly thought-provoking about the uses of writing in research.

CREATIVE METHODS FOR LISTENING TO CHILDREN IN RESEARCH

Chapter objectives

- To further develop the idea that research can involve children directly as participants
- To consider what might be meant by the idea of 'creative methods'
- To think about a range of research methods that might directly elicit young children's views
- To reflect upon the possibilities and limitations of such methods

In Part 1 of this book, we discussed the development of research that involves listening to and engaging with children directly in research. This is linked to the growth of work, which stresses the need for children's views to be sought on matters that affect them, following the UN Convention on the Rights of the Child (see Chapter 4 especially). Crucially, the emergence of participatory research can be viewed as a challenge to thinking that has positioned children as *passive* in research (Veale, 2005). Indeed Malewski (2005: 221) argues that children often offer the 'cleverest voices' in research.

The development of research in this area can be seen in the increasing number of publications that focus on the use of children-centred methods that involve children *directly* in the research process as well as research that reports on studies that have been carried out *with* children. You will read about a few of these studies as you work through the chapter.

Our purpose in this chapter is to outline some of the creative approaches to listening to young children in research that have been developed – with a focus on *early* childhood. In doing this, we recognise that there has been significant growth in this area over the past few years and there are likely to be many other interesting methods that have been used but not reported here. We include a discussion about children's drawing and photography *here* rather than in the chapter that looks at using documents in research because here we want to focus on using these tools as an *active* strategy rather than what Robson (1993: 272) describes as an 'unobtrusive measure'.

LISTENING TO YOUNG CHILDREN IN RESEARCH: DEVELOPING AN INCLUSIVE APPROACH

We begin this chapter by reiterating our commitment to the development of strategies that involve young children as *participants* in research. Before looking more directly at methods that might be used in order to do this, we will outline what 'creative listening' might mean. We will then think about this in relation to research carried out with young children and make the case for developing inclusive methods in research.

Roberts-Holmes (2005) links the notion of 'creative listening' to young children to the Hundred Languages of Children – a term used in Reggio Emilia to denote the many ways that children 'speak' to us about their experiences, perceptions and concerns using music, talk, sculpture, painting and suchlike. He argues that researchers need to be receptive to these many languages in order to elicit children's perspectives.

A commitment to not only listening but to *hearing* young children is a theme that also runs throughout Soto and Swadener's (2005) edited book on research with children. With this in mind, Malewski (2005: 219) argues for 'precocious methodologies' in research with children. By this, he is referring to methods that *empower* children and youth and offer a challenge to traditional practices in research that have had a tendency to ignore the lived experiences of particular children in particular sociocultural contexts. For Veale (2005), participatory or creative methods that involve children in research offer a challenge to traditional ideas about research, such as positivism, because they combine both scientific rigour with imagination and creativity.

Before we move on to discuss some of these creative methods, it is important to note that we are aware that the development of innovative approaches to involving young children in research can also be criticised, at times, for falling into the trap of being a 'gimmick approach' (Dockett and Perry, 2007: 50). As with any methods chosen, they need to be 'fit for purpose'. It should also be noted here that we believe that interviewing children continues to be a significant method in early childhood research, once young children are able to do this. Similarly, we think that observation continues to be a key research tool, particularly when carrying out research with very young children and babies. Chapters 9 and 10 looked at these research tools respectively.

Malewski (2005) is critical of methods that are underpinned by a belief that children's perceived unpredictability and naivety should be compensated for in some way. It is important that creative methods for involving young children in research are not perceived as such. While we agree that researchers should not underestimate children's abilities, we do think the researcher has a responsibility to develop methods that are suited to children's current or persistent interests and their perceived level of knowledge and understanding. This has particular resonance for *early childhood* research owing to the vulnerability of young children and, on occasions, their parents (Langston et al., 2004). An example of this might be that we would not expect a child aged 2 years to be able to participate in an interview that includes questions worded with an older, more experienced person in mind. Similarly, we would not expect a 2-year-old child to sit in one place for a length of time for an interview as we might most adults. This also links to Alderson's (2005) work on ethical research with children and her belief that it is wrong to put children in a position which is difficult for them – one that possibly highlights what they do not know and cannot do as opposed to what they do know and can do. Therefore, the researcher needs to ensure that the methods they choose to use are appropriate for the *particular* children participating in the research (Greene and Hill, 2005).

We would also want to add here that what might work with one group of children or child on one occasion, might not be a successful research strategy on another occasion. For those of you who have had direct experience of caring for young children, this might seem like a truism. This is not an argument for the 'special' or different nature of young children here, but a recognition that adults and children alike are not fixed entities, with fixed emotions and fixed ideas. Research participants, like the researcher and the context in which the research is carried out, are ever changing.

〰 **Reflection point**

What challenges does the argument that people and contexts are changeable hold for researchers?

In thinking through the question raised in this reflection point, you may have reflected that the changeable nature of human ideas, feelings and behaviours is problematic for researchers working within the positivist **paradigm**, who aim for uncovering 'truths' **G** about the world.

So far we have made the case that researchers might employ a range of creative methods in order to involve children directly as *participants* in research. Before looking at some of these methods, it is important to stress the importance of developing research methods that are inclusive of *all* children. This can be difficult in research where collective participation is the chosen approach, such as in the use of drama and role play, because inequities can be masked by the research process (Veale, 2005). An example might be a child that does not participate equally in a particular aspect of a research project owing to differentials in class, gender, ethnicity or ability in comparison with other group members. As with any method employed in research, if some children – and indeed adults – are unable to participate in the research for some reason, this may result in a silencing of their perspectives. This, in turn, is likely to impact on the **validity** of the research findings. **G**

What follows in this chapter is a discussion of a range of creative methods that might be employed when carrying out research that involves children *directly*.

PHOTOGRAPHY

Photography is a tool that has been employed creatively in research projects with young children. Cook and Hess (2007: 32), in their discussion of three research projects involving children using cameras, summarise the key benefits as:

- Using cameras is an engaging strategy for children.
- Acceptable results can be produced by young children with modern equipment.
- As young children are able to operate many modern cameras, they are able to be in control of what they take pictures of. Thus, the resulting pictures are likely to reflect the children's interests and concerns.
- Using photographs is a more tangible strategy than direct interviewing, particularly if the topic under

discussion is complex or abstract. This is an important point to consider in research with young children.

- Photographs enable the researcher to return to a topic at a later date as they act as a visual prompt for the children.
- Photographs can be used when writing up a research project, making the resulting work accessible and interesting to the children.

However we need to be cautious in using cameras. Roberts-Holmes (2005) argues that a delay in printing out photographs can mean a loss of interest in the subject matter by the children. He points to the ethical issues involved in taking photographs of children, advising that permission is sought from practitioners (including the manager), parents and carers and children themselves. In addition, when thinking about photography, the researcher should also consider *ownership* of the photographs. Children should be given a copy of photographs they have taken or that have been taken of them.

 Case study

Anna's research for her Early Childhood Studies degree project aimed to look at the benefits of using a forest school on a weekly basis for a term with a reception class. She decided to adopt a multi-method approach to address issues of triangulation, including using children's drawings, observations of the children, discussions with the children in small groups, parent questionnaires before and after the forest school programme, interviews with practitioners, and making use of digital cameras with the children.

Anna encouraged the children to use the digital cameras to take photographs of the things they were interested in on their visits to the wooded area. She used the photographs as points for discussion on return to the classroom, asking the children to tell her why they had taken a particular picture. Here are some examples of comments children made:

- Daniel had taken a photograph of a large red flower. He said 'I like it – it's really beautiful'.
- Seema had taken a photograph of some rubbish and stated 'there shouldn't be rubbish in *our* wood'.
- Thomas had taken a photograph of a pile of sticks and assorted materials with a group of children building a den from them. He observed that the picture was of 'my friends making a den'.
- Hamdi had taken some photographs of children jumping from a large log, noting, 'I like jumping off the logs'.

From these comments and other data gathered with the children, such as drawings and interviews, Anna began to identify a few themes. These were as follows:

- Children appreciated the aesthetic quality of the wooded area.
- Over the period of the project, the children began to talk of the wood as '*our* wood' as opposed to '*the* wood'. Anna saw this as important in children's developing sense of ownership and stewardship towards the natural world.
- The children enjoyed having the opportunity to work together on mini-projects such as building dens, which encouraged a cooperative approach to learning.

- The children appreciated the opportunity for physical challenge that the wooded area offered.

Alongside writing up her project for an adult audience, Anna made a book with the children based on the children's participation in the project and this is now kept in the book area so the children can look at it and recall what they had done. In this way, Anna had thought through how the findings of her project could be disseminated to the child-participants as well as for the adult audience. We will be looking at data analysis as well as writing up a research project in the final part of this book.

DRAWINGS

Children's drawings have a history of being used as a tool employed to assess their cognitive and/or emotional functioning (Veale, 2005). Some of you may be familiar with the 'draw-a-man' test devised by Goodenough (1926), for instance. But drawings can also be regarded as a tool that might be employed creatively in early childhood research.

Roberts-Holmes (2005) argues that drawings are a powerful means through which children represent their feelings and explore and learn. Moreover, they offer a means for children to communicate meanings about topics that have meaning for them. Veale (2005), for instance, comments on their usage in research with children in countries that have been affected by war and violence, such as Croatia and Rwanda.

Young children of many abilities seem to enjoy painting and drawing, therefore they may be useful inclusive and participatory tools to employ in research (Roberts-Holmes, 2005). However they are unlikely to be useful as a method in research with babies and very young children, for instance.

Drawings made by others might also be employed as a research tool. Veale (2005) discusses the use of a drawing of a happy girl and boy and a drawing of a sad girl and boy in encouraging children to discuss what the drawn figures might be thinking. She points out that the youngest children in her study tended to prefer free drawing as opposed to a drawing session (or indeed other activities) structured by adults. The youngest children in her study were 7 years old – at the top of the age range that might be considered 'early childhood'. Thus, while we would not want to make generalisations to all children based on age, we should always be mindful of the ages of the child participants when we examine published research.

In addition to this, we should remember that employing the use of children's drawings has other limitations – like any other method. One such criticism is that children need to be familiar with drawing as a medium of expression in order for it to be employed effectively (Veale, 2005). After all, we should remember that drawing is only one of the 'hundred languages' or means through which children represent their lives. Another charge that could be levelled at their use is that drawings might be open to multiple interpretations. However, as we have noted elsewhere in this book, this could also be said of observation

Ⓖ and interview **data** for instance. Therefore it is crucial that researchers employing drawing as a method encourage children to *talk* about their drawings. Not to do so, would mean that any analysis of the drawings would be purely on the basis of the researcher's interpretation of what they may or may not signify and this is likely to be problematic. It also seems to go against the spirit of *listening* to children in the research.

🔍 Research in focus

Angelides and Michaelidou (2009) carried out research using children's drawings as a tool to help them to understand young children's feelings of marginalisation. The use of drawings and the children's talk about them was viewed as a key strategy in 'giving voice' to children's experience of marginalisation and exclusion. The researchers define 'marginalisation' in terms of whether a child occupies a position that is marginal *academically* or *socially* (ibid.: 30).

The research was conducted in a class of 22 children aged 5 years in Cyprus, with the researchers visiting the school twice a week for a four-month period. After spending time getting to know the children and staff, Angelides and Michaelidou spent time with the children in small groups engaging them in drawing using a range of media. They were given a topic, 'the break', as a basis for their drawing, chosen to enable the children to express the feelings they had towards break times. The resulting drawings were discussed with the children who had drawn them. Alongside this strategy, all children were interviewed.

When analysing the data from these phases in the research, Angelides and Michaelidou identified six children who seemed to be saying that they had experienced marginalisation. These children were then asked to draw whatever they wanted. Figures 14.1 and 14.2 are two of the drawings that came from this study and a synopsis of what was said about them.

Figure 14.1 'It's break time and the rabbit is playing. It is playing with the games … they do not want it to be their friend' (Angelides and Michaelidou, 2009: 39 reproduced with permission)

The child who drew the picture in Figure 14.1, Peter, told the researchers that he had only drawn one rabbit because no one wanted to be its friend. Angelides and Michaelidou suggest that he is expressing his own feelings of isolation at break times, projecting his own feelings of marginalisation into his drawing of a rabbit. They had noted that Peter was a quiet child in the class, who often had games taken away from him and rarely participated in activities or class discussions with his peers.

Figure 14.2 'The sun plays with Maria' (Angelides and Michaelidou, 2009: 42 reproduced with permission)

The child who drew the picture in Figure 14.2, Maria, was new to the school and seemed to have difficulties in making friends. A constant theme in her pictures was a sun playing with a girl. In this picture, we can see *two* girls. Maria told one of the researchers that the girl (who is closer to the sun in the picture) is playing with the sun. When asked whether the other girl was also playing with the sun, Maria replied 'No, she is Christiana, and she is far away in Greece. Only this girl is playing with her friend the sun' (Angelides and Michaelidou, 2009: 42). When asked further about this, Maria told the researcher that the girl is playing with the sun because she has no friends – her friends being in Greece. Maria seems to have projected her feelings of isolation onto the girl playing with the sun, far away from the friends she had known and still misses.

Angelides and Michaelidou (2009: 43) do not propose any grand theory based on their research nor do they argue that their research strategy could reveal each instance of children's marginalisation. However, they maintain that 'children's drawings and discussions with their creators revealed many hidden dimensions of children's school life', amounting to a 'deafening silence'. As inclusion is an important concept in education, it would seem that strategies that enable children to express their experiences of isolation and marginalisation are vital in helping everyone involved in early childhood education better recognise, understand and address these issues in their practice.

PLAY AS A RESEARCH *STRATEGY*

Malewski (2005) argues that educational research methods have tended to downplay the significance of playfulness and imagination. Edmiston (2005) is a researcher who embraces play as a strategy that children and adults can participate in *together*, as opposed to play being seen as the preserve of young children to be observed at a distance by adults. By participating in children's play, Edmiston argues that researchers can share authority with children and, in so doing, raise and explore a range of issues that are important to them *both*.

 Research in focus

Edmiston (2005) carried out research over a number of years with his son, from when he was 2 years to 7 years. Unlike other researchers who eventually leave the field once the research has finished (see Corsaro, 1985, for instance, and the discussion of 'leaving the field' in the ethnography chapter), Edmiston acknowledges that in researching play with his son he had, and indeed still has, an ongoing relationship with the research participant.

Edmiston used play and his inquiry into it to enable him to explore his different understandings about play as well as his understandings of himself as an 'adult-father-researcher' (ibid.: 58). The vehicle of play enabled him to disrupt usually held perceptions of what adult–child relationships should be. For instance he was able to take on a range of non-hierarchical and/or 'silly' roles in play and both he *and* his son were able to direct and interpret the play events.

At the age of 4, his son became fascinated by the story of Dr Jekyll and Mr Hyde, and this became a constant theme in his play with his father. The play increasingly challenged Edmiston's strongly held views as a pacifist, such as whether it is acceptable to kill someone in certain situations, as he encountered a range of perspectives on this issue through the adoption of different roles in relation to the story. Play opened up a space for Edmiston and his son to explore different ideas and possible meanings around a range of issues of importance to them. Crucially, through play, by sharing authority with his son and using the potential of play to disrupt their understandings of particular issues, they came to far deeper understandings, but Edmiston recognises that any understandings reached are temporary and not conclusive.

Edmiston was therefore able to explore a range of issues that relate to children's play. These included reflecting on questions such as 'should adults follow children's imaginative play wherever it leads?' or 'should children be taught during play?' or 'is play emotionally dangerous?' (ibid.: 72). In exploring questions of such significance to early childhood practice, it would seem that the action of playing and being playful with children is a valuable tool for research, not least because the direction of the research is *shared* between the adult and the child rather than decided upon in advance by the adult researcher. In this way, the approach could be regarded as similar to the notion of 'play-partnering' where adults and children alike might lead or follow the direction of the other (Bruce, 1991) but here is applied to a research context.

In reading about Edmiston's approach, you may have made links to some of the ideas about participant observation and ethnography in earlier chapters.

STORY-TELLING AND NARRATIVE APPROACHES

Drawings, photographs and play are not the only strategies that can be used to gain children's perspectives. Hyder (2002) discusses the use of Persona Dolls, which enable children to talk about their feelings in an engaging way. Persona Dolls are used to encourage children to explore issues of equality and inclusion as each doll has a personal story attached to it. Hyder also recommends puppets as another tool that can be used to encourage children to discuss their feelings.

In addition to this, storytelling is a strategy that is appealing for young children as you will see in the following 'Research in focus' section.

 Research in focus

In the research *It Hurts You Inside*, Willow and Hyder (1998) employed the use of a community artist to create a book with a character known as 'Splodge', who did not know about smacking. After hearing a story about Splodge, the children, who were aged between 4 and 7 years, were encouraged to talk to the character about smacking using a range of open-ended questions to structure the discussion. The resulting discussions provide a powerful message about children's perspectives on this issue as the title of the research indicates.

Children's *own* stories can also provide a focus for research. Some of you may be familiar with the work of Paley, who has written numerous books that document the stories, and enactments of them that have taken place in her kindergarten classroom (Paley, 1981; 1990). Paley uses the medium of story because she believes it enables her to gain a window into children's thinking about a wide range of enduring concerns, such as the meaning of friendship. The children's collaborations, through storying, seem to demonstrate their desire to explore the complexity of these abiding human issues. An example of this can be seen in the title *Bad Guys Don't Have Birthdays* (Paley, 1991).

Sylva (1999) argues that Paley provides an ethnographic account that emphasises *authenticity* but cannot make claims about the impact of the storying approach on long-term development or be generalised to *all* classrooms. In thinking about the children's stories, which Paley transcribes on a regular basis, Paley reflects on what they mean for classroom practice and her own role as a kindergarten teacher. If you have not read any of her work we thoroughly recommend it as thought-provoking and very readable.

THE MOSAIC APPROACH

We finish this chapter with a discussion of the Mosaic Approach to listening to young children as it encompasses a range of different tools that piece together to form a fuller picture of young children's perceptions of their early childhood setting, for instance. It is an approach devised by Clark and Moss (2001) that aims at improving the work of early childhood settings by ensuring that the views of *all* the participants in the setting are included – adults and children alike. A strong emphasis is placed on a range of documentation processes including, for example, narrative observation, children's drawings, role play, discussions with the child's family and key person, and the use of cameras and walking tours.

The use of cameras in the Mosaic Approach aims to encourage children to document the people, places and events that have particular meaning for them. Walking tours may also include the use of cameras. Walking tours may involve one child and an adult or a group of children and an adult (or adults). A tour involves the child or group of children in taking an adult on a tour of a given space, taking photographs along the way of what interests them or has particular meaning for them. The adult role on the tour is to allow the child(ren) to choose where to go and what to focus upon and take photographs of along the way. Once finished, the child(ren) may be encouraged to make their own drawing or map and place their own photographs on it (Clark and Moss, 2001). During the process of the tour and the possible resulting representation by the children, adults should be asking questions that are sensitive to the child(ren)'s concerns. In this sense, Roberts-Holmes (2005: 131) likens a walking tour to an 'interview on the move'.

To conclude this chapter, one of the most important factors in developing creative methods that encourage the participation of young children is the ability of the researcher to engage the children with the process (Veale, 2005). It is possible therefore, that personal and/or professional experience of caring for young children might be an advantage for researchers hoping to research in this way. This is because they are likely to have a greater understanding of the types of activities children enjoy as well as experience of interacting with children in relation to a range of child- and adult-initiated activities including play. Furthermore, early childhood practitioners may be particularly well placed to employ methods that involve leading a group, such as encouraging children to respond collectively to a group story, owing to their experience in leading similar sessions in their professional work.

Possibly of more significance than the creative methods discussed in the chapter is having an ongoing relationship with a child or group of children as it can alert the researcher to children's persistent concerns and current interests. Such a relationship might develop if a researcher was carrying out the research with children in his or her care or if the researcher was engaged in an ethnographic study involving extensive fieldwork. In both instances there is time for a relationship to develop between the researcher and the child(ren). A powerful example of this was outlined in this chapter, when we looked at Edmiston's research with his own son. Thus *time* is a factor as it supports the development of the kinds of close relationships in which the creative methods outlined in this chapter might be employed successfully.

But it is important to note, in concluding this chapter, that 'hanging out' with children over time – hardly a novel method of research! – is likely to reward the researcher with greater insights into their lives as it allows the researcher to take advantage of those moments of *naturally* occurring talk and play as and when they happen (Lahman, 2008:

296). This point is further exemplified by Davis et al. (2008) who emphasise the use of *everyday* cultural practices in order to elicit children's perspectives rather than supposedly more 'innovative' practices.

Key points from the chapter 🔑

- There has been a growth in creative methods employed in research with young children.
- The development in creative methods for engaging children *directly* in research can also be allied to the idea that children are experts on their own lives and are able to act as *participants* in research. Thus, it is allied to the children's rights perspective.
- There is a wide variety of creative methods that might be used when researching with children. Here, we have focused on using photography, drawings, play and a range of other strategies as well as an approach that combines methods, known as the Mosaic Approach (Clark and Moss, 2001).
- Creative methods for involving young children in research may work best if employed by someone with experience of caring for young children as s/he is likely to have some knowledge of the kinds of activities that young children will find engaging as well as the ability to present them.
- We should never forget that 'hanging-out' with children over time is a useful strategy that may reward the researcher with an insight into issues of importance to those children.

Further reading 📖

Angelides, P. and Michaelidou, A. (2009) 'The deafening silence: discussing children's drawings for understanding and addressing marginalisation', *Journal of Early Childhood Research*, 7(1): 27–45. A thought-provoking article, which exemplifies the use of drawings as a research tool.

Clark, A. and Moss, P. (2001) *Listening to Young Children: The Mosaic Approach*. London: NCB and JRF. A significant book on the subject, not just for early childhood research but of importance to practice too.

Soto, D.S. and Swadener, B.B. (eds) (2005) *Power and Voice in Research with Children*. New York: Peter Lang. A more challenging text than the others here. This book contains a range of fascinating chapters such as Edmiston's featured as a boxed entry in the chapter.

PART 4
CARRYING OUT A RESEARCH PROJECT

In this part of the book, we look at how to put together a small-scale piece of research, perhaps for an undergraduate dissertation, or for a work-based project. The previous three parts of the book will hopefully have prepared you for undertaking your *own* research project and Part 4 aims to build on these by encouraging you to apply what you have already learnt to this task.

Chapter 15, 'Research design', takes you through all the stages that you will undertake to complete a research project. We take you from the beginning, when you are trying to decide on a suitable topic, through to choosing an appropriate research design and choice of methods, to issues that need to be considered when choosing your participants. Throughout this chapter we will be looking at the decisions that have to be taken at the design stage to ensure that your research is *reliable* and your findings *valid*. Each project is different and the decisions that you make in the planning stage will depend on the context of your research, your underpinning attitudes and beliefs about early childhood, and the research paradigm within which your research is located. Each step in the decision process should be taken logically and in such a way that you can fully justify your decisions. Above all, we would hope that you will have enough information to be able to plan research that is *worthwhile*, rather than purely an academic exercise.

Reviewing the literature is an essential part of the research process because it locates your study in the context of what is *already* known in that area. By reviewing the literature you will gain an understanding of what is known already about your chosen research topic. Chapter 16 will guide you through the process of structuring and writing your literature review and contains practical advice about finding sources of information, so that you can avoid common pitfalls.

As you conduct your research project, you may generate a mass of information in the form of observations, questionnaires, transcripts of interviews and journal entries. Chapter 17, by necessity a very long chapter, discusses how to order the data so that it is ready for analysis. You will learn that quantitative data and qualitative data are analysed and presented differently, but that the overall aim is the same; that is to discover *themes* and *patterns* in the data and relate these to your overall research question, hypothesis or area of investigation. Data analysis is a dynamic and personal process, guided, as for all other aspects of the research process, by your underlying beliefs and attitudes. In the same way, writing up your research is not a neutral process.

Chapter 18, the final chapter, outlines some of the choices that have to be made to enable you to tell your research 'story' in a way that is appropriate to the research that you have undertaken. A piece of research stands or falls by the way that it is written up, after all it is the only chance you have of persuading your 'audience' that the decisions and choices you have made throughout the research process have been based on a thorough understanding of the literature as well as research methodology and methods, and that your findings are reliable, valid and worthwhile.

15 RESEARCH DESIGN

Chapter objectives

- To outline the stages in planning a research project
- To explore ways of turning an area of interest into a research question, area of investigation or a hypothesis
- To gain an understanding of how to choose the methodological approach and methods of data collection best suited to your research
- To reflect on the concepts of reliability and validity when applied to research design
- To investigate different ways of choosing your participants (sampling)
- To discuss how to write a research proposal and consider the most effective ways of working with a research supervisor

So far in this book we have looked at the **paradigms** and principles behind research in early childhood, and looked at some of the most commonly used approaches methods employed to collect **data**. Although it is unlikely that you have read this entire book chapter by chapter, starting from Chapter 1, you are already likely to have come across some of the issues that we will be describing in more detail here. In this chapter we will look at how *you* can start planning to undertake a piece of research into an aspect of early childhood. For some of you this will be a piece of small-scale research as part of a module in an early childhood studies degree, for others it may be a more major piece of work for a project, dissertation or thesis. This chapter will take you *step by step* through the process of planning a piece of research, explaining the decisions that have to be made along the way. Throughout this chapter we will be referring to a hypothetical student called Kerry, who is beginning her research project for her Early Childhood Studies Degree.

THE STAGES OF PLANNING A RESEARCH PROJECT

It is not unusual for students to feel intimidated at the thought of starting a piece of independent research. Many are aware that this is a hurdle that has to be negotiated before they can achieve their degree and have wondered how they will complete this task in the time they have available. There are steps that can be taken, even before deciding on a research topic that will give you an idea about what will be required. These include:

- *Examining the course/module requirements.* As with any other aspect of study, you should have a good understanding of exactly what is required of you. It goes without saying that you should make attending any teaching sessions about this aspect of the course a priority.
- *Looking at examples of other students' work.* It is usually possible to look at completed research projects from previous years. Often these are in the teaching institution's library.
- *Talking to students who have successfully completed their research.* If possible talk to someone who has successfully completed their research. Very often the advice they give is invaluable, especially if they have overcome difficulties in reaching completion.

Although the requirements for the independent research element of a course varies from institution to institution, and the focus of the research will inevitably vary from researcher to researcher, there are common stages in planning a research programme that have to be undertaken. At first sight, planning and executing a piece of research may look like a linear process, with one stage needing to be completed before another begins. Green (2002: 102), for example, suggests the following stages in planning a piece of research:

- choosing a subject area
- writing aims and objectives
- setting out a **hypothesis** or research question
- setting parameters
- selecting an appropriate approach to the research
- identifying ethical considerations
- identifying an appropriate time management plan.

However Blaxter et al. (1996) see the preparatory stages in planning a piece of research as not being separated from the actual processes of data collection and analysis, but an integral part of a *cyclic* research process. From this conceptualisation, the research process is seen to be a never-ending process that can be entered at any point as Figure 15.1 shows on page 185.

DEVELOPING AN AREA OF INVESTIGATION, RESEARCH QUESTION OR A HYPOTHESIS

There are several stages that need to be worked through before reaching a 'workable' hypothesis, area of investigation or research question. These stages include choosing an area of interest, narrowing down the focus of interest, deciding on the general aim of your research and formulating your hypothesis or research question.

Choosing an area of interest

The first decision to be made is the topic of your research. The following questions may help you in your decision-making process.

1. What topics have interested you during your course?
2. Have any of your previous assignments generated ideas for future research?
3. If you are a practitioner, is there an aspect of your own practice that you want to improve, or a new initiative that you want to implement? Undertaking a piece of action research may give you that opportunity.
4. Are there some topics that you can obtain information about more easily than others?

When you have settled on an area of interest you are in a position to start to think about what exactly it is that you want to find out.

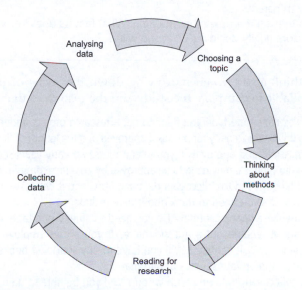

Figure 15.1 The research cycle (adapted from Blaxter et al., 1996: 10)

Narrowing down the focus of interest

The topic you have chosen is very likely to be very wide. For example, you may know that you want to focus on the social and emotional development of children, or may be interested in how children with special educational needs are supported in early childhood settings. However, at the moment, these areas are too broad. The following suggestions may help you decide exactly what aspect you want to be the focus of your research.

• Create a *mind map* (Buzan, 2007), spider graph, topic web or list, to identify different aspects of your topic.

Activity

Kerry, a student about to embark on her undergraduate project, has decided that she is interested in partnership with parents. Draw a topic web of all the different areas that this might include.

- Discuss your area of interest with colleagues in your setting, if you are a practitioner, to see if there is an aspect of this that needs investigating or developing.
- Talk to your project supervisor.

 Reflection point

Kerry works with children aged 3 to 5 in a private day nursery. Her colleagues have suggested that she could look at developing ways to improve the way that the nursery works in partnership with parents.

Kerry has two terms to complete her research. What factors does Kerry have to take into consideration before finally deciding what she will do?

Other factors to think about when narrowing down the focus of interest include the length of time available to complete the study and the resources that might be needed.

- *Time.* It always takes more time than you think to get a research project under way. You will need to consider how long it will take to get your proposal approved and the length of time it may take to gather the necessary permissions and approvals if you intend to use an early years setting. In some settings, such as hospitals, your proposal may have to be approved by an ethics committee. You will need to estimate the length of time needed to collect your data and how long it will take to write up the research.
- *Resources.* The questions you need to think about here include:
  – Will your study involve a financial outlay? Do you need a camera, or a tape recorder? Will you need to pay for postage if sending out a questionnaire? If you are in employment, will you need to request unpaid leave to visit settings? Will you have to buy specialist books and materials?
  – Have you access to appropriate sources of information?
  – Where will you collect your data and with whom? Will you be able to gain access?

Deciding on the general aim of your research

 Reflection point

Kerry decides to undertake an exploratory study to find out what ways both practitioners and parents suggest that their partnership with the nursery could be improved.

After reading Part 1 of the book, try to answer the following questions.

1. What methodological approach is she likely to be using?
2. Is she likely to be using a hypothesis?
3. What ethical issues need to be considered?

 It is likely that Kerry will be using a design, which employs **qualitative methodology** and because her study is exploratory, she will not be testing a hypothesis. As you may recall from Chapter 3, in any piece of research there are ethical issues to be considered. Here are a few issues that Kerry would need to think about (but it is not an exhaustive list): she would need to reflect on the powerful position of the practitioners in relation to the parents – parents may tell her what they think she wants to hear as their own children attend the setting; they may fear repercussions if they express negative views. In addition, Kerry may find herself in a difficult position if parents tell her negative things about other members of staff.

From the above you can see that Kerry has a general aim for her research, that is, in general terms she knows what she wants to find out and why, although at this stage she may not have a clear idea of the methods she will be using.

Once you have an overall aim this can be set out in formal terms. Kerry's aim might look like this: '*The aim of this piece of research is to investigate ways in which partnership with parents can be improved in a private nursery.*'

Formulating the area of investigation, research question or hypothesis

Whether or not you will have an area of investigation, research question or a hypothesis depends, to some extent, on your underlying research paradigm. In Chapter 1 we saw that a positivist, scientific approach may involve the use of a hypothesis, a statement that can be tested using **quantitative** scientific methods, derived from a theory. If the findings from your research do not support your hypothesis then the conclusion is that the theory is either untrue, or needs modifying.

Hypotheses should be written in such a way that there is no ambiguity (Cardwell et al., 1996), the variables are stated clearly, and how the hypothesis is to be tested is clear. For example, in Chapter 1, we looked at an imaginary scenario where a teacher had a theory that children learned better in the morning than the afternoon.

〜 **Reflection point**

Look back at Chapter 1 and remind yourself of the research that the teacher planned to undertake into children's learning. Her first attempt at writing a hypothesis was, 'Children will learn spellings more efficiently in the morning than the afternoon'. Later on she changed it to: 'Children learning a list of five spellings in the morning will remember more spellings 24 hours later than children who learn a list of five spellings in the afternoon.'
What changes have been made and why?

The hypothesis stated in the reflection point is a *prediction* that there will be an effect present, that is, that there will be a change in the dependent, or outcome, variable (the number of spellings learned) because of a manipulation of the **independent variable** (the time of day). This is called the **alternative hypothesis**. It is convention, in quantitative research, for the hypothesis to also be given in terms that suggest that no effect will be present. This is the **null hypothesis**. In our example the null hypothesis will look like this: '*There will be no significant difference in the number of words recalled, 24 hours later, between children learning a list of five spellings in the morning and children who learn a list of five spellings in the afternoon.*'

In the example we are looking at we may find that 100 per cent of the children who learn the spellings in the morning remember all of them 24 hours later, but only 75 per cent of the children who learn the spellings in the afternoon remember all of them. If this is the case, can we reject the null hypothesis and accept that the alternative hypothesis is true? Do the results *prove* that learning spellings in the morning results in more spellings being remembered? Could the results just be due to chance alone? If you repeated the experiment over and over again and averaged out the results, would no effect be seen? To answer these questions we can subject the results to statistical analyses, known as *tests of significance*, which tell researchers if any effect is likely to be due to chance or not. The tests tell us what the probability is that a particular result will occur.

Probability is measured on a scale, with something that is not possible being given a probability level of 0, and something that must or always happens being given a probability of 1 (Coolican, 2004). Generally, if the probability that our results would occur by chance alone is less than 0.05, the null hypothesis can be rejected and the alternative hypothesis accepted.

Our experience of working with students on early childhood studies courses is that it is *very rare* for them to do research that involves the testing of hypotheses and the use of tests of significance. This is due to the difficulties that are encountered in conducting *worthwhile* research involving the rigorous control of variables outside of a laboratory situation. Furthermore, a high level of statistical analysis is involved. For students who want to research in this way we recommend that they look at Field (2009), *Discovering Statistics using SPSS*.

Sometimes, still within the positivist paradigm, it is not appropriate to use a hypothesis because a prediction is not being made, or there is no underlying theoretical model that is being tested. The aim of the research may be to investigate or explore a phenomenon. In this case a quantitative research question is used instead. '*How often do 3-year-old children show acts of empathy?*' is an example of a quantitative research question.

Most students undertaking a small-scale research project will not be operating within a positivist paradigm; it is more likely that they will be taking an interpretivist approach, which is less concerned with confirming or refuting theory, in a way that allows findings to be generalised out to a wider **population**, and more concerned with looking at making sense of the researcher's immediate world. In these situations the use of a hypothesis or a quantitative research question would be inappropriate, and a more general, qualitative research question is likely to be used.

Qualitative questions are generally more open ended; often they are more like the aims discussed earlier on in the chapter. They tend to ask questions about a process, issue or phenomenon to be explored (Johnson and Christensen, 2008: 79). Previously, we looked at Kerry's research into parental partnership. She formulated her aim as follows: '*The aim of this piece of research is to investigate ways in which partnership with parents can be improved in a private nursery.*'

Reflection point

Kerry's first attempts at writing her research question were as follows:

1. What can the nursery do to make parents attend parent consultation sessions?
2. Why do parents not communicate well with the nursery staff?

On reflection Kerry decided that neither of these questions was appropriate. What do you consider to be the problem with these questions?

In the reflection point activity you may have realised that, in both cases, the *parents* were seen to be the 'barrier' to effective partnership, perhaps reflecting a deficit model of parental partnership being held by Kerry and her colleagues. This would be a 'conforming' model of parental partnership (MacNaughton and Hughes, 2003). Beginning the research with such a negative view point raises ethical issues (see Chapter 3). In addition the questions are very *narrow* in focus and may limit the amount of valuable data that could be obtained.

After consulting her project supervisor Kerry amended her research question. Her final version was: '*What do parents and early years practitioners, at a private day nursery in London, perceive to be the benefits and barriers to an effective partnership between parents and practitioners? What suggestions do they have for improving the partnership?*'

CHOOSING A RESEARCH DESIGN

Once a concise hypothesis, area of investigation or research question has been reached, decisions need to be made as to the strategy that will be used to investigate the issue. Traditionally, the concept of a **research design** belongs within the *positivist* tradition and, in Chapter 1, we looked at one of the main positivist research designs, the *experiment*. However, if it is considered that a research design 'is the process by which the topic is turned into a researchable project' (Hayes, 2001: 77), then qualitative or mixed modes of research will also have a 'design'.

Kumar (2005: 93) suggests that it is useful to classify research design according to three perspectives:

1. The number of contacts with the study population
2. The reference period of the study
3. The nature of the investigation.

We will look at each of these in turn.

Study design based on the number of contacts

This classification looks at how many times the participants are involved in the research.

- *Cross-sectional study*. This is probably the most common form of research whereby the participants are investigated at a single point in time, or during a brief time period. Most commonly, data are collected from more than one group of participants. For example, the teacher's memory experiment in Chapter 1 had a cross-sectional design. In this study she looked at two groups of children, one group in the morning, and another group in the afternoon. The main advantage of the cross-sectional study is that it is possible to conduct research in a short space of time, and participants are not likely to drop out of the study (Coolican, 2004). Most undergraduate students will be conducting cross-sectional studies primarily because of the time factor involved in doing something that takes longer to complete. The disadvantage of this design is that it is not possible to follow individual participants to see if there are any changes *over time*.

- *The before and after study design* (pre-test/post-test). The before and after study design can be used in both quantitative and qualitative research and is typically used to assess the effect of an *intervention* on a group of participants. For example, two groups of reception-aged children could be weighed and measured at the beginning of the school year to find out their body mass index (BMI). During the course of the year, one group would be given an intervention aimed to increase their levels of physical activity during school hours. At the end of the school year both groups of children would be weighed and measured again.

    The disadvantage to this design is that it takes longer to collect data and, between the first contact point and the second contact point, participants may have dropped out. Another problem with the design is that, unless a control group is used, as in the example discussed above, it is difficult to work out if any observed change at post-test is due to the *intervention*, or to other variables. For instance if no control group was used in the example discussed, any reduction in BMI could be due to a reduction in the calorific value of school meals. If investigating children, the interval between pre- and post-test may itself introduce a source of variance, as young children can change *dramatically* in a few months. Of course, in using a 'control' group, the researcher would also have to be mindful about Robson's (1993) concern about withholding the possible benefits of research to a group of participants.

- *The longitudinal study design*. This is the design of choice for looking at patterns of change *over time*, and as such is not a design that students are likely to use. In the longitudinal design a group of participants are investigated at several points, over an extended period. The disadvantages of longitudinal studies are similar to those of the before and after design, but more exaggerated as the likelihood that participants will be 'lost' to a study is far greater if the study is undertaken over decades (Kumar, 2005).

Study designs based on the reference period

Some studies look back at past events and some look forward to what might happen in the future.

- *Retrospective designs* investigate issues that have happened in the past, using data available from the time, or relying on the memory of participants.
- *The prospective study design* is one that is designed to wait until the future to find out the outcome of an event/intervention or the effect of a variable, for instance.

Study designs based on the nature of the investigation

The paradigm and methodological approach within which you are working will affect your choice of research design.

Quantitative designs include:
- *Experiments*: here the researcher tries to control as many variables as possible while only altering the independent variable. There are a variety of ways that experiments can be designed and some of these were discussed in Chapter 1.
- *Quasi-experiments*: often it is not possible or ethical to conduct experiments on children. For example, it would not be ethical to conduct a *true* experiment about the effects of passive smoking on children, as it would be wrong to deliberately expose children to smoke to investigate the outcome. However, it *is* possible to investigate the effects on children who are born into households where the parents smoke.
- *Non-experimental designs*: these would include **correlations**, as discussed in Chapter 1.

Qualitative designs include:
- *Case studies*: Greig et al. (2007: 145) define a case study as 'an investigation of an individual, a family, a group, an institution, a community, or even a resource, programme or intervention'. Case studies are looked at in depth in Chapter 7.
- *Action research:* 'Action research is designed to improve practice or to deal with a problem or an issue' (Kumar, 2005: 108). We looked at this in Chapter 8. In our experience, it is a common research design used by practitioners who are studying for a degree in early childhood.
- *Ethnography:* this is an approach that is designed to describe the culture of a group of people in detail. An ethnographic study tries to take a holistic approach, and as such will be interested in documenting things like 'shared attitudes, values, norms, and practices, patterns of interaction, perspectives, and language of a group of people' (Johnson and Christensen, 2008: 49). Ethnography is described in more detail in Chapter 6.

CHOOSING APPROPRIATE METHODS

Part of planning your research project involves choosing the methods that will be used to collect your data. These need to be 'fit for purpose' (Sylva, 1999). We have looked at the most commonly used methods in Part 3 of this book. Here we will briefly describe eight questions devised by Blaxter et al. (1996: 73), which will help you choose the most appropriate methods for your study.

1. *What do you need or want to find out?* Your research question may already point to a suitable method.

Before you read the following text, please look at the reflection point on the next page.

In the reflection point example, you may have considered that Kerry could choose to use interviews or questionnaires, interviews being the preferred option as detailed information is more likely to be obtained. However, this decision will be affected by the number of parents and practitioners that Kerry decides to include in her sample and the time available.

 Reflection point

Earlier on in the chapter we discussed Kerry and her proposed research into parental partnership. Her research question was:

'*What do parents and early years practitioners, at a private day nursery in London, perceive to be the benefits and barriers to an effective partnership between parents and practitioners? What suggestions do they have for improving the partnership?*'

What methods could Kerry use to find out the opinions of the parents and practitioners?

---

2. *What skills do you have?* For example, face-to-face interviews demand a high degree of interpersonal skills.
3. *How will your methods affect the answers you get?* Some methods are more suited to particular situations than others. For example, *structured* questionnaires are a good method to use if the researcher wants relatively straightforward information from many people. However, if the research is aiming to look at an issue in *depth*, exploring participants' underlying attitudes and beliefs, then an in-depth, open-ended interview is the best choice. The choice of *who* to include in a study will also profoundly affect the results, and this will be discussed in the section on **sampling** later on in the chapter.
4. *How will **you** affect your research?* All the decisions made about the aims of the research, formulating the research question, deciding on the research design, choice of participants, analysis of the data and suchlike are influenced by the self of the researcher (Scheurich, 1997). We noted this in Chapter 2 of this book. You may recall that research that falls within the *positivist* paradigm tries to counteract these effects by rigorous control of variables. Interpretivist researchers recognise that they are an integral part of the research process and the **reliability** of findings can be corroborated by a process of **triangulation** (see Edwards, 2001).
5. *Which methods are acceptable?* There are two issues to be considered here: ethical considerations, which are discussed in Chapter 3, and external constraints. Blaxter et al. (1996) discuss how a choice of methods may be influenced by others. For example, the use of particular methods may be written into your assignment brief, or you may be working within an institution or setting, which takes a particular approach to research.
6. *Do you need to use more than one method?* Some research projects will use more than one method. Action research may entail collecting information from staff, parents and children, so you may decide to interview staff, give a questionnaire to parents and observe children. In addition, the need to triangulate (see question 4) may indicate the use of different methods. Also, as previously discussed, the exploratory phase of research may indicate the need for different methods than the confirmatory phase.
7. *Do you need to change methods?* Sometimes, you may start off using one particular method and find that you are not getting the information you want or expected. For example, it is not unknown for students to distribute questionnaires and find out that there is a very poor response, or that the child you had in mind for a case study has changed settings. When things like this happen you will need to take stock and think about alternative methods.

RELIABILITY AND VALIDITY

When undertaking research, the overall aim is to collect information (data) about an issue and to draw *conclusions* using this information. It is, therefore, important that you can trust that this data will actually allow you to make appropriate conclusions, and to allow this to happen your methods must be both *reliable* and *valid*. The concepts of reliability and **validity** have different meanings depending upon whether a quantitative or qualitative approach is being taken (Greig et al., 2007) as well as the paradigm within which the research is located.

Reliability

When using *quantitative* methodology, reliability is concerned with the stability of the measurements you are collecting. If a method of obtaining information, such as a test, rating scale, observation or questionnaire is to be *reliable* it must give the same results when administered on different occasions or administered by different people. Atkinson et al. (1996) identify two sorts of reliability: temporal stability and internal consistency.

A method of obtaining information is said to have temporal stability if the results obtained from a group of participants on one occasion are replicated if the procedure were to be repeated under similar circumstances, on another occasion. For example, in Chapter 1, we looked at an experiment on memory conducted by a teacher. Her way of assessing memory was the number of words correctly spelled from a five-word list recalled after 24 hours. To be reliable the scores obtained from the group would need to be similar if the experiment was repeated on a second occasion.

 Reflection point

Can you think of a problem about establishing temporal stability in a test of memory, if the outcome is number of words correctly spelled?

Your reflections upon the memory experiment may have led you to conclude that if the same list of words was used for the second test, then the children's scores should be better as they will have had another chance to learn them. To get around this problem, researchers, wishing to check the validity of a test, will often produce two tests that are of comparable difficulty, and use a different test the second time around.

Internal consistency is the degree to which items in a test measure the same thing. For example, one can use personality tests to assess an individual's level of extraversion or introversion. One way to test this is to give the test to a group of individuals and to score the first half and second half of the test separately. If the test is reliable then the scores for the first half should be very similar to the sores for the second half. Devising reliable tests is a skilled business and demands knowledge of statistics. Because of this, researchers often do not make up their own tests, but use pre-prepared tests (Field, 2009). Any student considering the use of a test in this way should seek the help of their supervisor as this is not an approach we would advise many students to take.

When using qualitative methodology the issue of reliability is slightly different. This type of research does not involve statistically devised tests, but may be using methods such as in-depth interviews to elicit the participants' underlying attitudes and beliefs. Siraj-Blatchford and Siraj-Blatchford (2001a) suggest that reliability in these situations is the degree that the researcher's theoretical analysis and conclusions 'fit' or correspond to the actual data that was obtained.

Cohen et al. (2000: 120) reiterate this viewpoint, suggesting that the criteria for reliability for quantitative and qualitative research differ and that in qualitative methodologies, 'Reliability includes fidelity to real life, context and situation specificity, authenticity, comprehensiveness, detail, honesty, depth of response and meaningfulness to the respondents'.

Validity

A valid data-gathering instrument is one that measures what it sets out to measure. For example, Eysenk (2004) describes historical attempts to measure intelligence in terms of an individual's intelligence quotient or IQ. Although popular at one time, the idea that a person's intelligence could be measured and reduced to one number has been discredited. There were great concerns about the validity of such tests, as not all areas of intelligence were measured and the amount of education and the cultural background of the participant impacted upon the test results.

 Research in focus

Walsh and Gardner (2005) describe the creation and validation of an assessment instrument designed to assess the quality of early years classrooms from the perspective of the child's experience. The items from the observation schedule, known as the Quality Learning Instrument, were given to a panel of experts to ensure that they were an *appropriate* and *valid* way to make judgements about the quality of settings.

The paper describing how the assessment instrument was devised is available online – see http://ecrp.uiuc.edu/v7n1/walsh.html (accessed 30 November 2008).

In qualitative research, validity is viewed differently but is nonetheless important. *Authenticity* is of paramount importance. As Edwards (2001: 124) notes, 'Validity in qualitative research is a matter of being able to offer as sound a representation of the field of study as the research methods allow'.

The researcher needs to able to say that their research is as truthful an account of the area of study as is possible. For some researchers, this is reached through careful *triangulation*. This might be done through using a variety of sources of data; multiple methods; different theoretical perspectives; or more than one researcher looking at the issue under study (Denzin, cited in Edwards, 2001: 124).

For researchers working within a *post-structuralist* paradigm, the idea of triangulation implies the identification of a fixed point that can be reached with certainty and is in opposition to their position of multiple and ever-changing realities. Richardson and Adams St

Pierre (2005), for instance, employ the metaphor of a *crystal* as it helps them to highlight the way that *how we see* depends on the *position from which we are viewing*. Moreover, as a crystal grows, it represents the *changing* nature of reality. Guba and Lincoln (2005) note how the notion of arriving at a position of 'truth' itself is seen as questionable for researchers working within this paradigm, especially as they often aim at problematising commonly held 'truths'. They maintain that for some post-structuralist researchers, being 'transgressive' in this way is how validity is reached. For others, validity is seen as occurring through the ethical relationships developed in the course of the research and the degree to which the researcher supplies a reflexive account of their study (Guba and Lincoln, 2005). These ideas are complex, but are included here to show how validity is viewed differently according to the paradigm within which the researcher has positioned their research.

CHOOSING A SAMPLE

One of the decisions that has to be made when planning a research study relates to the people who are to be included as participants in the study. If you are intending to undertake a piece of research in an early years setting, the decision may, in part, be already taken. For example, in Kerry's investigation of parental partnership, she may decide to interview every practitioner, but only a selection of the parents, as she has not got sufficient time to interview everyone. Kerry will choose a few participants, or elements, from the wider population of parents who use the nursery. The process of choosing who will be your participants is called sampling. In qualitative studies, the population is likely to be relatively small because the findings of these studies are often designed to apply to a restricted group such as an early years setting. In quantitative studies, where the findings are often designed to be applied to whole populations, the sample is likely to be much larger.

Not everyone (or every element) in a population will be accessible to be part of a study. In Kerry's research, she wants to conduct interviews. This means that her sample can only include parents who are accessible to be interviewed during school hours, or have a telephone so they can be telephone interviewed in the evening. If Kerry worked in a nursery with many parents who were not yet proficient in spoken English, she would have to decide if she were going to use translators or leave these parents out. The parents whom Kerry decides could be included in her study form the **sampling frame**. It is from this group of parents that the sample will be drawn.

 Reflection point

The decisions made about who will be in the sampling frame can affect research findings. If Kerry is only able to interview parents during the day, she may not find out the opinions of parents who work (the majority of her parents). Similarly, if she can only interview parents who are proficient in speaking English, parents who are not proficient will be excluded. How will this affect her results?

The next decision to be made is *who*, or what elements, from the sampling frame will constitute the sample for the research study. In research influenced by the positivist paradigm, the control of variables is of prime importance. So when sampling, the researcher tries to choose a group of participants (elements) that share the *characteristics* or *variables* of the population. Findings from the research involving this sample can then be used to make inferences about the wider population (Hart, 2005). There are various techniques for choosing a sample in an effort to control the effects of random variables (Cardwell et al., 1996; Johnson and Christensen, 2008; Kumar, 2005), some of which will be described here. Siraj-Blatchford and Siraj-Blatchford (2001a) suggest that sampling methods can be split into two types:

1. *Probability sampling.* This type of sample is designed to be representative of the whole population and includes random sampling, systematic sampling, and stratified sampling.
2. *Non-probability sampling.* This is used when there is no requirement for the sample to be representative of the whole population, or when the sample is chosen to include specific categories of individual. This includes opportunity, self selected and snowball sampling.

Random sample

In a random sample, every person or element in a sampling frame is given the same chance of being selected for inclusion. The larger the sample, the more likely it is that the sample will be representative of the sample frame, although this is not guaranteed. There are various ways of obtaining a random sample. One is to write all the possible names on separate pieces of paper and shake them up in a container. Names are then drawn out one by one, at random, until the sample size is reached. This may be possible with a small sample frame, but is impossible if the sample frame is large. Another way is to give every possible participant a number and use computer-generated random number tables to tell you who to choose. If you intend to use random number tables it is suggested that you ask for specific guidance on how to use them as it is outside the scope of this text.

Systematic sampling

This is when participants are chosen from a list at fixed intervals. An example of this may be a researcher choosing a sample consisting of every twentieth person on the electoral register. Although not completely random, because not everyone has the same chance of being included in the sample, it is viewed as an unbiased way of sampling (Cardwell et al., 1996).

Stratified sampling

In this method of sampling the researcher decides beforehand what variables are likely to affect the outcome of the study, finds out the proportions of these variables within the population and then chooses a sample that reflects these proportions. For example, if you wanted to conduct a study looking at the extent to which parents support their children's education at home, it may be considered that social class of the family is important. The researcher would separate out the population according to social class and then draw a sample, at random, that reflected social class *in the same proportions* as the population.

Opportunity sampling

This involves the researcher choosing anyone who is available to take part in their research from a particular population. This is a common form of sampling used by students. For example, in Kerry's study on parental partnership, her sample of parents to be interviewed may have consisted of the parents she saw every day, with whom she had a good rapport, and who had the time to help her. This type of sampling is unlikely to be a truly *representative* sample and any possible effects of this need to be taken into account when attempting to draw conclusions from the findings of the research.

Self-selected sample

In this type of sampling, participants volunteer to take part in research. It is a method often used to test drugs or medical procedures and you may have seen advertisements for volunteers in newspapers. Students sometimes use this as a sampling method, for example, if you wanted to find out about early childhood studies' students' opinions on play, you could ask for volunteers in your class to help you. The disadvantage of this is that the sample may be very unrepresentative of the population as a whole. For example, if the population consists primarily of early years' practitioners, you will not have included students who are *not* practitioners and who may have very different views on play, which are not based on *professional* experience.

Snowball sampling

In snowball sampling, every participant recruited into a study is asked to identify others who may be appropriate or *willing* to be a participant. For instance, if Kerry had wanted to know about parents' views on parental partnership in general, rather than being specific to her workplace, she could have asked the parents from her nursery to ask their friends if they would be willing to be interviewed. This can be useful in gaining access to groups that might be deemed 'difficult to reach' (see, for instance, Standing's work, 1998, on lone mothers).

Theoretical sampling

This is a method of sampling used in some qualitative studies, where participants are chosen *as the study evolves*. Qualitative studies often take a cyclic approach to research with data being analysed and additional participants chosen according to the researcher's understanding of the theoretical strands that emerge. Theoretical sampling is similar to what Johnson and Christensen (2008) describe as *purposive* or *criterion-based* selection, where cases are chosen that provide the information needed for the purpose of the research.

WRITING A RESEARCH PROPOSAL

A proposal is a 'written document summarising prior literature and describing the procedure to be used to answer the research question' (Johnson and Christensen, 2008: 91). Some students are required to write a research proposal before they start their research project and this will form the basis of discussions with their project supervisors. A proposal will also be needed if the research needs to be considered by research/ethics committees and funding bodies (Hart, 2005).

Apart from being a possible requirement as part of a module, writing a research proposal will help you formulate your ideas and should act as a guide to steer you through the research process. Hart (2005: 367) suggests that a research proposal should identify:

- what you intend to research
- why that research is needed (including a brief review of the literature)
- how the research will be done
- when the research will be done
- what resources are needed
- who you will talk to
- where the data is
- how you will access the data
- how the data will be analysed
- what the outcomes may be.

There are many different ways to write a proposal and you may have one suggested to you by your institution. We would recommend that you do not use these bullet points as headings – a rationale; brief literature review; and proposed methodology are usually enough – and also recommend that you include detail about any ethical considerations associated with your proposed research.

KEEPING A RESEARCH DIARY OR JOURNAL

There are important reasons why keeping a journal is recommended:

- A journal can act as a record of *what you have done*, together with notes you make as you go long about *what has to be done*.
- A journal can be used to *record your ideas and feelings* about how the research is going, an approach particularly valuable in qualitative studies.

There are many ways to organise a research diary or journal. Some journals may look like a personal diary, some may be more structured. However you organise your diary or journal it will be invaluable when preparing for meetings with your supervisor and when you are writing up your project. If you wish to read more about this, please refer to Chapter 13, which looked at journaling in more detail.

WORKING WITH A RESEARCH SUPERVISOR

A research 'supervisor' is usually a member of the academic team in an institution such as a university, who has the responsibility of overseeing your project. Usually you will be allocated a supervisor because they have specialist knowledge in the area you have chosen. In addition, perhaps more importantly, your project supervisor will have a good understanding of the research *process* and the requirements of *your particular course*.

Academic institutions will all have different ways of organising supervision. It may be that it is *your responsibility* to make the first contact, or it may be the supervisor who contacts you to arrange a first meeting. Most meetings will be face to face, but if you are a distance learner you may have primarily telephone tutorials or email contact. Whatever the mode of contact, the first meeting is important. Ideally you will have some ideas about the topic you are interested in and have begun to think about your research question and methodology before you meet your supervisor. The first meeting will be concerned with setting parameters for the research process and may include:

- clarification of how many hours are available for supervision/how often the sessions will occur
- an exploration of the best ways to keep in contact (email/ telephone?)
- confirmation about the expectations in terms of hand-in date, word length and suchlike
- discussion about the topic, suitability of the research question and methodology
- action planning, such as thinking about timescale

The success of supervision relies both on the *skill* of the supervisor and the *motivation* and *openness* of the student. It works best when students are:

- independent
- keep appointments
- send draft sections/chapters to be looked at with *plenty of time for their supervisor to review them* before planned meetings, so that this time is used in *discussion* rather than reading
- tell the supervisor when there are problems, so there can be a discussion about how to deal with them.

Key points from the chapter

- Planning the research process is *key* to the success of your project and starts with finding and refining the topic you are interested in.
- Once the overall aims of your research have been decided upon, you are in a position to choose an area to investigate, formulate a hypothesis or develop a research question.
- Research design depends upon:
  – the number of contacts with the study population
  – the reference period of the study
  – the nature of the investigation.
- The methods chosen must be reliable and valid.
- Choosing participants for your research has to be undertaken with care. This is known as sampling.

- Once you have decided on how you are going to conduct your research a research proposal can be drawn up.
- Using a research diary or journal will help you keep on track with your research and will allow you to record ideas and reflections that will help you when writing up your research.
- Research supervisors are there to support you through the research process. Supervision works well if the student is motivated and proactive in keeping in contact with their supervisor.

Further reading

Blaxter, L., Hughes, C. and Tight, M. (1996) *How to Research*. Buckingham: Open University Press. Chapters 1 and 2 are helpful for students who are considering what they want to do for a research project.

Edwards, A. (2001) 'Qualitative research designs and analysis', in G. MacNaughton, S. Rolfe and I. Siraj-Blatchford (eds), *Doing Early Childhood Research: International Perspectives on Theory and Practice*. Maidenhead: Open University Press. The beginning of this chapter looks at some key issues in designing a qualitative study.

16   REVIEWING THE LITERATURE

Chapter objectives

- To develop an understanding of the purpose of a literature review in a piece of research
- To consider what makes a successful literature review
- To develop systematic ways of searching for and organising information

This chapter looks at an important part of any research project: conducting a literature review. All research projects will draw upon literature that relates to the area under investigation and tutors who are marking student projects will be looking not only at a student's ability to plan a project using methodological tools that are 'fit for purpose', they will also be looking at a student's ability to position their research within a wider body of work in a similar area. This chapter, then, aims to encourage you to think carefully about this area of your research project.

WHAT IS A LITERATURE REVIEW?

When we think about the term 'literature review' it would be easy to imagine that a literature review is a place for discussing what you have read and the extent to which you have enjoyed it. Many of you will have read newspapers and magazines that have reviewed new books on the market and recommended them as 'good reading' or not. This is fine when you are considering whether to buy a particular novel for reading on the beach but in terms of academic research in early childhood this would be quite wrong.

In a piece of research, the researcher is not writing about the *quality of the writing style* of a particular author, they are reviewing their *ideas* and their contribution to the area of study being undertaken. A literature review, then, is a critical analysis of related literature in a relevant field to that of the research being undertaken. It is a key part of any research project because it outlines the subject content and academic knowledge *relevant* to the topic of research.

It is sometimes easier to gain an understanding of the nature of a literature review if you consider how it sits within a research project as a whole. In general, a research project will have the following structure:

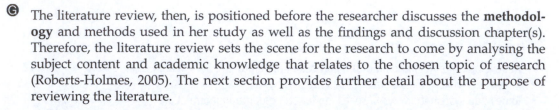

Abstract
1. Introduction
2. Literature review
3. Methodology
4. Findings and discussion (sometimes two chapters)
5. Conclusion
Bibliography
Appendices

The literature review, then, is positioned before the researcher discusses the **methodology** and methods used in her study as well as the findings and discussion chapter(s). Therefore, the literature review sets the scene for the research to come by analysing the subject content and academic knowledge that relates to the chosen topic of research (Roberts-Holmes, 2005). The next section provides further detail about the purpose of reviewing the literature.

WHY IS IT IMPORTANT TO CONDUCT A LITERATURE REVIEW?

A crucial role for the literature review is to contextualise a piece of research into research that has been carried out before. No matter what area is chosen for research, there will always be an established body of research and writing that the researcher's current research fits into. Bell (1993) suggests that even in small-scale research, you will need to read what other people have written about your chosen area; some of which will support, others of which will refute your written-up research project.

Campbell et al. (2004: 66) argue that conducting a literature review enables the researcher to be 'Guided by previous research in the area, the methods they used, problems they encountered and the suggestions they may well have made for further research'. They suggest that research needs, at times, to replicate previous studies as well as build on previous studies in the chosen area of focus. Bell (1993) maintains that by reading around the topic you have chosen, ideas may be gleaned that will be of use to your own analysis and interpretation of **data**. However, while developing knowledge about your chosen area is important, Robson (1993) warns that it is easy to become blinkered by the way others have carried out their research.

WHAT MAKES FOR A SUCCESSFUL LITERATURE REVIEW?

This section aims to encourage you to think about what makes a successful literature review. Generally, a successful literature review will have the following features:

• evidence of wide and relevant reading
• discussion of key terminology
• critical analysis of the topic under discussion
• clear structure

- well-written
- correct referencing.

This section will now go through each of these areas in turn, in order to clarify your thinking in this area.

Evidence of wide and relevant reading

While it would be impossible to review every piece of literature on a given topic, especially at degree level, a successful literature review demonstrates evidence of wide reading that is *relevant* to the aims of the research or the research question. This is because generally, the greater the reading undertaken, the greater the depth of understanding of the topic.

〰 Reflection point

Think about the range of texts you have probably encountered and read over the past week. These might include:

- text messages
- policy documents
- websites
- books and journal articles
- shopping lists
- magazines
- recipe books
- tickets

Think about why some of these texts are regarded as 'academic' and others not.

Try to consider the type of writing you are referring to. It might be one of the following:

- a piece of journalism
- government policy
- writing based on first-hand research
- writing based on a resume of other people's research and ideas
- a philosophical inquiry.

Inevitably, a literature review should aim to look primarily at the latter items on the above bullet-pointed list. Academic journals are a good source of material because the articles published are usually peer reviewed before publication by other researchers in a similar field. Thus, there have been checks on the quality of writing and research carried out. Journal articles, then, draw upon a range of sources and will discuss the research methods used in the study. In other words, they are scholarly pieces of work.

This can be contrasted with journalism. An article in a newspaper or magazine is unlikely to have gone through such thorough reviewing and is unlikely to draw upon the range of reading or expertise. This is not to say that journalism has no place in a literature review but, rather, that it needs to be recognised for its limitations. Journalism is useful, for instance, in gaining a sense of the media issues that are prominent at a given time. Debbie Albon's research into young children's food and eating (Albon, 2007; 2009), for instance, has been carried out at a time when there is a huge amount of media reporting and policy initiatives relating to the issue. Thus, her research needs to be seen as part of a bigger picture; a picture in which food and eating are the subject of much policy and media interest.

There may also be occasions when you might draw upon literature that is 'outside the box'. By this, we mean outside the early childhood studies' canon. As early childhood studies has always drawn upon a range of disciplines, owing to the multidisciplinary nature of the field, it may well be appropriate to draw upon an eclectic range of literature. The key deciding feature is its *relevance* to the topic under study.

 Case studies

Here are some examples of ways in which some students have incorporated literature beyond the 'usual' early childhood studies' readings.

- A student researching using a local allotment as a stimulus to her reception class children's learning, incorporated a small amount of reading about the history of allotments and their place in communities into her study. This was justifiable because she was highlighting the importance of using the allotment to enhance children's developing sense of citizenship.
- A student looking at the views of West African parents about nursery education in her local area incorporated some reading in relation to West African history to help her to contextualise her study. This was important in highlighting the legacy of colonialism in West Africa as well as the type of early childhood provision that developed. This in turn, she argued, may have impacted on the views West African families have of nursery education on entry to the UK.

In this sense, a whole range of literature *may be* relevant – we say *may be*, because it is up to the researcher to demonstrate the relevance of any literature used to the study undertaken. When writing a literature review, it is very easy to drift away from the point, so when deciding what to include and what to exclude, try to think about the following:

- What type of writing is this? Is it a reliable source?
- Is it relevant to *my* study, that is, does it link to my research question or research aims?
- Does it help to contextualize *my* study, that is, does it help me in telling the story of *my* research?

Campbell et al. (2004) suggest four types of literature that the researcher might use in a study:

1. Previous research in the chosen area.
2. Methodological texts (but these will mostly be employed in the methodology chapter).
3. Literature about theory and practice in the area of study. Here, the researcher might be drawing upon work that locates their study within a broader body of sociological or psychological writing, for instance, that helps to inform their understanding of some of the underpinning issues relevant to their own study.
4. Finally, there are many other sources that could be of use. As noted earlier, these may be eclectic, such as from historical and philosophical writings, literature, and possibly film or television. Campbell et al. (2004: 67) maintain that this area is unlikely to be the first or major source of information that will be drawn upon. However, they argue that sources such as these, alongside discussions with other interested parties in the research, might 'add to the theoretical argument, provide insight to the analytical process, illuminate the analytical frame or simply enliven the writing'.

Key terminology discussed

In many research projects, there is likely to be key terminology, which on the face of it seems unproblematic, but on deeper reading may well prove to be more complex. In order to exemplify this further, consider the following terms:

- disability
- poverty

In the first example, there are different perspectives as to how disability might be viewed. A medical model of disability focuses on the child as an individual and the problems their condition might present, whereas a social model of disability is a perspective that looks at the structural conditions that impact on the experience of people with disabilities, such as people's attitudes towards disability and the environment. Thus, the second model sees *society* as crucial in *disabling* the person with a disability (Olsen and Clarke, 2003).

In the second example, you would need to consider whether you are thinking about the issue of poverty as absolute or relative. Absolute poverty refers to the kind of poverty where people have little or no access to running water, food and shelter, whereas relative definitions of poverty see poverty in relation to other people in society (Townsend, 1979). Therefore, you could be considered as living in relative poverty if you cannot afford a television or a telephone if most people living near to you, who want these things, have them.

In these examples, a critical discussion of the terminology you will be using is significant in positioning your research. This is because, if written well and drawing upon a range of reading, you will be arguing *why* you are adopting a particular definition. You will notice that we are not suggesting that you obtain dictionary definitions here; a literature review needs to explore definitions from relevant literature in order to highlight the complexity of trying to form a definition of the terminology used.

Critical analysis of the topic under discussion

It would be very easy, when carrying out a literature review, to *describe* an aspect of an author's or a group of authors' work. However, description on its own is unlikely to make for a successful review of the literature. Silverman (2005: 295) argues for seeing a literature review as 'dialogic rather than a mere replication of people's writing'. In doing this, the researchers should view the review as helping them to answer a series of relevant questions to their research.

Clough and Nutbrown (2007: 101–2) argue for a 'radical reading', interactive approach to the literature. They advocate that you ask yourself questions such as the following as you read:

- What is the author trying to say?
- To whom is the author speaking?
- What is the author trying to achieve?
- What evidence does the author offer to support their claim(s)?
- Do I accept this evidence – does it relate to what I know of the world? What reasons do I have for this?

We would also like to add that you should try to gain a sense of the particular contribution a writer has made to the field. In addition, when reviewing the literature, you may find that different writers appear to be saying something similar about a given issue. Try to ask yourself what it is about their work that leads you to think they hold a similar position. Are they writing within a similar theoretical frame, such as drawing upon psychoanalytical perspectives to support their arguments? Conversely, there may be authors, whose thinking on a given issue differs. Try to think about where their ideas differ, and why they might differ. Sometimes, these differences will be very subtle.

Wherever possible, we would recommend that you try to read people's work in the original, rather than relying purely on other people's understandings of that work (although you need to refer to this too). Different writers hold different views of key theorists, for instance. If we take Piaget as an example, look at the following two quotations about his work: 'Although Piaget's theory has been criticized and found wanting in some respects, there is no theory that has been so supportive to practice in this respect because it is the most over-arching so far in relation to motor play' (Manning-Morton and Thorp, 2003: 52) or 'The net effect of Piagetian frameworks has been to devalue what children know, and hence their knowledge' (Mayall,1996: 45). As you can see, there is a range of viewpoints in relation to key theorists such as Piaget and, if relevant to your study, you might need to argue why you are adopting a particular position with references to the authors that think that way.

Silverman (2005) argues that some reading will be more important to your study than others and this should be a guiding principle in the amount of attention that is paid to the text in the literature review. While a sentence may be sufficient in describing a text that acts as background information, key texts need greater critical analysis, such as a critique of the theoretical frame used by the writer or the research methods employed by the writer in their research. In doing this, Silverman argues for an approach that is both respectful of the writer as well as advancing the reader's thinking about that literature.

Finally here, the way that you organise the review will also provide evidence of analysis, because although you will be collecting lots of information from a range of sources, these need to be organised and classified into a 'coherent pattern' (Bell, 1993: 34). If this is not done, Bell (1993) argues that a literature review can read like a catalogue or list of items. Thus, structure is an important component in demonstrating critical analysis too.

Clear structure

Another important way that a literature review can show evidence of critical analysis is in the way that themes or issues are developed as an organising feature of the chapter (MacNaughton and Rolfe, 2001). In reading about the topic related to your research, you are likely to notice similar points being raised by different authors. You might try to assign a title to these different themes or issues.

∿ **Reflection point**

It might be helpful to see how other people have structured their reviews:

In Albon's (2005) review of approaches used in the study of children, food and sweet-eating, she organises her paper around the following themes:

- bio-medical approaches
- structuralist approaches
- materialist approaches
- post-structuralist approaches
- children's culture.

In doing this, Albon summarises the contribution each theoretical perspective has made to the study of children, food and sweet-eating, arguing – among other things – that sweet-eating should be positioned as a popular cultural artefact as opposed to a food.

Alternatively, in reviewing the literature around playtimes, Towers (1997) uses the following themes:

- the neglect of playtime
- playtime's recognition
- the 'romantic' view
- the 'problematic' view
- the value of the playtime experience
- the future direction of playground research.

In doing this, Towers is able to outline a range of perspectives on the issue of playtimes. In writing this review, Towers makes clear that she believes playtimes are an important area for consideration.

While you need to develop a range of themes around which to organise the review, it is also important to think about introducing and concluding the chapter. One of the differences many students find when writing up a research project is that it is organised into chapters. Book chapters will usually begin by outlining what the reader will expect in the chapter and will conclude by reiterating some of the key themes from the chapter. This is no different to a literature review (and, indeed, the other chapters in a student research project). We discuss the importance of structure further in the final chapter.

Well written

Communicating ideas clearly is an important part of any research project in the same way as it is in an essay. For many of you, writing a project will be one of the longest pieces of writing you will have undertaken thus far. For BA students it is likely to be approximately 10,000 words, and for MA students, around 20,000 words, although this varies between institutions. Good writing will keep your audience, that is, the readers of your research, interested. While one aspect of this is ensuring there is a clear structure, spending time on the grammar and spelling is very important.

Another, sometimes less-discussed, area of writing that can improve clarity of communication is signposting. By 'signposting' we are talking about the words and phrases that serve to guide the reader through your work, sometimes reminding them of what has been written previously, sometimes foregrounding points that are going to be made (Northedge, 1990). In a long piece of work, such as a research project, signposting assumes greater importance.

Activity

Try to access a published literature review such as those discussed earlier. Use a highlighting pen and mark the words and phrases that link points together, introduce new topics or tell the reader that the next section of writing contrasts with what has just been written.

Correct referencing

While individual colleges and universities are likely to have their own student guidance about referencing, they will all share the view that this is an important aspect of a student's work. Not only this, but referencing is part of the process by which academic knowledge is disseminated as well as acting as respectful acknowledgement of the origin of the ideas you are discussing.

The literature review will not have a separate bibliography. All the references used throughout the research project as a whole will be incorporated in alphabetical order in one bibliography at the end of the project. Some key things that you can ensure are as follows:

- Ensure that all the references you use in the text have a corresponding reference *in full* in the bibliography.

- Ensure that the bibliography is in alphabetical order by first author's last name. (It is likely that the referencing system used in your college will require this. In this book, we are using a system called 'Harvard referencing'. It is commonly used in early childhood books and journals.)
- Ensure that Internet references have the date of retrieval clearly referenced in the bibliography.
- Ensure that you include the publisher and place of publication as part of the full reference in the bibliography.

When referencing a chapter in an edited book, it might look like this:

Allen, G. (2005) 'Research ethics in a culture of risk', in A. Farrell (ed.) *Ethical Research with Children*. Maidenhead: Open University Press.

When referencing a journal article, it might look like this:

Angelides, P. and Michaelidou, A. (2009) 'The deafening silence: discussing children's drawings for understanding and addressing marginalisation', *Journal of Early Childhood Research*, 7(1): 27–45.

When referencing a book, it might look like this:

Arnold, C. (2003) *Observing Harry. Child Development and Learning 0–5*. Maidenhead: Open University Press.

When referencing from the Internet, it might look like this:

British Nutrition Foundation (2007) *Healthier Packed Lunches*. www.nutrition.org.uk/ (accessed 28 November 2008).

You are likely to have student guidelines that help you with referencing in your college or university. Follow this guidance carefully as it is very frustrating to lose marks for poor referencing.

HOW TO GO ABOUT REVIEWING THE LITERATURE

Undertaking a search for literature can be a daunting process for the novice researcher. This section aims to give you some ideas in order to make this more manageable.

Where to find relevant literature

The previous section argued that it is important to refer to key readings relating to your chosen topic. Sometimes, as a new researcher, it might be difficult to decide who the key writers are in the field of study under exploration. Some helpful ideas in this area might include:

- *Look at relevant module reading lists.* Bell (1993) notes that books and articles considered to be 'required reading' for modules may well be useful as a starting point. It may be that some of the reading you did for a particular module motivated you to carry out your own research.

- *Ask your allocated research project tutor.* Usually you will be allocated a tutor, who will support you with your project. This person may have specialist knowledge of your chosen research area, and is certainly likely to have a wide knowledge of early childhood studies. This person may be able to steer you towards the most important sources. However, it is important to note, that as a student–researcher, one of the key things your college or university will be hoping is that you develop the independent study skills necessary to carry out a research project. One way of demonstrating this is in a thorough literature search and a well-written review.

- *Look at the bibliographies of recently published material.* If you look at recently published material in your chosen area, you will often find that this writer has drawn on a range of sources that you might like to explore. Look at the bibliography and note the full reference and try and get hold of the source yourself.

- *Use your college or university library.* Most university libraries will have an online catalogue enabling you to search according to author/title/key word. This type of system is useful not only in locating relevant books and journals, it will usually show you whether these books are available in the library at the present time as well as whether you can reserve them. You may even be able to do this from home online. Journals are likely to be catalogued in terms of the journal title, so you will probably have to search within these. In some instances, the journal title will clearly have relevance to your study; for example, if you are searching for information about promoting healthy eating, the journal *Health Education* is likely to have relevant articles within it in some or many of the editions. However, there may well be articles that are relevant in journals such as *Early Child Development and Care*, which contains articles on a wide range of topics relating to early childhood. The advantage of journals such as this is that you will know that the article will be explicitly related to early childhood. The *Health Education* journal will contain articles relating to all age groups. Finally, you may have a subject librarian at the institution where you are studying and s/he will be able to help you access resources.

- *Carry out an online search.* When carrying out an online search, it is important to ensure that the material you are hoping to use is reliable. When you are looking at an article in a journal, you can usually be confident that it has undergone some kind of peer-reviewing process, which acts as a 'quality control' on the material that is published in that journal, as we noted before. But when looking at an Internet site, what checks are there on the **reliability** of the material?

Obviously, there are peer reviewed journals available online – we are not talking about these – here, we are focusing on *websites* that could be useful. If the website has .gov.uk at the end of the web address, it means that it is a government website, therefore it may contain important information about policy (although not a critique of it). If the website has .org.uk at the end of the web address, it usually means that it is a website for a group such as a voluntary organisation. There are some very useful websites that fall into this bracket, such as the National Children's Bureau (www.ncb.org.uk). An address that has .ac.uk at the end of it means that it comes from a university in the UK. The university we both work in, for instance, has the web address www.londonmet.ac.uk

More problematic are websites that have .com or suchlike as part of the web address. This is because they may be trying to sell you something rather than disseminating information that has undergone a rigorous review process. At worst, information found on the Internet could potentially be wrong – after all, you can set up a website and put information onto it without having to go through a process of verification or reviewing by others who have expertise in the field. This is important to bear in mind in any piece of work.

- *Use specialist libraries, if appropriate.* For some of you, there may be occasions when it might be useful to make use of a library beyond your local library or university library. The National Children's Bureau, for instance, has an excellent library, which contains reports, books and journals in areas such as children's rights, children's health and well-being, and services for children and young people, to name but a few. Specialist libraries such as this may charge a fee unless you are working or studying at an institution that has library membership (you would need to check). In addition, unlike local or university libraries, do not assume that you can just turn up and use the library; you may be expected to reserve a time to ensure that it does not get too crowded.

We might liken carrying out a literature search to being a detective. It may be necessary to work hard to track down relevant material, but the pleasure when a useful source is found can make this worthwhile. Try to enjoy it! Presumably you will have chosen an area that excites you in some way, therefore reading around it and developing expertise in the area should not feel like a chore.

Keeping it manageable

It is easy to feel overwhelmed when carrying out a literature search, especially if you are searching for too broad a topic. This is where the planning of your study is so important, especially refining your research question. In order to think about this further, try to imagine the number of references there might be for a topic on 'parental involvement' as compared to 'involving parents of children under five years in promoting healthy eating'. Therefore, try to do the following:

- Define the *parameters* of the study (Bell, 1993). By doing this, you will be able to carry out a key word search for your chosen area.
- As noted earlier, you could start your literature search by looking at more recent material then widen your search. Newly written material is likely to summarise and discuss previous work in the area and may therefore be a useful starting off point. However, it is important not to preclude the use of older material in your literature search. An example might be that in a study looking at attachment, the work of Bowlby (1969) would be very relevant, yet his research was carried out and written many decades ago. We think it is important, where relevant, to examine some of the work of key theorists in your chosen area *in the original* if possible.
- Green (2000) maintains that another useful strategy for keeping a literature search manageable is to limit the search by country. In other words, if your research is looking at involving parents in promoting healthy eating in a nursery class, you might limit your search to looking at studies carried out and published in the UK or Europe. We would like you to think very carefully indeed about this. This is because to limit your search in this way suggests an ethnocentric bias in your work. In other words, the underlying assumption behind this appears to be that there is nothing significant to be gained from looking at non-European countries. Also, by doing this, you may well be eliminating significant sources of information from your study; there are a number of very interesting Japanese

studies that highlight the importance of food and eating in early childhood settings for instance (for example, Ben-Ari, 1997).

- Be systematic about selecting sources (Bell, 1993).

Whatever strategies you adopt for keeping the actual searching for material manageable, inevitably, carrying out a literature search takes time. There is no 'quick-fix' for this and the tutor(s) who supports and marks your completed research project will recognise the efforts you have gone to in order to get hold of relevant material.

Organising notes

It is important to keep careful notes when conducting a literature search. In doing this, it is important to be systematic. Of initial importance is ensuring that a full reference is always put with any notes made.

Some writers argue that it is helpful to keep a personal index system in order to record the books, articles and reports read for the study. Campbell et al. (2004: 68–71) suggest a format that looks something like this

Author(s)
Title
Year of publication
Publisher
Place of publication
Key words
Points of interest
Useful quotation(s)

This format would look slightly different according to whether you were recording key points of information from a book, a chapter from an edited book, a journal article or another source, such as a radio programme or CD-ROM. Ideally, Campbell et al. (2004) suggest that maintaining an electronic database is most useful because this enables you to cut and paste information to form the bibliography or to paste in quotations that are important to include. This could be done using an Excel spreadsheet for instance.

There are now purpose-made packages that help to facilitate this, such as End Note, which is compatible with Microsoft Word and enables the user to maintain and order a database of relevant references; reformat references; import data from national and international bibliographic databases; and enable the user to import information directly into the text of their work. A non-computing strategy would be to use a series of index cards containing the relevant information.

It should be noted that however you decide to keep track of the material you have looked at, this is *not* a substitute for your note-taking – it is more of an aide-memoire. You will still need to ensure that you take notes in greater detail, especially if the book or article that you are taking notes from is significant to your own study.

Key points from the chapter 🔑

- The literature review is a key part of any research project.
- It helps you to tell the story of your own research.
- It involves critical analysis of relevant reading around your chosen topic.
- It positions your own research within an established body of previous research and writing.
- It should be clearly linked to your chosen study. This does not mean you cannot make use of literature that is seemingly 'outside the box' but does mean that you need to demonstrate how it is relevant.
- As with any other area of writing, take due care of referencing, structuring and writing as these will also help to create a good literature review.
- Be systematic about looking for sources, taking notes and keeping track of your sources.

Further reading 📖

Campbell, A., McNamara, O. and Gilroy, P. (2004) *Practitioner Research and Professional Development in Education*. London: Paul Chapman Publishing. Chapter 5 is useful on managing a literature search.

Clough, P. and Nutbrown, C. (2007) *A Student's Guide to Methodology*. 2nd edn. London: Sage. Chapter 5 is especially useful in relation to critically analysing texts as part of a literature review.

17

ANALYSING AND PRESENTING DATA

Chapter objectives

- To explore the meaning of 'analysis' in research
- To consider how to analyse and present quantitative data
- To consider how to analyse and present qualitative data

When **data** has been collected, the next stage is to process the information so that the data can be reviewed to see if there is an answer to your research question, discover if you have proved or disproved your **hypothesis**, or to see what has been learnt about the research topic – depending on the type of research undertaken. Even before data have been collected; at the design stage, it is advisable to have thought ahead about how you will process and analyse the information obtained. In this chapter we will be looking at how to process and analyse data to enable you to present your findings and discuss them in relation to your original research aim(s).

We will see how the process of analysing data is dynamic; that there are decisions to be made that will reflect your underlying beliefs and feelings about the nature of research. These decisions will be informed by the underpinning **paradigm** which has guided your research, whether you are operating under a positivist paradigm, using **quantitative methodology** or being guided by an interpretivist or post-structuralist paradigm, using primarily **qualitative methodology**. In this chapter, we will be looking at the two different approaches to analysing data, the *quantitative* approach, which concentrates on making sense of numerical data and the *qualitative* approach that aims to come to an in-depth understanding of the topic under study. This chapter is designed to be an *introduction* to the subject as entire books are devoted to the subject. When we look at how to analyse quantitative data we will be restricting the explanation to a discussion of **descriptive statistics** only.

WHAT DO WE MEAN BY ANALYSIS?

Once data have been collected using the methods chosen, such as interviews or observations, you may find yourself with a wealth of data. Somewhere in all of this data, organised or not according to the way you work, is to be found the answer to your research question, new insights into the area of investigation, or the proof or not of the hypothesis you are testing. Blaxter et al. (1996: 173) describe research 'as a messy process', and it is at this stage that you may feel it is at its most messy.

Data analysis is a way of summarising and describing your findings, and then seeing if you can find common patterns or themes (Roberts-Holmes, 2005). *Quantitative* approaches to research, which generate numerical data, lend themselves to statistical analysis; that is, the application of techniques that can process large amounts of numerical data and reveal trends. *Qualitative* approaches to research lend themselves to non-statistical techniques, aimed at revealing patterns in the information gathered, allowing you to understand the topic under study in greater depth.

GETTING ORGANISED

Blaxter et al. (1996) differentiate between two different styles of working. Some students are highly organised; they have a clear action plan and timescale, they have all their notes filed and referenced, their questionnaires are filed all in one place and their observations and interviews are already neatly transcribed. Other students may be more chaotic; their notes and files are in disarray, they may not be sure where they have put their completed questionnaires and they have not started transcribing their interviews or writing up their observations. Students should aim to be organised, not least because they have an *ethical responsibility* to ensure that the data they have obtained is stored securely. Moreover, data analysis requires that the information you have collected during your research is *organised* before you start. This might involve the following examples:

- *Typing up* information from notebooks or handwritten notes of observations, making sure that all the relevant details are included.
- *Transcribing* any electronic recordings of interviews and making sure relevant details are recorded on all observations.
- *Checking* that you have actually got all the information you require. Kumar (2005) suggests that even the most *experienced* researcher forgets to ask questions, record a response or write legibly. It may be that you have to go back to a particular respondent to get additional information. This is particularly the case with qualitative research, where ongoing analysis of data may indicate further avenues of research.
- *Numbering* each completed schedule if using a questionnaire. For example, if you have 20 questionnaires, number them 1–20. This will help with the analysis later on.
- *Keeping your research journal up to date*. During data collection, you will have thoughts and ideas about what the information is telling you, which will be very useful when it comes to analysing the data more systematically. This is especially important in qualitative research.

A review of these suggestions shows that you do not have to wait for *all* your findings to come in before you start organising the data. Research does not always fit into neat time lines and sensible researchers transcribe interviews and write up observations as they do them. Later in the chapter we will see that, for qualitative studies, data analysis may progress even before all the information is collected. Students are often dismayed to find out how long this aspect of research actually takes, so it makes sense to start as early as possible.

QUANTITATIVE METHODS OF DATA ANALYSIS

It is difficult to find answers to your research question or see if your research hypothesis can be accepted or rejected, with data in its *raw* form. There needs to be some way of summarising this data and presenting it in a way which helps you to understand the findings. There are four levels of quantitative analysis:

- descriptive statistics, which describe the data in terms of frequencies, averages and ranges
- inferential statistics, used when you are investigating to see if the difference between two groups is due to chance or not, by using tests of significance

- investigation of simple relationships between two variables such as **correlations**
- multivariate analysis, which looks at the effects of more than two variables (Blaxter et al., 1996: 195).

In this chapter we will be looking at how you can use *descriptive statistics* as a tool for analysing numerical data.

〰 **Reflection point**

Review Part 3 of this book, which is concerned with *methods* of data collection. Which methods might involve the collection of *numerical* data?

At first glance, it may seem that only structured questionnaires, structured interviews and some types of observations such as time samples contain numerical data, but open questions in semi-structured questionnaires can be reduced to numerical data as well. For example, in a questionnaire about parents' satisfaction with the degree to which an early years setting communicates with them, there may be an open question at the end that asks '*What suggestions do you have that may improve the communication between the setting and parents?*' Although there will be a variety of responses, you are likely to find that the participants' responses fall into similar categories. For instance, you may find four parents who mention after-hours meetings, two may suggest communication by email and six may suggest newsletters.

One method of analysing the number of times a word appears in a document or a particular image appears on the television is content analysis.

Content analysis

This approach arises primarily from the positivist position in relation to research, and tends to be quantitative in nature (Jupp and Norris, 1993). It might involve counting the number of times certain words or phrases are used in a text. At the time of writing this chapter, the inauguration of President Barack Obama has just taken place. The newspapers the following day were full of analyses of his inaugural speech, counting the number of times he used certain words such as 'global' or 'together'.

As Jupp and Norris (1993: 41) note, 'content analysis is typically concerned with the *manifest* content and surface meaning rather than with deeper layers of meaning' (original emphasis). Therefore, it is likely to look at *what is said* rather than *why people said it*, for instance. Importantly, the requirement in this type of research, as you will recall from Chapters 1 and 2, is that the variables are controlled in such a way that any researcher would arrive at the same results with the same set of documents (Silverman, 2005), be they newspaper headlines, minutes of meetings or sets of photographs.

Activity

You can carry out a simple piece of content analysis by doing something like the following:

- Take a given number of books in a nursery book area – let us say 100 – and count the number of times there is an image of a child with a physical disability
- Alternatively, you could look at a children's television channel for a given period of time (as another form of 'text') – let us say 2 hours – and, again, count the number of times you come across an image of a child with a physical disability.

In both instances, you would be controlling the number of books looked at or the period of time watched (known as the **independent variable** as manipulated by you – the researcher. You may recall this terminology from Chapter 1). The number of images of children with a physical disability would be the **dependent variable** as this is what you – the researcher – are measuring. You can imagine, we are sure, how this approach to looking at documents can be applied to many different areas of focus, beyond that of images of children with a physical disability.

In doing this, consider what the data would be able to tell you and the limitations of this. As you know, there are always possibilities and limitations with any method chosen in research.

While content analysis has its uses, Silverman (2005) argues that qualitative research can offer much more than merely coding and counting data. He argues that qualitative researchers should aim for a deeper analysis of the texts that form the data set. One such approach to analysing texts is **discourse** analysis, which is described later in the chapter.

Coding quantitative data

Transforming raw data into a numerical form, as in the example just described, is called 'coding' and is undertaken as early as possible in the research process. Sometimes coding decisions are made when the data-collecting instrument is being designed, for example, some structured questionnaires and interviews have the responses pre-coded, so findings can be input directly into the computer. You may be familiar with questionnaires containing items such as the following example. Here each response is given a code number, making analysis more straightforward.

> Q1. *What is your highest level of qualification or status relating to early years care and education? Please tick the appropriate box.*
>
> 1. Early years practitioner (NVQ level 2 or equivalent) [ ]
> 2. Early years practitioner (NVQ level 3 or equivalent) [ ]
> 3. Early years practitioner (NVQ level 4 or equivalent) [ ]
> 4. Early years practitioner (Foundation Degree or equivalent) [ ]
> 5. Early years practitioner (Early Childhood Studies Degree) [ ]
> 6. Early years professional (EYPS) [ ]

The following guidelines for coding information in quantitative analysis are suggested:

- *Codes must be mutually exclusive.* In other words, a response should only be able to be placed in one category. In the example we looked at that asked practitioners about their early childhood qualifications, it was important that they were asked to give their *highest* level of qualification, to ensure that the categories were mutually exclusive (Blaxter et al., 1996; Kumar, 2005).
- *The categories should be exhaustive.* When coding the findings from open questions, every response should be placed in a category. Previously we discussed an open question: '*What suggestions do you have that may improve the communication between the setting and parents?*' As we discussed, responses will vary, but it will be possible to group suggestions into categories, which can be coded. For example, some respondents may mention newsletters; some may suggest home/setting books; other respondents may request meetings after hours; whilst others may mention email contact. Each of these categories should be coded, with no suggestions left out (Blaxter et al., 1996; Kumar, 2005).
- *Codes must be applied consistently.* Thus, if coding a particular response in a particular way at the start of data analysis, all subsequent, similar responses should be given the same code (Blaxter et al., 1996). This is vital in terms of **reliability**.

In order to further exemplify how to code an open question in a semi-structured questionnaire, we will be using as an example the question, '*What suggestions do you have that may improve the communication between the setting and parents?*'

1. Draw up a chart similar to that in Table 17.1. You could do this straight onto a computer if you want, or use a sheet of paper.
2. Go through the responses for the question for the first respondent (R1). Write down the suggestions made in the 'suggestions' column, and indicate with a tick in the R1 column that these suggestions belong to R1.
3. Take the second questionnaire and look to see if this respondent has made similar suggestions. If yes, then indicate with a tick in the R2 column. If the respondent has suggestions not on your list add them to the suggestion column and put a corresponding tick in the R2 column.
4. Carry on in the same way for every questionnaire.

Table 17.1 An example of how to code an open question

Q.10 What suggestions do you have that may improve the communication between the setting and parents?

Code	Suggestion	R1	R2	R3	R4	R5	R6	R7
1	Newsletters	✓	✓		✓			✓
2	Email	✓		✓		✓		
3	Meetings in evening	✓	✓		✓			✓
4	Meetings during day		✓		✓			
5	Telephone contact			✓		✓		
6	Home/setting book							✓

Grouping the data

Once all the responses have been coded, the next task is to group data together. For example, you may have wanted to find out how many babies younger than 6 months of age are in day-care settings in a particular locality. You send a questionnaire to each setting and as they are returned you record the findings:

> **Number of babies below six months of age in each setting**
>
> 0 3 1 3 5 2 0 2 1 5 2 0 0 1 4 6 4 1 0 3

In this format it is difficult to discern much of a pattern, so the first thing you could do is to arrange the data in to some sort of order. Denscombe (2007: 258) calls this 'constructing an array of the raw data'.

> **Number of babies below six months of age in each setting**
>
> 0 0 0 0 0 1 1 1 1 2 2 2 3 3 3 3 4 4 5 5 6

Immediately, it is easier to see that most settings have very few infants who are below 6 months of age. Denscombe (2007: 259) suggests that a further refinement is to convert the data array into a tally of the frequency, or number of times that particular values occur.

Number of babies below six months of age in each setting	
Number of babies	Frequency
0	5
1	4
2	3
3	3
4	2
5	2
6	1

> ### ⟶ **Reflection point**
>
> Think about the data set that we have been using. Do you think we have all of the information we need to come to any sensible conclusion about the number of young babies in early years' settings?

I expect you have concluded that just knowing *how many* very young babies there are in a setting does not tell us very much. For example, we are not given the details about the kind of setting; nursery classes in primary schools or pre-school settings probably only take children from about the age of 3, so some of the settings with no very young babies may never take them. Even in settings where they are set up to care for babies of this age, the number they take depends upon the size of the establishment. A small nursery may only have places for one or two young babies. It is likely that this information is to be found within the questionnaires somewhere, and should be used when grouping the information. For example, the data set could be based on the percentage of children in a setting under 6 months of age, and data from nursery classes and pre-schools could be left out. Decisions about what data to process and how to process it have a real impact on the *usefulness* of your findings.

Levels of measurement

One decision to be made is the type of measurement being dealt with. Different types of measurement give rise to different sorts of data. There are four main classifications: nominal, ordinal, interval and ratio (Coolican, 1990; Denscombe, 2007; Harrison, 2001). We will look at each of these in turn.

- *Nominal measurement*. This involves classification of data according to a named category, for example, male/female. In the excerpt from the structured questionnaire outlined in the previous section, practitioners were asked to tick a box to indicate their qualifications. When using nominal data, each respondent can only be assigned one category. That is why the question asked for the practitioners' *highest* qualification.
- *Ordinal measurement*. This level of measurement describes position, or order, in a group. In ordinal measurement it is not assumed that the interval or gap between each rank is exactly the same. For example, you could rank order a group of infants according to the ages that they began to walk. One may have started walking at 32 weeks, another at 40 weeks, the next at 53 weeks, another at 58 weeks and so on. In this example you could assign each infant a rank, but the gap (in weeks) between each child varies. Scales which ask respondents to assign an item to a point on a scale are another instance of ordinal measurement. An example of this would be a question that asks parents to indicate their level of satisfaction with an aspect of provision according to a scale, where 1 indicates a high level of dissatisfaction, 3 indicates neither satisfaction nor dissatisfaction and 5 indicates a high level of satisfaction.
- *Interval measurement*. In interval measurement, a scale is used that has an equal interval, such as number of items recalled in a memory test, or years of post-compulsory education (Harrison, 2001).

- *Ratio measurement.* Interval scales that have a zero point are known as ratio measures. Examples would be time, distance and age.

It is important to know the level of measurement you are using if you are going on to use inferential statistics, and this will also impact upon the way that you present your data. For example, you can only present your data in the form of a line graph if you are using interval measurement.

Measures of central tendency

One way of describing a group of numbers, or data set, is to calculate the number that is *most* representative of that data set. You will be familiar with the most common measure of central tendency already. This is the average, or mean, in statistical terms.

Activity

Look at any newspaper and identify how many times the term 'average' is used. What are the journalists trying to explain when they use the term 'average'?

The three most commonly used expressions of central tendency used in statistics are the mean, median and the mode. We will look at these in turn.

- *The mean.* This is the average of a set of numbers and is achieved by finding the sum of all the numbers in a data set and dividing by the number of items in the data set. In the data set we have about number of babies under 6 months, in early years settings, the mean will be calculated as follows:

Calculating a mean

To find the mean number of babies below six months of age in each setting:
- Add up 0 0 0 0 0 1 1 1 1 2 2 2 3 3 3 4 4 5 5 6
- $0 + 0 + 0 + 0 + 0 + 1 + 1 + 1 + 1 + 2 + 2 + 2 + 3 + 3 + 3 + 4 + 4 + 5 + 5 + 6 = 43$
- Divide by the number of settings (20)
- $\frac{43}{20} = 2.15$

The mean number of babies under six months in each setting is 2.15 (although this may not be a very useful way of describing data in this case!).

- *The median.* This is the middle point of a set of numbers, and for this you need to put the data in rank order and identify the middle number. If you have an uneven set of numbers in your data set, then the median is easy to identify, but with an even set of numbers the median will fall halfway between.

Finding the median

The following is a set of marks (percentages out of 100) given to a group of 15 students.

35, 36, 42, 43, 48, 49, 50, **53**, 56, 60, 65, 66, 75, 77, 81

The median is the middle score: 53

If there were 16 students with the following marks

35, 36, 42, 43, 48, 49, 50, 53, * 56, 60, 65, 66, 75, 77, 81, 85

the median will fall in the middle of 53 and 56. To find the median you add 53 and 56 together and divide by 2.   53 + 56 = 109

$$\frac{109}{2} = 54.5$$

In the example we have been looking at, where nurseries have been asked the number of babies they have younger than 6 months, the median is calculated as follows.

0 0 0 0 0 1 1 1 1 2 * 2 2 3 3 3 4 4 5 5 6

The median falls between two '2s' so the median is 2.

- *The mode.* This is the most frequently occurring value in a data set.

Calculating the mode

Consider the data set of the number of babies aged under 6 months in early years settings:

0 0 0 0 0 1 1 1 1 2 2 2 3 3 3 4 4 5 5 6

The most frequently occurring value is 0.

It is now possible to compare the mean, median and mode for our data set on the number of babies in early years settings:

- The mean is 2.15.
- The median is 2.
- The mode is 0.

 This tells us that the data within the *range* is not distributed evenly because most settings have few babies. With a small data set such as the one we have been using as an example, you may be forgiven for thinking that this is *obvious*, just by looking at the data set, without resorting to calculating the mean, median and mode. However, if you are dealing with *hundreds* of values, then calculating measures of central tendency is a good way of analysing data. You would only use such calculations if doing so would contribute to your understanding of the data you have collected. This is a very basic look at quantitative research analysis and you would also need to know about other statistical processes such as normal distribution and standard deviation. A good book on this subject is Field (2009) *Discovering Statistics Using SPSS*.

Using percentages

In the data set we discussed previously, consisting of student's marks, the marks were expressed in percentages. A percentage means 'out of one hundred'. For example, if we had 100 children and 10 of them were left handed we could say that 10 per cent (10%) were left handed. If you are dealing with large amounts of numbers, it sometimes helps to express them in terms of percentages because it is easier to understand what they mean. For example, if we found out that 731 early years' practitioners out of 986 had an NVQ level 3 as their highest qualification, this might mean less to us than if we said that 75 per cent of the workforce were qualified to NVQ level 3.

The choice to express raw data in terms of percentages has to be made *carefully*. With a small data set, using percentages can be misleading. For example, if you have a setting with five members of staff and three were qualified to NVQ level 3 that would be 60 per cent, if just one more member of staff became qualified to NVQ level 3 the percentage would jump to 80 per cent. This means that one person can produce a 20 per cent change. Although there are no hard and fast rules about when to use percentages, we suggest that ideally you need a data set of approximately 100 before you should consider using percentages. However, each situation is different and it may be that you consider it appropriate to use percentages with far fewer participants. The activity about the time sample later on in the chapter may be a case in point.

How to calculate a percentage

$$\frac{\text{Given amount}}{\text{Total amount}} \times 100$$

Consider this example: 250 out of 500 children have brown eyes.
Divide the given amount (250) by the total amount (500) and multiply the result by 100, that is, $\frac{250}{500} \times 100 = 50\%$ of children have brown eyes.

Consider this example: Out of 122 parents, 31 came to a parent consultation meeting. Divide the given amount (31) by the total amount (122) and multiply the result by 100, that is, $\frac{31}{122} \times 100 = 25.4\%$ of parents attended a parent consultation.

PRESENTING QUANTITATIVE DATA

When you are writing up your research you need to consider how you are going to present your findings. There are two main methods in quantitative research: tables and charts (Denscombe, 2003). There are no hard and fast rules as to when to use charts and tables, except that the aim should be to:

- choose the methods that most *clearly* present your data. In some cases this may be a choice between a table and a chart, while in some instances it helps to have a table followed by a chart
- keep your presentation as *simple* as possible. Adding layers of complexity will not help you or the reader understand your findings. Clear communication is the key.

Using tables to present your findings

Presenting data in the form of a table makes it easier to see any emerging patterns, both for yourself and the people who will be reading your report. In the example we have been using about the number of very young children in early years settings, the data could easily be presented in a table (see Table 17.2).

Table 17.2 Example of a frequency distribution

Frequency distribution of numbers of babies under 6 months of age in early years settings

Number of babies in the setting	Frequency
0	5
1	4
2	3
3	3
4	2
5	2
6	1
	Total 20 settings

When using a table, Green (2000: 88) suggests the following:

- all rows and columns must be clearly labelled
- all units of measurement must be given
- if rows and columns are totalled, this must be indicated on the table
- every table should have a title.

If you are using more than one table it should be numbered. In the table we have just used as an example (Table 17.2) the title and number tells us that:

- it is a table, not a chart
- it is in Chapter 17

- it is the second table in Chapter 17
- it is an example of a frequency distribution.

Activity

Rugina, a student on an Early Childhood degree course, has a placement in a nursery class within a primary school. Throughout the day, the children have free access to all areas of the nursery. It seems to Rugina that the boys tend to spend more time in the outside play area when compared with the girls. She decides to undertake a time sample to look at this more systematically. Every 15 minutes she will count the number of boys and girls inside and outside. She decides to start at 9.45 in the morning and continue until 11.45 when all the children have to come in for lunch.

There are 30 children altogether, who at any one time are either inside or outside. There are 15 boys and 15 girls. During the morning, if she is inside she counts the children inside, and if she is outside she counts the children outside. Her data sheet looks like this:

9.45 outside 7 boys 3 girls
10.00 outside 6 girls 8 boys
10.15 inside 10 girls 6 boys
10.30 inside 3 boys 13 girls
10.45 inside 10 boys 12 girls
11.00 inside 9 girls 10 boys
11.15 outside 12 girls 10 boys
11.30 outside 6 girls 8 boys
11.45 inside 13 boys 14 girls

Using these figures, draw up a table showing the number of boys and girls inside and outside at each point in time.

1. What is the mean number of girls playing outside in the morning?
2. What is the mean number of boys playing outside in the morning?
3. What is the range of the data for boys playing inside during the morning?
4. What is the range of the data for girls playing inside during the morning?
5. With equal numbers of boys and girls it is easy to make simple statements about whether boys or girls use the outdoor area predominantly. The situation is a little more complex with unequal numbers of boys and girls. What could she do to get around this problem?

In thinking about this task, you might also reflect that the information gained is very *simplistic*. After all, it does not tell you anything about the resources put out indoors and outdoors or children's perceptions of the activities on offer. It also does not pick up on whether it is the *same* group of boys outdoors, that is, there may be some boys that *rarely* use the outdoor space – the time sample would not pick this up and might simplify what is a very *complex* issue.

In the activity feature about the number of boys and girls playing inside and outside during a morning, the mean number of girls playing outside is 4.9. The mean number of boys playing outside is 7.3. The range for the number of boys playing inside is 3–13 and the range for the number of girls playing inside is 3–14. This is a good example of when one needs to know both the range and the mean of a set of scores to make sense of the data, as the two ranges are similar, but the means for the sets of scores are quite different. If there were unequal numbers of boys and girls it may be more helpful to convert raw scores to percentages so that a true comparison can be made, even though there are relatively low numbers of children involved.

Graphical representations of data

A graph is a pictorial way of showing numerical data and as such, is a good way of showing patterns and relationships. In a graph there are usually two intersecting lines called axes:

- The X axis is the bottom horizontal line and usually represents what is being measured or counted.
- The Y axis is the left hand vertical line that represents the frequency of what is being counted.

There are many different sorts of graphs or ways of representing data pictorially and we will be looking at line graphs, bar charts and pie charts.

Line graphs

Line graphs are used to show changes in quantities or 'progression in a sequence of data' (Denscombe, 2007: 278) and are commonly used to plot changes over time. In experimental studies, line graphs are often used to show changes in the dependent variable as a result of manipulating the independent variable.

The line graph in Figure 17.1 is drawn from an imagined set of results showing the progress made in implementing a positive behaviour management plan for a child.

Of course, in doing a study such as this, it is important to define what you mean by 'challenging behaviour' beforehand because there may be a range of practitioners noting these incidents and there needs to be a shared understanding of the issue.

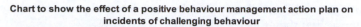

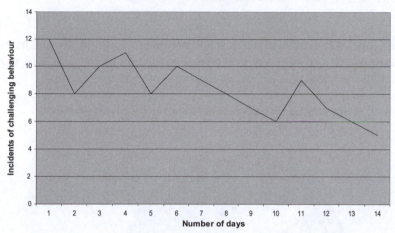

Figure 17.1   A line graph to show the number of incidents of challenging behaviour shown over a two week period

Bar charts

Bar charts, sometimes called bar graphs are where vertical bars are used to represent nominal data (data that is in the form of categories). In Table 17.1 we saw the suggestions that parents made for improving communication between them and the setting. This type of information is ideal for a bar chart (see Figure 17.2).

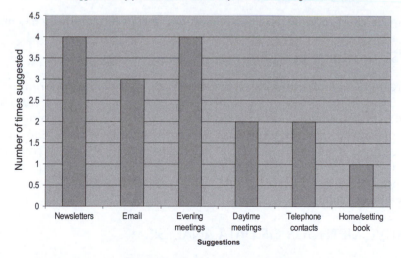

Figure 17.2   Bar chart to show the type and frequency of parents' suggestions as to how to improve communication between parents and the setting

Histograms are similar to bar charts, but use interval data and the columns are set close together so that they touch each other.

Pie charts
Pie charts are one of the most effective ways of indicating proportions. Each 'slice of the pie' represents a category and is represented as a percentage of the whole. Figure 17.3 is an example of a pie chart.

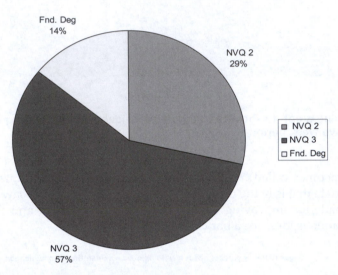

Early childhood qualifications of staff in ten private nurseries

Figure 17.3   Pie chart to show level of qualifications of staff in ten private day nurseries

Using SPSS or similar programmes

You can create both tables and charts on your computer, using programmes such as Microsoft Excel. If your computer skills need developing in this area, many institutions hold classes where you can learn how to do this. For more complex analysis, there are specialised computer software packages such as SPSS. SPSS is a statistical package designed specifically for social scientists and is primarily concerned with analysing and presenting quantitative data. To use SPSS properly you have to have a level of understanding of statistics that is beyond that which is presented in this chapter (see Field, 2009).

QUALITATIVE METHODS OF DATA ANALYSIS

We have already seen that when analysing data, there are decisions to be made about what data to include and what techniques to use to aid analysis. However, in analysing *quantitative* data the aim should be to keep the influence of the researcher to a minimum; two different researchers should be able to separately process the data and come up with similar findings. In qualitative studies the influence of the researcher, on both what is collected and recorded as data and the way that this information is analysed and understood, is profound and in some cases fundamental to the process (Coffey, 1999). Denscombe (2007) describes two ways in which researchers deal with the involvement of self. One way is for researchers to endeavour to identify how their ideas, attitudes and beliefs could affect their interpretation of findings, and to guard against this (as far as possible). The other approach is to recognise that, *inevitably*, a researcher's identity, beliefs and values will have an effect on the way data is interpreted and to discuss this in relation to any conclusions that are made (Guba and Lincoln, 2005). You may recall that this is linked to the notion of **reflexivity**. Fontana and Frey (2000) warn that often researchers are not sufficiently reflexive about interpreting their findings. They point out that in the past there has been pretence that:

- data reported tends to flow nicely
- the data is not contradictory
- no data is excluded
- improprieties never happen.

In reality, Fontana and Frey (2000: 661) suggest that researchers frequently become buried under a 'mountain of filed notes' and other information. The process of imposing some sort of order is often problematic, contradictory and, by *necessity*, influenced by the researcher. Johnson and Christensen (2008) point out that although qualitative methods have been used since the early twentieth century, agreement about how to analyse the data is only slowly evolving.

Preparing qualitative data for analysis

At the start of the chapter we discussed the importance of preparing data before analysis. In this section we will look in more detail about what this means for qualitative data. Denscombe (2007: 289) gives the following suggestions:

- Try to get all the information in a similar format (A4 paper or record cards for example).
- When you collect data, try to do it in a way that allows comments and reflections to be recorded alongside. This may mean leaving a column for reflection at the side of observations and transcripts of interviews.
- Each item that you have collected (observation, interview and suchlike) should be given a reference number so that it is easy to identify and file in a logical way. For example, observations could be referenced by the child's initials and the date.
- Keep copies of all your original materials for the duration of the research project. This not only involves the transcripts of your interviews, for example, but also copying the actual recordings. Your original material is *irreplaceable*.

Interim data analysis

In quantitative research it is usual to have two distinct phases, data collection and data analysis. In qualitative studies researchers tend to enter a more *cyclical* process of data collection, analysis and additional data collection. As research progresses, and the researcher's understanding of the material collected deepens, new themes and patterns may emerge that require additional questions to be asked. Denscombe (2007: 292) describes this as a '*data analysis spiral*'. This process continues until the point of theoretical saturation (Johnson and Christensen, 2008) when the researcher concludes that the topic being investigated is understood as fully as is possible. Practical considerations such as lack of time or resources may also bring this phase of research to an end.

Ⓖ It is at this stage of analysis that issues of **validity** and reliability need to be re-addressed. You would have already thought about these concepts in the design stage (see Chapter 15), but, once the data starts to be collected and the first steps towards analysis are undertaken, there are decisions to be made that may affect the reliability and/or validity of your findings. For example, you may have a preconceived idea about what you will uncover or a common theme may be emerging. If some of your data is not in keeping with your emerging theme, the temptation may be to include only the data that fits in with your ideas. Silverman (2005) suggests that far from ignoring this data, or the 'Deviant Case', the researcher should return to the participant to obtain additional information, which may facilitate a greater depth of understanding.

Silverman (2005: 152) suggests that as the first items are analysed, you should be asking yourself if your methods of data collection and of data analysis are still appropriate.
Ⓖ Often the **research design** will need to be changed at this stage. Interim analysis enables the researcher to begin to see what categories their *participants* are using. For example, in a qualitative study about parental involvement in their children's education, initial perusal of interview transcripts may reveal a theme about parental guilt if they work during school hours and cannot join in with trips and outings. Future participants may be specifically asked about this theme to see if it is a common feeling.

Silverman (2005) recommends that data analysis is begun as soon as it is collected. He also cites Wolcott (1990: 20) as suggesting that 'you cannot begin writing early enough'.

Stages in analysis

There are many different ways to approach the analysis of qualitative data, but, although they differ in approach, generally analysis proceeds in stages. Denscombe (2007) outlines the following stages:

1. *Becoming familiar with the data.* This involves reading and re-reading text data, looking at any images that are being used, and using any field notes or journal entries to help you put the information into context. As you look through the data you should look for 'implied meanings' or information that you would expect to see but is missing.
2. *Coding the data.* In the section looking at quantitative analysis we looked at how to code the responses to an open question. In the example, participants' responses were placed into similar cat-

egories, which were given a name and assigned a code number. A similar process is undertaken with qualitative data, where segments of text are identified, which have specific meaning for your research study. Johnson and Christensen (2008: 534) suggest that a segment could be 'a word, a single sentence, or several sentences, or it might include a larger paragraph or even a complete document'. In qualitative analysis codes can be a simple category label or a more complex idea. As the researcher reads through the text, identifying and coding the segments, a list of codes and their meanings is drawn up; this is known as the **coding frame** (Barbour, 2008). Segments that include similar ideas, attitudes, thoughts and feelings are given the same code. It is important that the coder demonstrates **intra-coder reliability**, meaning that the codes are applied consistently, with similar segments being assigned the same code. Coding is a highly subjective process and, in studies using more than one coder, training is usually given to achieve intercoding reliability.

Barbour (2008) describes the coding of meaningful segments derived from participants' words and concepts as having its origins in Glaser and Strauss's (1967) concept of 'Grounded Theory'. This method of coding is also known as **inductive coding**, in contrast to **a priori codes** that have been developed prior to the data being collected (Johnson and Christensen, 2008).

3. *Categorising the codes.* Once you have developed a coding frame you can look to see if certain codes seem to 'fit' together.

Activity

Gill wanted to find out early years practitioners' views on the Early Years Professional Status. The following are some of the responses given and the codes that they were assigned.

Code	Response
1	At last we are being recognised.
1	We can progress in our career without being a teacher.
2	I'm a bit worried about the Maths and English.
3	I don't think that they will have the same status as teachers.
2	It's still a long haul; we have to have a degree first.
4	No one here wants to do more training.
5	What will happen if the nursery hasn't got an EYPS practitioner?
6	I can't afford to pay for an EYPS practitioner.
1	I have had my early childhood degree for a while. It's a chance to progress.
5	Will nursery classes stop employing teachers now?
5	I don't think that the government has got this all sorted out yet.

Codes: 1 Happy: career progression
2 Worries about needing further training
3 Still won't have same status as teachers
4 Reluctance to undergo training
5 Uncertainties about implications
6 Cost implications

- As we have mentioned previously, coding is very subjective. Would you have coded differently?
- Can you see any codes that seem to fit together to form a category?

4. *Identifying themes and relationships among the codes and categories.* Here the researcher looks at the codes and categories that have been generated and looks to see if broad themes can be developed that reflect the underlying meaning of the participants' responses. For example, in the practitioners' responses about the Early Years Professional Status, we might reflect that there is an underlying theme about how it might increase the status of early years work offering greater opportunities for career progression. Another theme might be a general worry about the future, and the added demands that may be made on both individual practitioners and managers.

   In thinking about generating themes, it is important to consider how they can be applied across the different types of data, such as observations and interviews. In addition, once codes have been identified, they need to be assigned back to the data to see if they work well (Denscombe, 2007).

5. *Develop concepts and arrive at some generalised statements.* This is the process which involves relating the themes generated back to the original research question. Do your findings allow you to make generalised conclusions about the topic being studied? You may develop suggestions that point the way towards further research. Some researchers may even be able to suggest an underpinning theory. For most students doing their undergraduate research project, this stage will involve developing a *narrative explanation* of the findings (Denscombe, 2007).

   Silverman (2005) suggests that researchers should go back to the participants in the study with the tentative findings and ask them if the conclusions are an accurate reflection of what they perceive to be the 'truth' – sometimes known as 'respondent validity' (Silverman, 2005). He warns that participants may not have the *whole* picture and that their comments should be treated as an *additional* source of data, rather than being a true validation process.

 Research in focus

In Debbie Albon's (2009) study, which looked at challenges to improving the uptake of milk in a nursery class (children aged 3–4 years), she observed 72 nursery snack times, interviewed the three practitioners who worked in the class, talked to parents and used laminated examples of the children's drink wrappers as a stimulus to elicit the children's perspectives directly. Only 9 of the 39 children had school milk, despite the fact that 37 of the families were eligible for free milk.

From the wealth of data generated, Albon (2009) reported on two general themes 'A link with personal identity' and 'A link with home and the drama of family life'. Here are *some* examples of data that seemed to 'fit' into these themes:

Theme 1: A link with personal identity
Data obtained from talking to children with laminated drinks' labels as a stimulus:

'I have blackcurrant drink but B (her brother) has orange. He doesn't like blackcurrant.' (child B) (p. 146)
'This is a mango one. My sisters – they have mango juice at their school. This is nice one – *my one*. This one right … is my brother's right! He loves it.' (child S1) (p. 146)

Data obtained from observation:

At snack times, the children, who had bought drinks from home are given their drinks first.

These drinks have the children's names on which are written as a shared activity with their parents at the beginning of the session. Milk does not have the children's names written on them – despite the use of children's written names being very affirming – and is *always* given out last.

There was virtually no data from 72 snack time observations to support the idea that the milk provided by the *school* was linked to a sense of personal identity.

Theme 2: A link with home and the drama of family life
Data obtained from observations of snack times:

Child J says 'Mummy shouted at daddy 'cos daddy forgot to buy me some juice and mummy was cross and he had to go and get some for me.' (p. 147)
Child M says that her brother 'cried 'cos there was only apple juice and he wanted orange. Mummy went to the shop to buy him orange.' (p. 147)

There were many observations noting that when children forgot a drink from home and had to have milk, the practitioners apologised for this and seemed to reinforce the view that drinking milk was a result of their parents' 'negligence'. One example was a practitioner saying 'your mummy didn't bring you a drink today so I *am* sorry but you'll have to have a milk today.' (p. 147)

Data from parent conversations:

'It makes it easier to bring him in if he has something he can bring in from home.' (Child B's mother) (p. 148)
'She cries if I don't let her bring it (Ribena) in. I and H bring in a drink so she wants to be the same.' (Child F's mother) (p. 148)

In writing up her findings Albon (2009) weaves the different sources of data together under the two themes. She concludes by encouraging practitioners to recognise the importance of snack times and to pay attention to the minutiae of their practice in order to make healthier drinks' choices an attractive option for children and families.

Discourse analysis

Discourse analysis is a more critical look at texts than previously discussed and is used in a range of disciplines such as psychology, sociology and literature. Rather than merely focusing on counting words that are used in texts, discourse analysis is more concerned with the social relations within which language is 'produced, reproduced and sometimes reshaped' (Jupp and Norris, 1993: 47). Very simply, discourses should be seen as narratives that shape our ideas about the world such as what we see as appropriate behaviour in given situations or the role(s) we might take in social life (Woolfitt, 2008). Discourse analysis can be applied to texts such as interview transcripts but also, more broadly, to other forms of 'texts', as we will see.

Foucauldian discourse analysis tends to focus on issues of power. Foucault is a post-structuralist theorist who is interested in exploring how *power* is exercised through texts as opposed to what texts tell us about their *author(s)* (Jupp and Norris, 1993). In doing this, he explores the way that some discourses dominate and privilege particular ways of seeing and acting in the world and, in so doing, legitimise the power of particular groups of people and the perpetuation of particular ideas. We should also note that in thinking about 'texts' Foucault interprets this widely to include 'meaningful events, processes or objects that can be interpreted' (Woolfitt, 2008: 450).

🔍 Research in focus

This idea that almost anything can be read as a 'text' has early childhood applications. Mitchell and Reid-Walsh (2002) carried out research looking at the style of children's bedrooms, arguing that they can be read as 'cultural texts'. Children's bedrooms, they argue, are to a certain extent controlled by adults in terms of design, but they also have a *regulatory* function, observed in phrases such as 'go to your room' and 'clean up your room' (p. 113). Mitchell and Reid-Walsh look at the kind of information children's bedrooms contain, that is, bedrooms denote a *separate* sleeping space for children, which is a relatively new and/or middle-class, minority world phenomenon; they denote a *place for play* and the emerging idea of the 'companionable family' (p. 121) and the idea of the *individualism of the child* as important. As children get older, the bedroom becomes an increasingly 'private play zone' (p. 124) away from the prying eyes of adults.

Mitchell and Reid-Walsh look at bedroom décor such as strongly gendered baby bedrooms in pale blues or pinks, and explore in some depth a Winnie the Pooh themed bedroom – chosen by parents owing to its possibly more 'gender-neutral' theme (despite the character being male). They argue that the choice of artefacts in baby's bedrooms reflects not only the identity of the babies, but the identity of their parents. They maintain that bedrooms are a site where children 'grow into' popular culture and ask the reader to consider what children's bedrooms tell us about the nature of *childhood* itself. The authors extend their analysis to looking at how children's bedroom décor changes as children get older and gain greater control over their own space. In doing this, they argue that, owing to increasing concerns about children's activity outside the home owing to safety fears, children's bedrooms (in minority world countries) have assumed greater importance in children's lives as a place to express their sense of self. However, there are new fears now, which are linked to children's increased use of virtual spaces such as the Internet.

Using computer packages for data analysis

Just as there are computer packages that have been developed to assist researchers with *quantitative* analysis, there are computer packages such as N-Vivo and ATLAS-ti that are designed to help analyse *qualitative* data. In the same way that using SPSS demands a high level of understanding of statistics, the use of computer packages for qualitative analysis should only be attempted by researchers who have a good grounding in the area. Barbour (2008: 195) advises that if researchers do not know the principles of qualitative analysis first, there is a possibility the analysis is 'driven by the properties of the package rather than the other way round'.

PRESENTING QUALITATIVE DATA

Presenting findings from a quantitative study is relatively straightforward compared with presenting qualitative data, but the aim is the same; you are presenting the evidence upon which you are basing your conclusions clearly. Bogdan and Biklen (1998: 195) suggest that 'the qualitative researcher, in effect, says to the reader, "Here is what I found and here are the details to support that view"'.

A quantitative researcher would not present raw, unprocessed data in a results' section. Similarly, qualitative researchers present their *analysis* of the data, rather than complete transcripts of interviews or observational material. This will involve presenting their interpretations of what the data is telling them in terms of the main themes. This was seen in the 'Research in focus' section, which looked at Albon's (2009) research. The interpretations should be supported by sufficient excerpts from the data to allow the reader to see that your interpretations are based on *evidence*. It is usual to use direct quotes from interviews, excerpts from observations and excerpts from your field notes or reflective journal to allow the reader to get close to the participants and situations you are describing (Johnson and Christensen, 2008).

Continuing with the examples of Albon's (2009: 148) research outlined in the 'Research in focus' section, she presents the data in the following way:

Parents seemed to stress the link between drinks and home explicitly. Child B's mother stated:

'It makes it easier to bring him in if he has something he can bring in from home ... Does he have a milk as well?'

Without the observations and quotations as *evidence* to support the point she is making, there would be no reason to believe the claims she is making for her research.

Key points from the chapter ⚷

- Data analysis involves looking at your data to uncover patterns and themes.
- Quantitative analysis involves the manipulation of numerical data and the use of statistics.
- Content analysis can be used to analyse texts.
- Quantitative data can be presented graphically using tables, charts and graphs.
- Qualitative data analysis uses non statistical techniques to help us to understand the meaning of the data. In qualitative research, interim analysis can begin as soon as the first information is collected.
- A coding frame can be set up to allow categories to emerge and the identification of themes and patterns.
- Discourse analysis is an interesting approach to analysing texts.

- There are a variety of ways to present findings in qualitative research, but all require that evidence in the form of excerpts from the data are presented to support your arguments.

Further reading

Field, A. (2009) *Discovering Statistics Using SPSS*. 3rd edn. London: Sage. This text describes the statistical analysis of quantitative data, using the computer software SPSS. It is easy to read and has a companion website. It goes far beyond what we have been able to cover in this chapter.

Silverman, D. (2006) *Interpreting Qualitative Data: Strategies for Analysing Talk, Text and Interaction*. 3rd edn. London: Sage. This is an excellent text which gives an overview of qualitative research methods by a leading authority in the area. It is particularly useful for practical advice on how to analyse texts, naturally occurring talk and visual images.

18   WRITING UP

Chapter objectives
- To develop skills in writing up of a piece of research including how it might be structured
- To consider how conclusions and implications for early childhood practice might be drawn from a piece of research
- To reflect on issues of power and voice in relation to writing up research
- To think about how a piece of research might be presented to a wider audience

In this final chapter, we will be looking at writing up research, building on the previous chapter, which looked at analysing and presenting **data**. This is an area of importance because it is the stage in the research process where you will put your ideas forward in a way that is both clear and, hopefully, good to read. We will also be thinking about how you might draw tentative conclusions from your research – we say 'tentative' because it is important to be cautious about any claims you make for your research. This is something that is important for *all* researchers to consider. In addition, we will develop the idea that writing up research is not a neutral act; there are still issues of *ethics* to consider.

WRITING UP A RESEARCH PROJECT

We begin this chapter by looking at writing up a piece of research. For many of you, this may be the longest piece of writing you have been asked to do – on average, a BA dissertation or project is about 10,000 words in length. It may be as long as 20,000 words if you decide to do a Master's degree. While this may seem daunting, the *structure* of the written up research can be helpful in making this seem more manageable. The usual structure suggested for writing up a piece of BA research is as follows:

- Introduction
- Literature review
- Methodology
- Findings and discussion (sometimes two chapters)
- Conclusion.

You should note that each institution may have differences in the way they would like student projects to be presented and there can be some flexibility in this. For instance, sometimes it is useful to include a chapter that discusses the development of policy prior to the literature review chapter. Gilbert (2008b: 501) argues that it is acceptable to 'break the rules' on occasions as long as 'the message you want to convey is nevertheless communicated effectively'. The rationale for the structure of your work should be based on what helps *you* to tell the story of *your* research most effectively.

The introduction is usually preceded by an abstract that outlines the aims of the study, the way(s) in which it was carried out, the key findings and possibly the implications for early childhood practice. Although the abstract is usually about 250–300 words in length, it is an important part of the overall research project as it should entice the reader to want to read more. Although it is one of the last pieces of writing you will do in relation to your research, try not to leave it until the last minute. It can take time to write a good abstract.

Activity

Look at an academic journal such as the *Journal of Early Childhood Research*. You will notice that at the beginning of each paper there is an abstract or short piece of writing that acts as a synopsis of the research as a whole.

If you choose to look at a journal such as *Health Education* you will notice that the abstract is highly structured. This is sometimes the practice in science-related journals. It is interesting that each discipline seems to have a particular style of presenting research.

In thinking about the dissertation – or written-up piece of research for a student project – Hart (2005: 102) offers a useful way of conceptualising its structure. He encourages students to think of its structure as a kind of story. This works in the following way:

Beginning
- *There was once this issue or problem* … (the rationale for the topic and introduction to the dissertation)
- *Which some researchers believed was important* … (the literature review)

Middle
- *That I thought might be a suitable topic* … (aims and objectives of the research)
- *So what I did was* … (the **methodology** and data collection tools)

End
- *And I found out* … (the results and findings)
- *Which means we now know this* … (the conclusions and recommendations)
  (Based on Hart, 2005: 102).

Clough and Nutbrown (2007: 221) also discuss writing up research in terms of story, arguing that, at first, you need to ask 'what is the research story I wish to tell?' then 'how can I best construct my research account?' We will now take you through the parts of a typical research project and discuss what each should usually contain.

Introduction

The introductory chapter should outline the *rationale* for the study. It might contain your personal interest in the topic, your professional interest in the topic (if applicable), and will give a sense of *why* the topic is significant. After all, you want to try and convince the reader that the area is an *important* one. If we take an example of a research project entitled '*How are children with English as an additional language (EAL) supported during literacy hour? A case study of a year one class*', the introduction might also outline some smaller aims or *research objectives* that fall within this topic, such as:

- To investigate the roles of the different adults who support children with EAL.
- To find out whether there are any particular resources used to support children with EAL – if so, what are these and how are these employed?
- To explore the perceptions of this group of year one children of their EAL support during literacy hour.

Like an essay, the introduction to a piece of written-up research should set the scene, giving the reader a sense of what is to follow. If you are looking at an issue using a particular theoretical lens, such as psychoanalytical theory, this could be flagged up in the introductory chapter. It may also be useful to introduce the reader to some information about *where* the study was conducted and describe the group of participants. Thus, continuing the previous example of some research into literacy hour and the way children with EAL are supported, it would be useful to briefly outline some information about the school in which the class is situated and the number of children with EAL in the school. More information about the 'case' and participants, in this example, would be provided in the methodology chapter.

Literature review

We have devoted an entire chapter to conducting a literature review, so we recommend that you revisit Chapter 16. The literature review should discuss relevant literature to the research topic and helps to contextualise your own research within a wider body of research and writing that previously exists.

Methodology

In this chapter, you will need to discuss the **paradigm**, methodology and methods used in your research project. In doing this, try to demonstrate the following:

- An understanding of the paradigm and methodology, which underpins the study. In the example of a research project entitled '*How are children with English as an additional language (EAL) supported during literacy hour? A case study of a year one class*' and the objectives outlined earlier, it would

(G)   be important to show how the research is located within the interpretivist paradigm, using a **qualitative** methodological approach.

(G) • Continuing with this example, there would need to be a discussion of **research *design*** – in this instance, a case study approach to research. Details would need to be given about the 'case', without breaching issues of confidentiality and an argument presented as to *why* a case study approach was appropriate for this particular research project.

   • The methodology chapter needs to contain *anonymised* details of the participants, details about how
(G)   the *sample* was chosen for the research, as well as how the sample fits into the **population** as a whole.

   • A discussion of the *methods* used in the research. In the hypothetical research example we have been looking at so far, the researcher might have carried out classroom observations, interviews with staff and children, as well as examining relevant documents. Again, it is important to make the argument for your choice of methods. *Why* were they appropriate?

   • A discussion of ethical issues that relate to the research. It is imperative that there is a discussion of *ethics* in the methodology chapter. Try to think about the ethical issues that you had to address all the way through the research process. Here are *some* of the issues that it would be important to include: How did you gain access (to the setting and/or individuals)? How did you ensure people were informed about what you were doing? If involving children in the research, how was the consent of their parents obtained and how did you gain the children's consent? How did you store the data and ensure anonymity of settings and/or individuals? In what ways did you (or will you) share the findings of the study?

   • Information about how you went about *analysing* the data. Given that the hypothetical example we have been thinking about falls within the umbrella of qualitative research, it is likely that the researcher would have used an inductive approach to analysing the data, possibly identifying themes that emerge through the data.

You will note that throughout the chapter we are suggesting that you are *creating an argument* to support the decisions made about how you went about conducting the research. In doing this, you should aim to support your arguments with reference to literature about research methodology just as you would support points made in an essay with reference to reading. The methodology chapter should *not* be a hypothetical exercise about research, it should be a discussion of *what you did* and *why*, supported by relevant literature. However, different institutions may have other expectations in relation to this.

Findings and discussion

In some institutions, students are encouraged to present their findings as a discrete chapter and then have an in-depth discussion of the findings separately. In other institutions students are encouraged to discuss their findings in relation to relevant literature as the data is presented, that is, as they go along. It may also depend on the type of research project undertaken. In positivist research there is a tendency to present the findings then discussion separately. This is something to check with your supervisor. Whatever the approach suggested, there needs to be a detailed discussion of the findings *somewhere*.

By the time you have completed your data analysis you are likely to have generated a number of themes or generalised statements, and will need to decide how to write up your findings. Chenail (1995) suggests that there are many different ways of deciding how to 'tell your story', including:

- *Natural.* The topic being studied shapes the way the findings are presented. For example, if your research is about the implementation of a new initiative, then the data will be presented in a sequential order, re-creating the history of the initiative. This can be useful in writing up action research projects.
- *Most simple to most complex.* The simplest theme uncovered is presented first, with more complex themes being presented later.
- *First discovered/constructed to last discovered/constructed.* This way of presenting findings re-creates the journey made by the researcher as the analysis progresses, with the initial findings presented first.
- *Narrative logic.* Findings are presented in the way that you would tell a story, so that themes and exemplars are ordered and there is a logical flow from one concept to another.
- *Most important to least important or from major to minor.* Here the most important findings are presented first with the least important findings being presented later.
- *Dramatic presentation.* Unforeseen discoveries and 'surprises' are presented last, to give maximum dramatic effect.

Once you have decided on the order that you will present your findings, you need to give consideration to how you will structure each section and how you will bring in the evidence from your data. Chenail (1995) suggests the following format:

- Section heading
- Present the distinction or finding
- Introduce the first data exemplar of this distinction
- Display the first data exemplar of this distinction
- Comment further on the first data exemplar of this distinction
- Make transition to second data exemplar of this distinction
- Display the second data exemplar of this distinction
- Comment further on the second data exemplar of this distinction
- Make transition to the next data exemplar of this distinction and repeat the pattern until the closing of this section.

For some of you reading this, Chenail's (1995) format may appear too mechanistic, for others of you it may be very useful. Whatever format you use, it is likely that the findings chapter will be the longest chapter in the piece of written-up research.

Let us continue with the hypothetical example of a research project entitled *'How are children with English as an additional language (EAL) supported during literacy hour? A case study of a year one class'* and consider how the findings' chapter might be structured. Possibly, in analysing the data from interviews, observations and key documents, the following themes *might* emerge (you will note that the previous chapter looked at data analysis in some depth):

- The value of being able to speak more than one language
- Professional training
- The importance of teamwork
- Listening to children – an inclusive approach.

These themes would also work well as sub-headings within the findings' chapter and would allow you to present your findings in a clear and organised way. In writing up the findings, it is also important to include a *deeper* discussion of what they seem to signify, linking the findings to relevant literature. As previously noted, in qualitative research studies there will often be a discussion of the findings in relation to the literature *within* the chapter. In **quantitative** research within the positivist tradition, the findings and discussion may be presented *separately* – often as two chapters.

Conclusion

The concluding chapter will remind the reader of the *story* of the research. By this we mean that it is worth re-stating the main aims of the study, how the study was carried out and the key findings of the study. There should also be a discussion about the *implications* of the study for our understandings of early childhood and early childhood practice. There may be recommendations that you would like to put forward based on the research findings. If you do this, it is important to be *tentative* and try not to claim too much for your research. In the hypothetical research example we have looked at in this section, it would be important to note that the research was carried out in one setting and the findings may not be generalisable to all year one classes.

It is also appropriate to indicate how you might have carried out the research *differently*, reflect on any personal learning that has happened as a result of carrying out the research, and make suggestions, if you have any, about future research that might be conducted in the area looked at. It is not a sign of *failing*, to reflect that the research might have worked better had you done something differently; it will demonstrate that as a new early childhood researcher, you are able to reflect on how you might make improvements to your research practice. You will need to review the **validity** of the study and the **reliability** of the methods used. This will stand you in good stead for any future research projects you might get involved in.

 Case study

Nadiya looked at early years practitioners' views on the value of the outdoor area as an environment for learning for her early childhood studies research project. She carried out 12 semi-structured interviews with practitioners from four different settings.

Nadiya found that the training practitioners received seemed to have an impact on the importance they placed on the outdoor area as a learning environment, with practitioners who had attended a course on outdoor play in their local authority appearing to have the most positive attitudes and greater confidence in articulating why the outdoors is important. She also found that fears about children having accidents and the possible reaction of parents to this seemed to impact on the degree to which practitioners encourage children to take risks in their physical play outdoors.

In writing up her research, Nadiya was careful to use the language 'seems to suggest' as opposed to 'clearly demonstrates' when discussing the implications of her findings. In other words, she was *tentative* in the claims she was making. In making some recommendations for practice she stated '*whilst this is a small sample of practitioners and it is difficult to make generalisations based on this, the following recommendations are suggested:*

- *There seems to be a need for high quality in-service training showing practitioners how the outdoor environment can support all areas of learning*
- *Practitioners need to reflect on how they can support children's physical risk-taking with confidence and consider the benefits such risk taking affords'.*

In doing this, Nadiya was thinking about the implications of her research for early childhood practice but with the proviso that her sample size was very small. She went on to suggest that had she had more time, she could have interviewed practitioners from a range of local authorities, who possibly had different opportunities for in-service training around supporting outdoor play. She might also have broadened the types of early childhood settings the practitioners worked in and the ages of children worked with as well as the range of professional qualifications held. By doing this, Nadiya was recognising the limitations of her study.

References

All the material referred to in the research should be included in the reference section. These should be arranged in alphabetical order by author's last name.

Appendices

Appendices are useful in organising materials that would be cumbersome in the text. In a piece of written-up research, they might contain items such as:

- letter of access
- consent form (note: not each one that was signed – the pro forma)
- questionnaire (again, not each one but the exemplar)
- interview schedule
- observations.

You should note that this is not an exhaustive list.

It is important to ensure that all appendices are numbered clearly and referred to in the text. We often tell our students that we do not *weigh* research projects – all material should be *relevant* and if it is not, should not be included. Similarly, it is important to think of the reader when writing up a piece of research; if the reader has to constantly refer to appendices it can be incredibly annoying. Given that a key audience for your research is likely to be your supervisor, who is also *assessing* your work, this is a vital consideration.

FINDING A 'VOICE' WHEN WRITING UP RESEARCH

One of the key things a researcher needs to do when writing up is to find their own voice. Throughout your degree programmes, you have probably been engaged in writing and have developed a personal style. This takes practice. It is important to look at any suggestions for amendments your supervisor has made of draft chapters. You might also ask friends and family to help with reviewing your work, acting as 'critical friends'. In this sense, writing up your research should be viewed as both a *process* and a *product*, because in the initial draft phases you are writing to *think* and then towards the end you are thinking of the writing as being more *permanent*, that is, a finished product (Clough and Nutbrown, 2002). This is why it is important to start writing early.

One of the things that makes reading a student project rewarding is a sense of the *person* of the student-researcher. Charmaz and Mitchell (1997: 193) state: 'Voice is the *animus* of storytelling, the manifestation of the author's will, intent, and feeling [original emphasis]. Animus is not the content of stories but the ways authors present themselves within their work.' Like the Victorian perception of children needing 'to be seen and not heard' they argue that there has been a tendency to recommend that writers are 'seen (in the credits) and not heard (in the text)' (ibid.: 193).

The reader of a dissertation is likely to get a sense of *you*, the researcher, in any stated interest in the subject matter in the introductory chapter; the literature you refer to (and do not refer to) and the way it is discussed; the decisions you made as to methodology and methods; the discussion you present in relation to the research findings; and any personal reflections on the research in the conclusion. In *qualitative* research, it is likely that a sense of the *self* of the researcher will be stronger than in quantitative research as qualitative methodological approaches tend to embrace the way that the researcher's subjectivity impacts on the research, particularly if falling within the post-structuralist paradigm.

One way that researchers can find their voice is through the *judicious* use of the autobiographical 'I'. This may go against what some of you were taught when at school. You may have been taught to write *consistently* in the third person in order to ensure that your work retains objectivity – the view that it sounds more 'academic'. Letherby (2003: 141) makes an interesting point in relation to the use of 'I': 'Writing in the first person helps to make clear the author's role in constructing rather than discovering the story/knowledge.'

In using 'I', the writer is acknowledging that their knowledge is based on their own perspective on the world as, for instance, a Black, working-class woman, an early childhood practitioner or a person of a particular faith. If you are a practitioner working on an action research project, it is difficult to see how you can write up some aspects of the research without referring to yourself directly – indeed referring to yourself as 'the author' can appear strange in the text. However, as we noted in the chapter on journaling as a research tool, it can appear as overly self-indulgent and possibly relates to the research paradigm within which the research is located. It is very unlikely that positivist researchers would refer to themselves *directly* in the text. It is important to be clear about how your college or university regards the use of the personal pronoun in a research project as institutions may differ in this regard.

WRITING THE VOICES OF OTHERS

Inevitably, when writing up research, you will be referring to the voices of the research participants be it in the views encapsulated on a completed questionnaire, an observation, or in direct quotes from an interview for example. It is important to remember that in writing up, you are *representing* people's views or actions and that doing this carries an *ethical* responsibility. Therefore, as with all other stages of the research process, writing up is not a neutral act (Coffey, 1999; Standing, 1998). You may recall in the previous chapter we noted Silverman's (2005) discussion of 'respondent validation', in which the researcher goes back to research participants and asks them whether their analysis of the data is a 'true' representation of what took place or what was said (but review the chapter for the discussion of the limitations of this). However, some researchers go further than this in their discussion of writing up, arguing that writing up carries with it a responsibility as to *what* is represented, *who* is represented (or silenced) and the *way* that they are represented.

MacNaughton and Smith (2005: 121) ask various questions of researchers, including 'whose voices are silenced and whose voices are privileged in your research with young children?' Similarly, Standing (1998) looks at the issue of power when writing up her research into low-income, lone motherhood. She argues that as a researcher she was in a powerful position in analysing and writing the 'private' words of her sample of women for the 'public' world of academia. Moreover she maintains that in juxtaposing her own words, when writing with her academic voice, with the words of the women in her research – women, who do not have an *academic* background – she was reinforcing *unequal* power relations between them. Standing is concerned that in writing up, researchers might reinforce stereotypical constructions of different groups, such as 'depressed lone mothers'.

It should be noted that these concerns are not expressed by all researchers. Positivist researchers believe it is possible to present their findings in a way that objectively represents the 'truth'. Indeed, it may be seen as more ethical to objectively represent research findings as 'truthfully' as possible, avoiding bias. This is an area we suggest you reflect upon further.

SHARING WHAT YOU HAVE LEARNT WITH OTHERS

In this final section we will consider the ways in which researchers might share their findings with others. You may recall that in Chapter 3, which looked at ethics, we argued that it is important to share your findings with the research participants. We will be considering this as well as considering how research might be shared with a wider audience, such as through publication.

Clearly, if the research has involved human subjects then the researcher should share their findings with them in some way. This relates to the principle of 'giving something back' to those who have agreed to participate in a piece of research. It is also associated with ensuring that people's experience of research is a positive one – one they might consider participating in again if asked. If undertaking content analysis of newspaper articles on early childhood issues, for instance, there are no actual people directly involved in the research. If the research has involved an institution such as a nursery or a health clinic, then the researcher could make a copy of the findings available to the setting. Another strategy might be to provide a brief report of the main findings of the research for all the participants. This can be useful as understandably, not everyone will have the time and/or inclination to read through a 10,000-word dissertation if this is what you have written, but may be interested in reading an A4 synopsis of the findings. This might also be an important strategy when sharing research with people, who may find reading difficult in the language in which the dissertation has been written.

Alternatively, the researcher might employ a collective strategy for sharing his or her research findings. In the Froebel Blockplay Research Project (Gura, 1992), the parents, whose children attended Danebury School's nursery class (one of the settings that participated in the study), were invited to an evening event at the school. At this event, the findings of the research project were shared with the children's families and the event served as a celebration of the children's and the practitioners' learning. The video that was made to highlight the work of the project shows a snippet of this evening event. If you have the opportunity to view this snippet of the video, you will see Tina Bruce presenting the work of the research group to a packed audience of parents.

But so far we have only discussed sharing findings with *adult* participants. How, then, might findings be shared with young *children*? This might be especially important in research undertaken with children over time as children have got used to the researcher's presence. One such method might be to take photographs during the research process and make a book *with* the children or *for* the children, documenting what took place, the children's involvement in the study and some of its key findings. In Albon's MA research, she found that one of the children, aged 5 years, became interested in the writing-up process in itself.

 Research in focus

Debbie Albon's MA research looked at young children's sweet-eating. Years later, she wrote about the interest one of the children in the research showed in the writing-up process as he still asked to be shown where he was referred to in the dissertation (Albon, 2006). Ian was interested in the number of words she had to write, what would happen to her if she wrote too much or too little (enjoying thinking of punishments for transgressions), what his words looked like in the 'book' (that is, the bound dissertation), and the comments received from the marking tutors. He was also interested in the idea that she might not actually 'finish' her interest in the topic and may continue research in a similar area (for him, writing meant finishing something in the allotted time at school).

Albon (2006) reflects that other children may be interested in the way research that involves them is written up and argues that by *sharing* the writing-up process with a child (who is interested – not all children would be), she and Ian had an opportunity to learn from each other and possibly *temporarily* suspend the polarities of researcher/participant or teacher/pupil.

It may well be that you decide to try to share your research findings with a wider audience, that is, beyond the actual group of participants. One way that this might be done is through presenting your research findings to the wider team, if the research has taken place in an early childhood setting. An example might be a practitioner-researcher, who has carried out a study looking at how to improve the way scientific investigations are supported in the nursery class attached to a primary school, sharing his or her ideas with the rest of the school. The findings might also be shared with other practitioners in the local authority or cluster group of settings. This, in our opinion, does not seem to happen enough or only happens when the researcher has gained some recognition such as through publication of their work. Yet as McNiff and Whitehead (2006) observe, small-scale action research has the potential to *transform* both theory and practice.

You may recall that we discussed this in relation to Penny Holland's (2003) research into war, weapon and superhero play in Chapter 8. As many practitioners are now undertaking further study, such as early childhood studies' degrees, developing local forums where practitioners can share their research might offer a platform for new practitioner-researchers to share their ideas.

Of course, you may decide that you would like to try and publish your work more widely, especially if you have received a good mark for your work or if someone with experience of publishing their own work or reviewing the work of others for a publication recommends this. There are numerous journals that might be appropriate.

Activity

Investigate the range of journals that are published in the area of early childhood. You can usually do this by carrying out an online search. Look at the range and style of the articles published in the journals.

Choose one of these journals and find out about its aims and scope as well as its instructions for authors. This is usually inside the front or back cover if you are looking at a hard copy of the journal, or a space on the journal's homepage if carrying out an online search.

It is important to note that in academic journals, any paper that is sent to the journal's editor(s) is likely to undergo a peer review process. This means that two or sometimes more people with expertise in the area that you have written about will look carefully at your paper and decide on its suitability for publication. These people usually remain anonymous. This process can take as long as a few months. The peer reviewers will usually prepare feedback for the author of the paper and if it needs some work, the author is given some time to work on revisions. The paper may, of course, be rejected at an early or later stage in this process.

Key points from the chapter 🔑

- Writing up research involves structuring it in a way that communicates the ideas in the study clearly. Usually, this involves a chapter format that includes an introduction, literature review, methodology, findings, discussion, and conclusion.
- A well-written piece of research gives a sense of the *self* of the researcher, albeit unobtrusively. The

extent to which this happens *directly* in the text is linked to the paradigm and methodological approach within which the researcher is working.

- Writing up research is an act of representation that carries with it ethical responsibilities, that is, it can reinforce particular views of particular groups of people.
- Research findings can be shared with a wider audience. Researchers should think about how to share their research findings with participants, including children. In addition, findings can be shared with a wider audience, such as disseminating findings to practitioners in a local authority or through publication.

Further reading

Silverman, D. (2005) *Doing Qualitative Research.* 2nd edn. London: Sage. Part 5 of the book looks at issues relating to writing up research and publication in qualitative research.

Standing, K. (1998) 'Writing the voices of the less powerful: research on lone mothers', in J. Ribbens and R. Edwards (eds), *Feminist Dilemmas in Qualitative Research: Public Knowledge and Private Lives.* London: Sage. This thought-provoking chapter looks at the issue of representing the voices of research participants. It is an issue that is picked up elsewhere in this edited volume.

CONCLUSION

We hope that in reading this book you have learnt more about early childhood research and will feel inspired to carry out your *own* research. It is something that we think is both *personally rewarding* and *important* in terms of developing greater understandings of issues relating to young children and their families. Crucially, research is significant in further developing early childhood *practice*. We hope, too, that as you carry out research, you try to share what you have learnt in order to develop the understandings and practice of others in the field. But most of all, we hope that in carrying out early childhood research you are drawn to studying with and about young children 'through some intuitive sense of desiring to see the world through children's lives, attempting to improve children's lives, and simply experiencing joy when with young children' (Lahman, 2008: 296).

GLOSSARY

These definitions are meant as a simple aid-memoire, as opposed to a complex explanation of terms.

A priori codes Codes used in identifying segments of data in qualitative analysis that have been decided upon before the data has been collected.

Alternative hypothesis A statement that there will be an effect on the dependent variable by the manipulation of the independent variable.

Anthropology The scientific study of the origin, the behaviour, and the physical, social, and cultural development of humans in naturalistic settings.

Child study A case study based on observations of a single child, sometimes with the aim of recommending a course of action for the child, or with the aim of finding out more about child development in general.

Coding frame The list of codes used in analysing data.

Correlation A statistic used to demonstrate the relationship between two sets of paired measurements. One might say that there is a correlation between obesity and diabetes.

Data Facts or information that has been derived by observation or experiment.

Demography The statistical study of populations.

Dependent variable The variable whose measured changes are attributed to the manipulation of the independent variable.

Descriptive statistics Ways of describing numerical data with the aim of summarising or explaining the data.

Discourse Discourses should be seen as shaping our ideas about the world, such as what we see as appropriate behaviour in given situations, or the role we might take in social life. They are concerned with the social relations within which language is 'produced, reproduced and sometimes reshaped' (Jupp and Norris, 1993: 47).

Empiricism The idea that knowledge comes from experience.

Epistemology The branch of philosophy that looks at what knowledge is (its nature), the source of knowledge and the validity of knowledge.

Hypothesis A prediction based on theory: the alternative hypothesis.

Independent variable The variable that is being manipulated by the researcher to find out its effect on the dependent variable.

Inductive coding Codes used in qualitative data analysis used to identify segments of data developed from the participants' views and opinions.

Intra-coder reliability Consistency in coding demonstrated by an individual coder.

Methodology Ideas about how to approach research based on an underlying paradigm.

Modernist Modernity can be thought about as a historical period starting in Western Europe in the late 17th century (the Enlightenment period). The ideas that encompass what can be described as 'modernist' are ones that embrace 'truth' as something knowable, certain and value-free, with progress viewed as achievable through the application of science and reasoning.

Null hypothesis A statement that manipulation of the independent variable will have no effect on the dependent variable.

Oedipus conflict An aspect of Freud's psychoanalytic theory which suggests that infant boys become sexually attracted to their mothers. At the same time they become aware of their father's power and fear that they will be punished, specifically by castration.

Paradigm A theoretical framework that underpins how one sees the world.

Play therapy Therapy used for very young children with limited communication skills, aimed at helping them resolve emotional conflicts. The therapist uses play (often small-world play) as a medium of communication.

Population The large group to which the researcher wants the findings of the study to apply.

Praxis The idea that theory and practice are inseparable, with theory informing practice and practice informing the development of theory.

Psychoanalytic theory A theory of personality that emphasises the role of unconscious processes in personality development and motivation. Gave rise to 'Psychoanalysis', a talking therapy based on psychoanalytic theory.

Qualitative research is usually concerned with describing experiences, emphasising meaning and exploring the nature of an issue in some detail. It is less concerned with being able to make generalisations about the world than is seen in quantative research.

Quantitative research Researchers using a quantitative approach usually (but not always) concentrate on the *confirmatory* stages of the research cycle, that is the formulation of a hypothesis and the collection of numerical data to test this hypothesis. Thus quantitative methodology aims to measure, quantify or find the extent of a phenomenon.

Range The difference between the maximum value and the minimum value in a data set.

Reflexivity The impact of research on the researcher and the effect of the self of the researcher on the research.

Reliability Relates to how well research has been carried out. Findings are said to be reliable if other researchers can replicate the findings of a study by using the same methods.

Research design The strategy or plan that is used to investigate a research question or hypothesis. Experimental design is one particular aspect of this.

Sampling A set of elements taken from the larger population.

Sampling frame The elements (individuals) in the population of your research, who could be available to be included in your sample.

Triangulation The use of a variety of methods, researcher's perspectives, theories and methodological approaches to answer a research question, in order to corroborate results and increase reliability. Triangulation is used primarily with qualitative research.

Validity A questionnaire is said to be valid if it obtains information about what the researcher claims it does. For example, a questionnaire designed to find out how often parents give their children sweets may not be valid if the parents feel guilty about giving their children too many sweets and give an answer that reflects what they think they should be doing, rather than what they actually do.

BIBLIOGRAPHY

Abbott, L. and Langston, A. (2005) 'Ethical research with very young children', in A. Farrell (ed.) *Ethical Research with Children*. Maidenhead: Open University Press.

Acheson, D. (1998) *Independent Inquiry into Inequalities in Health Report*. London: The Stationery Office.

Ainsworth, M. and Bell, S. (1970) 'Attachment, exploration and separation: illustrated by the behaviour of one-year-olds in a strange situation', *Child Development*, 41: 49–65.

Ainsworth, S., Blehar, M., Walters, E. and Wall, S. (1978) *Patterns of Infant Attachment: A Psychological Study of the Strange Situation*. Hillsdale, NJ: Erlbaum.

Albon, D. (2005) 'Approaches to the study of children, food and sweet eating: a review of the literature', *Early Child Development and Care*, 175(5): 407–18.

Albon, D. (2006) 'Writing up research involving child participants: some reflections on Ian, aged 5 years', www.tactyc.org.uk/pdfs/albon.pdf (accessed 20 September 2007).

Albon, D. (2007) 'Exploring food and eating patterns using food-maps', *Nutrition and Food Science*, 37(4): 254–9.

Albon, D. (2009) 'Challenges to improving the uptake of milk in a nursery class: a case study', *Health Education*, 109(2): 140–54.

Alderson, P. (2000) 'Children as researchers: the effect of participation rights on research methodology', in P. Christensen and A. James (eds), *Research with Children: Perspectives and Practices*. London: Falmer Press.

Alderson, P. (2005) 'Designing ethical research with children', in A. Farrell (ed.), *Ethical Research with Children*. Maidenhead: Open University Press.

Alldred, P. (1998) 'Ethnography and discourse analysis: dilemmas in representing the voices of children', in J. Ribbens and R. Edwards (eds), *Feminist Dilemmas in Qualitative Research: Public Knowledge and Private Lives*. London: Sage.

Allen, G. (2005) 'Research ethics in a culture of risk', in A. Farrell (ed.), *Ethical Research with Children*. Maidenhead: Open University Press.

Anderson, G. (1998) *Fundamentals of Educational Research*. 2nd edn. London: Taylor and Francis.

Angelides, P. and Michaelidou, A. (2009) 'The deafening silence: discussing children's drawings for understanding and addressing marginalisation', *Journal of Early Childhood Research*, 7(1): 27–45.

Angrosino, M. (2005) 'Recontextualising observation: ethnography, pedagogy, and the prospects for a progressive political agenda', in N.K. Denzin and Y.S. Lincoln (eds), *Handbook of Qualitative Research*. 3rd edn. London: Sage.

Angrosino, M. and Perez, K.A.M. (2000) 'Rethinking observation: from method to context', in N.K. Denzin and Y.S. Lincoln (eds), *Handbook of Qualitative Research*. 2nd edn. London: Sage.

Anning, A., Cottrell, D. Frost, N., Green, J. and Robinson, M. (2006) *Developing Multiprofessional Teamwork for Integrated Children's Services*. Maidenhead: Open University Press.

Arnold, C. (2003) *Observing Harry. Child Development and Learning 0–5*. Maidenhead: Open University Press.

Athey, C. (1990) Extending Thought in Young Children. London: Paul Chapman Publishing.

Athey, C. (2007) *Extending Thought in Young Children*. 2nd edn. London: Sage.

Atkinson, R.L., Atkinson, R.C., Smith, E., Bem, D. and Nolen-Hoeksema, S. (1996) *Hilgard's Introduction to Psychology*. Fort Worth, TX: Harcourt Brace.

Aubrey, C., David, T., Godfrey, R. and Thompson, L. (2000) *Early Childhood Educational Research: Issues in Methodology and Ethics*. London: Routledge/Falmer Press.

Axline, V. (1971) *Dibs in Search of Self*. Harmondsworth: Penguin.

Backstrom, C.H. and Hursh-César, G. (1981) *Survey Research*. 2nd edn. New York: Macmillan.

Bandura, A., Ross, D. and Ross, S. (1963) 'Imitation of film mediated aggressive models', *Journal of Abnormal and Social Psychology*, 66(1): 3–11.

Barbour, R. (2008) *Introducing Qualitative Research: A Student Guide to the Craft of Doing Qualitative Research*. London: Sage.

Barker, J. and Weller, S. (2003) '"Is it fun?" Developing children centred research methods', *International Journal of Sociology and Social Policy*, 23(1–2): 33–58.

Bell, J. (1993) *Doing Your Research Project: A Guide for First-Time Researchers in Education and the Social Sciences*. Buckingham: Open University Press.

Bell, J. (2005) *Doing your Research Project, a Guide for First-Time Researchers in Education, Health and Social Science*. 4th edn. Maidenhead: Open University Press.

Bell, L. (1998) 'Public and private meanings in diaries: Researching family and child-care', in J. Ribbens and R. Edwards (eds), *Feminist Dilemmas in Qualitative Research: Public Knowledge and Private Lives*. London: Sage.

Ben-Ari, E. (1997) *Body Projects in Japanese Childcare: Culture, Organisation and Emotions in a Pre-School*. Richmond: Curzon Press.

Bertram, T. and Pascal, C. (2001) *Effective Early Learning: Case Studies in Improvement*. London: Sage.

Blaxter, L., Hughes, C. and Tight, M. (1996) *How to Research*. Buckingham: Open University Press.

Bogdan, R. and Biklen, S. (1998) *Qualitative Research Education: An Introduction to Theory and Methods*. Boston, MA: Allyn and Bacon.

Bolling, K., Grant, C., Hamlyn, B. and Thornton, A. (2007) *Infant Feeding Survey 2005*. London: NHS.

Bolton, G. (2001) *Reflective Practice: Writing and Professional Development*. London: Sage.

Bordo, S. (2003) *Unbearable Weight: Feminism, Western Culture and the Body*. Berkeley, CA: University of California Press.

Bowlby, J. (1969) *Attachment and Loss*. Vol. 1: *Attachment*. London: Hogarth.

Bowlby, J., Robertson, J. and Rosenbluth, D. (1952) 'A two-year old goes to hospital', *The Psychoanalytic Study of the Child*, 7: 82–94.

Brice-Heath, S. (1983) *Ways with Words: Language, Life and Work in Communities and*

Classrooms. Cambridge: Cambridge University Press.

British Educational Research Association, http://bera.ac.uk (accessed 2 March 2009).

British Nutrition Foundation (2007) *Healthier Packed Lunches*, www.nutrition.org.uk/ (accessed 28 November 2008).

British Psychological Society, www.bps.org.uk/the-society/code-of-conduct/code-of-conduct_home.cfm (accessed 2 March 2009).

British Sociological Society, www.sociology.org.uk/as4bsoce.pdf (accessed 2 March 2009).

Bromley, D. (1986) *The Case Study Method in Psychology and Related Disciplines*. Chichester: Wiley.

Brown, T. and Jones, L. (2001) *Action Research and Postmodernism: Congruence and Critique*. Buckingham: Open University Press.

Bruce, T. (1987) *Early Childhood Education*. London: Hodder and Stoughton.

Bruce, T. (1991) *Time to Play in Early Childhood Education*. London: Hodder and Stoughton.

Bruner, J.S. (2006) *In Search of Pedagogy. Vol. 1: The Selected Works of Jerome S. Bruner*. Abingdon: Routledge.

Buchbinder, M., Longhofer, J., Barrett, T., Lawson, P. and Floersch, J. (2006) 'Ethnographic approaches to child care research', *Journal of Early Childhood Research*, 4(1): 45–63.

Bunting, G. and Freeman, R. (1999) 'The influence of socio-demographic factors upon children's breaktime food consumption in north and north-west Belfast', *Health Education Journal*, 58(4): 401–9.

Buzan, T. (2007) *The Buzan Study Skills Handbook*. Harlow: BBC Active.

Campbell, A., McNamara, O. and Gilroy, P. (2004) *Practitioner Research and Professional Development in Education*. London: Paul Chapman Publishing.

Cannold, L. (2001) 'Interviewing adults', in G. MacNaughton, S. Rolfe and I. Siraj-Blatchford (eds), *Doing Early Childhood Research. International Perspectives on Theory and Practice*. Buckingham: Open University Press.

Cardwell, M., Clark, L. and Meldrum, C. (1996) *Psychology for A Level*. London: Collins Educational.

Carr, C. and Worth, A. (2001) 'The use of the telephone for research', *Nursing Times Research*, 6(1): 511–24.

Central Advisory Council for Education (1967) *Children and their Primary Schools*. The Plowden Report. London: HMSO.

Centre for Longitudinal Studies (2007) *National Child Development Study*, www.cls.ioe.ac.uk/text.asp?section=0001000200030016 (accessed 14 February 2009).

Centre for Longitudinal Studies (2008) www.cls.ioe.ac.uk/ (accessed 30 March 2008).

Centre for Longitudinal Studies (2008) *National Child Development Study*, www.cls.ioe.ac.uk/text.asp?section=000100020003 (accessed 10 February 2009).

Charmaz, K. and Mitchell, R.G. (1997) 'The myth of silent authorship: Self, substance, and style in ethnographic writing', in R. Hertz (ed.), *Reflexivity and Voice*. London: Sage.

Chenail, R. (1995) 'Presenting qualitative data', *The Qualitative Report*, 2(3), December, www.nova.edu/ssss/QR/QR2–3/presenting.html (accessed 8 March 2009).

Christians, C.G. (2005) 'Ethics and politics in qualitative research', in N. Denzin and Y. Lincoln (eds), *The Sage Handbook of Qualitative Research*, 3rd edn. London: Sage.

Church, A. and Waclawski, J. (1998) *Organisational Surveys*. Aldershot: Gower.

Clark, A. (2005) 'Ways of seeing: using the Mosaic approach to listen to young children's perspectives', in A. Clark, A.T. Kjorholt and P. Moss (eds), *Beyond Listening: Children's Perspectives on Early Childhood Services*. Bristol: Policy Press.

Clark, A. and Moss, P. (2001) *Listening to Young Children: The Mosaic Approach*. London: NCB and JRF.

Clough, P. and Nutbrown, C. (2002) *A Student's Guide to Methodology*. London: Sage.

Clough, P. and Nutbrown, C. (2007) *A Student's Guide to Methodology*. 2nd edn. London: Sage.

Coady, M.M. (2001) 'Ethics in early childhood research', in G. MacNaughton, S.A. Rolfe and I. Siraj-Blatchford (eds), *Doing Early Childhood Research: International Perspectives on Theory and Practice*. Maidenhead: Open University Press.

Coffey, A. (1999) *The Ethnographic Self: Fieldwork and the Representation of Identity*. London: Sage.

Cohen, L., Manion, L. and Morrison, K. (2000) *Research Methods in Education*, 4th edn. London: Routledge.

Cohen, L., Manion, L. and Morrison, K. (2007) *Research Methods in Education*. London: Taylor and Francis.

Connolly, P. (2008) 'Race, gender and critical reflexivity in research with young children', in P. Christensen and A. James (eds), *Research with Children: Perspectives and Practices*. 2nd edn. London: Routledge.

Cook, T. and Hess, E. (2007) 'What the camera sees and from whose perspective: fun methodologies for engaging children in enlightening adults', *Childhood*, 14(1): 29–45.

Coolican, H. (1990) *Research Methods and Statistics in Psychology*. London: Hodder and Stoughton.

Coolican, H. (2004) *Research Methods and Statistics in Psychology*. 4th edn. London: Hodder Arnold.

Corsaro, W. (1985) *Friendship and Peer Culture in the Early Years*. Norwood, NJ: Ablex.

Corsaro, W. (1996) 'Transitions in early childhood: the promise of comparative longitudinal ethnography', in A. Colby, R. Jessor and R.A. Schweder (eds), *Ethnography and Human Development: Context and Meaning in Social Inquiry*. Chicago, IL: University of Chicago Press.

Corsaro, W. and Molinari, L. (2008) 'Entering and observing in children's worlds: a reflection on a longitudinal ethnography of early education in Italy', in A. Christensen and A. James (eds), *Research with Children: Perspectives and Practices*. 2nd edn. Abingdon: Routledge.

Crowther, R., Dinsdale, H., Rutter, H. and Kyffin, R. (2007) *Analysis of the National Childhood Obesity Database 2005–06*. Oxford: South East Public Health Observatory.

Darte, P. (2007) *Children's scientists discover fundamental protein instrumental to brain development and repair*. Washington, DC: Children's National Medical Centre. www.eurekalert.org/pub_releases/2007–07/cnmc-csd070607.php (accessed 1 November 2008).

Darwin, C.R. (1877) 'A biographical sketch of an infant', *Mind. A Quarterly Review of Psychology and Philosophy*, 2(7): 285–94. http://darwin-online.org.uk/content/frameset?itemID=F1779&viewtype=text&pageseq=1 (accessed 24 August 2008).

David, T., Tonkin, J., Powell, S. and Anderson, C. (2005) 'Ethical aspects of power in research with children', in A. Farrell (ed.), *Ethical Research with Children*. Maidenhead: Open University Press.

Davis, J., Watson, N. and Cunningham-Burley, S. (2008) 'Disabled children, ethnography and unspoken understandings: the collaborative construction of diverse identities', in P. Christensen and A. James (eds), *Research with Children: Perspectives and Practices*. Abingdon: Routledge.

De Vaus, D. (2002) *Surveys in Social Research*. 5th edn. London: Routledge. This is a 'classic' text that takes the reader through the practical steps of designing a survey and analysing the results.

Deegan, M.J. (2007) 'The Chicago School of ethnography', in P. Atkinson, A. Coffey, S. Delamont, J. Lofland and L. Lofland (eds), *Handbook of Ethnography*. London: Sage.

Degotardi, S., Torr, J. and Cross, T. (2008) '"He's got a mind of his own". The development of a framework for determining mother's beliefs about their infants' minds', *Early Childhood Research Quarterly*, 23: 259–71.

Deming, W. (1960) *Sample Design in Business Research*. New York: John Wiley and Sons.

Denscombe, M. (2002) *The Good Research Guide for Small Scale Research Projects*. Rept edn. Maidenhead: Open University Press.

Denscombe, M. (2003) *The Good Research Guide for Small Scale Research Projects*. 2nd edn. Maidenhead: Open University Press.

Denscombe, M. (2007) *The Good Research Guide for Small Scale Research Projects*. 3rd edn. Maidenhead: Open University Press.

Denzin, N. and Lincoln, Y. (2005) 'Introduction', in N. Denzin and Y. Lincoln (eds), *The Sage Handbook of Qualitative Research*. 3rd edn. London: Sage.

Department for Education and Skills (DfES) (2007) *The Early Years Foundation Stage*. Nottingham: DfES Publications.

Department for Education and Skills (DfES) (2002) *Birth to Three Matters*. Nottingham: DfES.

Department of Health (DoH) (2008) *The National Child Health Measurement Programme*. www.dh.gov.uk/en/Publichealth/Healthimprovement/Healthyliving/DH_073787 (accessed 9 November 2008).

DeVault, M.L. (1997) 'Personal writing in social research: issues of production and interpretation', in R. Hertz (ed.), *Reflexivity and Voice*. London: Sage.

Dockett, S. and Perry, B. (2007) 'Trusting children's accounts in research', *Journal of Early Childhood Research*, 5: 47–63.

Donaldson, M. (1979) *Children's Minds*. London: Fontana.

Douglas, M. and Nicod, M. (1974) 'Taking the Biscuit: the Structure of British Meals', *New Society*, 30(637) 744–7.

Driskell, D. (2002) *Creating Better Cities with Children and Youth*. London: Earthscan/UNESCO.

Duffy, B. (1993) 'The analysis of documentary evidence', in J. Bell (ed.), *Doing Your*

Research Project. Buckingham: Oxford University Press.

Dunn, J. (2005) 'Naturalistic observations of children and their families', in S. Greene and D. Hogan (eds), *Researching Children's Experience: Approaches and Methods*. London: Sage.

Dwyer, G., Higgs, J., Hardy, L. and Baur, L. (2008) 'What do parents and preschool staff tell us about young children's activity: a qualitative study', *International Journal of Behavioral Nutrition and Physical Activity*, 5: 66. http://ijbnpa.org/content/pdf/1479–5868-5–66.pdf (accessed 14 February 2009).

Edmiston, B. (2005) 'Coming home to research', in D.S. Soto and B.B. Swadener (eds), *Power and Voice in Research with Children*. New York: Peter Lang.

Edmond, R. (2005) 'Ethnographic research methods with children and young people', in S. Greene and D. Hogan (eds), *Researching Children's Experience: Approaches and Methods*. London: Sage.

Edwards, A. (2001) 'Qualitative research designs and analysis', in G. MacNaughton, S. Rolfe and I. Siraj-Blatchford (eds), *Doing Early Childhood Research: International Perspectives on Theory and Practice*. Maidenhead: Open University Press.

Elfer, P., Goldschmeid, E. and Selleck, D. (2003) *Key Person Relationships in the Nursery*. London: Sage.

Elliott, J. (1991) *Action Research for Educational Change*. Buckingham: Open University Press.

Emerson, R.M., Fretz, R.I. and Shaw, L.L. (2007) 'Participant observation and fieldnotes', in P. Atkinson, A. Coffey, S. Delamont, J. Lofland and L. Lofland (eds), *Handbook of Ethnography*. London: Sage.

Englander, D. (1998) *Poverty and Poor Law Reform in Nineteenth Century Britain, 1834–1914: From Chadwick to Booth (Seminar Studies in History)*. London: Longman.

Etherington, K. (2004) *Becoming a Reflexive Researcher: Using Ourselves in Research*. London: Jessica Kingsley.

Eysenck, M. (2004) *Psychology, an International Perspective*. London: Psychology Press.

Farrell, A. (2005) 'Ethics and research with children', in A. Farrell (ed.), *Ethical Research with Children*. Maidenhead: Open University Press.

Farrell, A., Tayler, C., Tennent, L. and Gahan, D. (2002) 'Listening to children: a study of child and family services', *Early Years*, 22(1): 27–38.

Fawcett, M. (1996) *Learning Through Child Observation*. London: Jessica Kingsley.

Field, A. (2009) *Discovering Statistics Using SPSS*. 3rd edn. London: Sage.

Fielding, N. (2008) 'Ethnography', in N. Gilbert (ed.), *Research Social Life*. 3rd edn. London: Sage.

Fielding, N. and Thomas, H. (2008) 'Qualitative interviewing', in N. Gilbert (ed.), *Research Social Life*. 3rd edn. London: Sage.

Fine, M., Weis, L., Weseen, S. and Wong, L. (2000) 'For whom? Qualitative research, representations and social responsibilities', in N.K. Denzin and Y.S. Lincoln (eds), *Handbook of Qualitative Research*. 2nd edn. London: Sage.

Fontana, A. and Frey, J.H. (2000) 'The interview: from structured questions to negotiated text', in N.K. Denzin and Y.S. Lincoln (eds), *Handbook of Qualitative Research*. 2nd edn. London: Sage.

Fraser, S. and Robinson, C. (2004) 'Paradigms and philosophy', in S. Fraser, Lewis, V., Ding, S., Kellett, M. and Robinson, C. (eds), *Doing Research with Children and Young People*. London, Sage.

Fromkin, V., Krashen, S., Curtiss, S., Rigler, D. and Rigler, M. (2005) *The Development of Language in Genie: A Case of Language Acquisition Beyond the Critical Period*, www.ling.udel.edu/simyong/ling101/2005s/lecturenotes/genie.pdf (accessed 30 August 2008).

Gallagher, K. and Fusco, C. (2006) 'IDology and the technologies of public (school) space: an ethnographic inquiry into the neo-liberal tactics of social (re)production', *Ethnography and Education*, 1(3): 301–18.

Geertz, C. (1973) 'Thick description: toward an interpretive theory of culture', in C. Geertz (ed.), *The Interpretation of Cultures: Selected Essays*, New York: Basic Books.

Gilbert, N. (2008a) 'Research, theory and method', in N. Gilbert (ed.), *Research Social Life*. 3rd edn. London: Sage.

Gilbert, N. (2008b) 'Writing about social research', in N. Gilbert (ed.), *Research Social Life*. 3rd edn. London: Sage.

Glass, N. (1999) 'Sure Start: the development of an early intervention programme for young people in the United Kingdom', *Children and Society*, 13(4): 257–64.

Golding, J., Pembrey, M., Jones, R. and the ALSPAC Study Team (2001) 'ALSPAC–The Avon Longitudinal Study of Parents and Children', *Paediatric and Perinatal Epidemiology*, 15, Supplement 1 (January): 74–87.

Goodenough, F. (1926) *Measurement of Intelligence by Drawings*. New York: Harcourt, Brace and World.

Green, S. (2000) *Research Methods in Health, Social and Early Years Care*. Cheltenham: Nelson Thornes.

Green, S. (2002) *Research Methods in Health, Social Care and Early Years Care*. Cheltenham: Nelson Thornes.

Green, S. (2007) *BTEC National Children's Care, Learning and Development*. Cheltenham: Nelson Thornes.

Greene, S. and Hill, M. (2005) 'Researching children's experience: methods and methodological issues', in S. Greene and D. Hogan (eds), *Researching Children's Experience: Approaches and Methods*. London: Sage.

Greenwood, D.J. and Levin, M. (2000) 'Reconstructing the relationships between universities and society through action research', in N.K. Denzin and Y.S. Lincoln (eds), *Handbook of Qualitative Research*. 2nd edn. London: Sage.

Greig, A., Taylor, J. and Mackay, T. (2007) *Doing Research with Children*. 2nd edn. London: Sage.

Guba, E.G. and Lincoln, Y.S. (2005) 'Paradigmatic controversies, contradictions, and emerging confluences', in N. Denzin and Y. Lincoln (eds), *The Sage Handbook of Qualitative Research*. 3rd edn. London: Sage.

Gura, P. (1992) *Exploring Learning: Young Children and Blockplay*. London: Paul Chapman Publishing.

Hammersley, M. (2007) *Methodological Paradigms in Educational Research*. London: TLRP. www.tlrp.org/capacity/rm/wt/hammersley (accessed 2 November 2008).

Hammersley, M. and Gomm, R. (2000) 'Introduction', in R. Gomm, M. Hammersley, and P. Foster (eds), *Case Study Method*. London: Sage.

Harrison, L. (2001) 'Quantitative designs and statistical analysis', in G. MacNaughton, S. Rolfe and I. Siraj-Blatchford (eds), *Doing Early Childhood Research. International Perspectives on Theory and Practice*. Buckingham: Open University Press.

Hart, C. (2005) *Doing Your Masters Dissertation*. London: Sage.

Hatch, J.A. (1995) 'Studying childhood as a cultural invention: a rationale and framework', in J.A. Hatch (ed.), *Qualitative Research in Early Childhood Settings*. Westport, CT: Praeger.

Hayes, A. (2001) 'Design issues', in G. MacNaughton, S. Rolfe and I. Siraj-Blatchford (eds), *Doing Early Childhood Research: International Perspectives on Theory and Practice*, Maidenhead: Open University Press.

Heise, D. (1970) 'The semantic differential and attitude research', in G. Summers (ed.), *Attitude Measurement*. Chicago, IL: Rand McNally. www.indiana.edu/~socpsy/papers/AttMeasure/attitude.htm (accessed 1 March 2009).

Hendrick, H. (1997) 'Constructions and reconstructions of British childhood: an interpretive survey. 1800 to the present', in A. James and A. Prout (eds), *Constructing and Reconstructing Childhood. Contemporary Issues in the Sociological Study of Childhood*. London: Routledge Falmer.

Hobart, C. and Frankel, J. (2004) *A Practical Guide to Child Observation and Assessment*. 3rd edn. Cheltenham: Nelson Thornes.

Hodder, I. (2000) 'The interpretation of documents and materials culture', in N.K. Denzin and Y.S. Lincoln (eds), *Handbook of Qualitative Research*. 2nd edn. London: Sage.

Holland, D. and Lachicotte, W., Skinner, D. and Cain, C. (1998) *Identity and Agency in Cultural Worlds*. Cambridge, MA: Harvard University Press.

Holland, P. (2003) *We Don't Play with Guns Here. War, Weapon and Super Hero Play in the Early Years*. Buckingham: Open University Press.

Holland, P. (2004) *Picturing Childhood: The Myth of the Child in Popular Imagery*. London: Tauris.

Holmes, J. (1993) *John Bowlby and Attachment Theory*. London: Routledge.

Holstein, J.A. and Gubrium, J.F. (1995) *The Active Interview*. Thousand Oaks, CA: Sage.

Hood, S. (2001) *The State of London's Children Report*. London: Office of the Children's Rights Commissioner for London.

hooks, b. (1990) *Yearning*. Boston: South End Press.

Hopcroft, R.L. (2005) 'Parental status and differential investment in sons and daughters: Trivers-Willard revisited', *Social Forces*, 83(3): 1111–36.

Hughes, C. and Dunn, J. (1998) 'Understanding mind and emotion: longitudinal associations with mental state talk between young friends', *Developmental Psychology*. 34(5): 1026–37.

Hughes, P. (2001a) 'Paradigms, methods and knowledge', in G. MacNaughton, S. Rolfe and I. Siraj-Blatchford (eds), *Doing Early Childhood Research: International Perspectives on Theory and Practice*. Maidenhead: Open University Press.

Hughes, P. (2001b) 'From nostalgia to metatheory: researching children's relationships with the media', *Contemporary Issues in Early Childhood*, 2(3): 354–67.

Hutton, P. (1990) *Survey Research for Managers: How to Use Surveys in Management Decision Making.* 2nd edn. Basingstoke: Macmillan.

Hyder, T. (2002) 'Making it happen: young children's rights in action – the work of Save the Children's Centre for Young Children's Rights', in B. Franklin (ed.), *The New Handbook of Children's Rights: Comparative Policy and Practice.* London: Routledge.

Ili, S., Von Mutius, E., Lau, S., Bergmann, R., Niggemann, B., Sommer-feld, C. and Wahn, U. (2001) 'Early childhood infectious diseases and the development of asthma up to school age: a birth cohort study.' *British Medical Journal*, 322: 390–5.

James, A. (2007) 'Ethnography in the study of children and childhood', in P. Atkinson, A. Coffey, S. Delamont, J. Lofland and L. Lofland (eds), *Handbook of Ethnography.* London: Sage.

James, A. and Prout, A. (eds) (1990) *Constructing and Reconstructing Childhood: Contemporary Issues in the Sociological Study of Childhood.* Cambridge: Polity Press.

James, A., Jenks, C. and Prout, A. (1998) *Theorising Childhood.* Cambridge: Polity Press.

Jarvis, M., Russell, J., Flanagan, C., Gorman, P. and Dolan, L. (2004) *Angles on Psychology.* 2nd edn. Cheltenham: Nelson Thornes.

Jenks, C. (2000) 'Zeitgeist research on childhood', in P. Christensen and A. James (eds), *Research with Children: Perspectives and Practices.* London: Falmer Press.

Johnson, B. and Christensen, L. (2008) *Educational Research.* 3rd edn. Los Angeles, CA: Sage.

Jupp, V. and Norris, C. (1993) 'Traditions in documentary analysis', in M. Hammersely (ed.), *Social Research: Philosophy, Politics and Practice.* London: Sage.

Kasunic, M. (2005) *Designing an Effective Survey.* Pittsburgh, PA: Carnegie Mellon University. www.sei.cmu.edu/pub/documents/05.reports/pdf/05hb004.pdf (accessed 26 November 2008).

Keesing, R. (2008) *A Brief History of Isaac Newton's Apple Tree.* New York: University of York Department of Physics. www.york.ac.uk/depts/phys/about/newtons-apple-tree.htm (accessed 10 February 2009).

Kelan, G. and Weiss, S. (2001) 'Childhood infections and asthma: at the crossroads of the hygiene and Barker hypotheses', *Respiratory Research*, 2: 324–7.

Kellett, M. (2005) *How to Develop Children as Researchers: A Step by Step Guide to the Teaching Process.* London: Sage.

Kemmis, S. (2008) 'Critical theory and participatory action research', in P. Reason and H. Bradbury (eds), *The Sage Handbook of Action Research.* 2nd edn. London: Sage.

Kemmis, S. and McTaggart, R. (2005) 'Participatory action research: communicative action and the public sphere', in N.K. Denzin and Y.S. Lincoln (eds), *The Sage Handbook of Qualitative Research.* 3rd edn. London: Sage.

Kincheloe, J.L. (1991) *Teachers as Researchers: Qualitative Inquiry as a Path to Empowerment.* London: Falmer.

Kumar, R. (2005) *Research Methodology, A Step-by-Step Guide for Beginners.* London: Sage.

Lahman, M. (2008) 'Always othered: ethical research with children', *Journal of Early Childhood Research*, 6(3): 281–300.

Lancaster, P. and Broadbent, V. (2003) *Listening to Young People.* Maidenhead: Open University Press.

Langston, A., Abbott, L., Lewis, V. and Kellett, M. (2004) 'Early childhood', in S. Fraser, V. Lewis, S. Ding, M. Kellett and C. Robinson (eds), *Doing Research with Children and Young People*. London: Sage.

Lee, D. (2008) *Science Time Line*, www.sciencetimeline.net/index.htm (accessed 2 November 2008).

Letherby, G. (2003) *Feminist Research in Theory and Practice*. Buckingham: Open University Press.

Lincoln, Y.S. and Guba, E.G. (2000) 'Paradigmatic controversies, contradictions and emerging confluences', in N.K. Denzin and Y.S. Lincoln (eds), *Handbook of Qualitative Research*. 2nd edn. London: Sage.

Macdonald, K. (2008) 'Using documents', in N. Gilbert (ed.), *Researching Social Life*. 3rd edn. London: Sage.

Macdonald, K. and Tipton, C. (1993) 'Using documents', in N. Gilbert (ed.), *Researching Social Life*. London: Sage.

Mackenzie, N. and Knipe, S. (2006) 'Research dilemmas: paradigms, methods and methodology', *Issues in Educational Research*, 16: 193–205.

MacNaughton, G. (2001) 'Action research', in G. MacNaughton, S.A. Rolfe and I. Siraj-Blatchford (eds), *Doing Early Childhood Research: International Perspectives on Theory and Practice*. Maidenhead: Open University Press.

MacNaughton, G. and Hughes, P. (2003) 'Curriculum contexts: parents and communities', in G. MacNaughton (ed.), *Shaping Early Childhood Learners, Curriculum and Contexts*. Maidenhead: Open University Press.

MacNaughton, G. and Rolfe, S.A. (2001) 'The research process', in G. MacNaughton, S.A. Rolfe and I. Siraj-Blatchford (eds), *Doing Early Childhood Research: International Perspectives on Theory and Practice*. Maidenhead: Open University Press.

MacNaughton, G. and Smith, K. (2005) 'Transforming research ethics: the choices and challenges of researching with children', in A. Farrell (ed.), *Ethical Research with Children*. Maidenhead: Open University Press.

Malewski, E. (2005) 'Epilogue: when children and youth talk back', in D.S. Soto and B.B. Swadener (eds), *Power and Voice in Research with Children*. New York: Peter Lang.

Mandell, N. (1988) 'The least-adult role in studying children', *Journal of Contemporary Ethnography*, 16(4): 433–67.

Manning-Morton, J. and Thorp, M. (2003) *Key Times for Play: The First Three Years*. Maidenhead: Open University Press.

Mayall, B. (1996) *Children, Health and the Social Order*. Buckingham: Open University Press.

Mayall, B. (1999) 'Children and childhood', in S. Hood, B. Mayall and S. Oliver (eds), *Critical Issues in Social Research: Power and Prejudice*. Buckingham: Open University Press.

Mayall, B. (2008) 'Conversations with children: working with generational issues', in P. Christensen and A. James (eds), *Research with Children: Perspectives and Practices*. 2nd edn. Abingdon: Routledge.

McCoyd, J. and Kerson, T. (2006) 'Conducting intensive interviews using email: a serendipitous comparative opportunity', *Qualitative Social Work*, 5(3): 389–406.

McNiff, J. and Whitehead, J. (2006) *All You Need to Know About Action Research*. London: Sage.

Mies, M. (1993) 'Towards a methodology for feminist research', in M. Hammersley (ed.), *Social Research: Philosophy, Politics and Practice*. London: Sage.

Miller, T. (1998) 'Shifting layers of professional, lay and personal narratives: longitudinal childbirth research', in J. Ribbens and R. Edwards (eds), *Feminist Dilemmas in Qualitative Research: Public Knowledge and Private Lives*. London: Sage.

Mitchell, C. and Reid-Walsh, J. (2002) *Researching Children's Popular Culture: The Cultural Spaces of Childhood*. London: Routledge.

Moon, J. (2006) *Learning Journals: A Handbook for Reflective Practice and Professional Development*. 2nd edn. Abingdon: Routledge.

Moss, P. (1994) 'Defining quality: values, stakeholders and processes', in P. Moss and A. Pence (eds), *Valuing Quality in Early Childhood Services*. London: Paul Chapman Publishing.

Moss, P., Clark, A. and Kjorholt, A.T. (2005) 'Introduction', in A. Clark, A.T. Kjorholt and P. Moss (eds), *Beyond Listening: Children's Perspectives of Early Childhood Services*. Bristol: Policy Press.

Mukherji, P. (2001) *Understanding Children's Challenging Behaviour*. Cheltenham: Nelson Thornes.

Mykhalovsky, E. (1997) 'Reconsidering "table talk": critical thoughts on the relationship between sociology, autobiography, and self-indulgence', in R. Hertz (ed.), *Reflexivity and Voice*. London: Sage.

National Evaluation of Sure Start (NESS) (2008) *The Impact of Sure Start Local Programmes on Three Year Olds and Their Families*. Nottingham: DfES Publications.

National Health Service (NHS) (2006) *The Personal Child Health Record*. South Shields: Harlow.

Northedge, A. (1990) *The Good Study Guide*. Milton Keynes: Open University Press.

O'Grady, S. (2006) The big question: how much faith should we have in political opinion polls? *Independent on Sunday* 24 October. www.independent.co.uk (accessed 23 March 2008).

O'Kane, C. (2000) 'The development of participatory techniques: facilitating children's views about decisions which affect them', in P. Christensen and A. James (eds), *Research with Children: Perspectives and Practices*. London: Falmer Press.

Oakley, A. (1981) 'Interviewing women: a contradiction in terms', in H. Roberts (ed.), *Doing Feminist Research*. London: Routledge and Kegan Paul.

Office of Public Sector Information, www.opsi.gov.uk (accessed 5 May 2009).

Olsen, R. and Clarke, H. (2003) *Parenting and Disability*. Bristol: Policy Press.

Paley, V.G. (1981) *Wally's Stories: Conversations in the Kindergarten*. Cambridge, MA: Harvard University Press.

Paley, V.G. (1990) *The Boy Who Would be a Helicopter: The Uses of Storytelling in the Classroom*. Cambridge, MA: Harvard University Press.

Paley, V.G. (1991) *Bad Guys Don't Have Birthdays*. Chicago, IL: University of Chicago Press.

Patton, M. (1987) *How to use Qualitative Methodology in Evaluation*. Newbury Park. CA: Sage.

Platt, L. (June 2003) 'Putting childhood poverty on the agenda: the relationship between research and policy in Britain 1800–1950', *Research Report of Save the Children Fund*. London: Save the Children Fund.

Plowman, L. and Stephen, C. (2003) 'Developing a policy on ICT in pre-school settings: the role of research', paper presented at the British Educational Research Association Annual Conference, Heriot-Watt University, Edinburgh, 11–13 September. www.leeds.ac.uk/educol/documents/00003362.htm (accessed 25 August 2008).

Pole, C. and Morrison, M. (2003) *Ethnography for Education*. Maidenhead: Open University Press.

Prior, L. (2004) 'Documents', in C. Seale, G. Gobo, J.F. Gubrium and D. Silverman (eds), *Qualitative Research Practice*. London: Sage.

Qvortrup, J. (1994) 'Childhood matters: an introduction', in J. Qvortrup, M. Bardy, G. Sgritta and H. Wintersberger (eds), *Childhood Matters: Social Theory, Practice and Politics*. Aldershot: Avebury.

Reinharz, S. (1997) 'Who am I? The need for a variety of selves in the field', in R. Hertz (ed.), *Reflexivity and Voice*. London: Sage.

Richardson, L. and Adams St Pierre, E. (2005) 'Writing: a method of inquiry', in N. Denzin and Y. Lincoln (eds), *The Sage Handbook of Qualitative Research*. 3rd edn. London: Sage.

Roberts-Holmes, G. (2005) *Doing Your Early Years Research Project: A Step-by-Step Guide*. London: Sage.

Robertson, M. and Sundstrom, E. (1990) 'Questionnaire design, return rates, and response favourableness in an employee attitude questionnaire', *Journal of Applied Psychology*, 75: 354–37.

Robson, C. (1993) *Real World Research: A Resource for Social Scientists and Practitioner-Researchers*. Oxford: Blackwell.

Robson, S. (2006) *Developing Thinking and Understanding in Young Children: An Introduction for Students*. London: Taylor and Francis.

Rolfe, S. (2001) 'Direct observation', in G. MacNaughton, S. Rolfe and I. Siraj-Blatchford, *Doing Early Childhood Research. International Perspectives on Theory and Practice*. Buckingham: Open University Press.

Rolfe, S., and MacNaughton, G. (2001) 'Research as a tool', in G. MacNaughton, S. Rolfe and I. Siraj-Blatchford (eds), (2001) *Doing Early Childhood Research. International Perspectives on Theory and Practice*. Buckingham: Open University Press.

Sachs, J. (1999) 'Using teacher research as a basis for professional renewal', *Journal of Inservice Education*, 25(1): 39–53.

Scheurich, J.J. (1997) *Research Methods in the Postmodern*. London: Falmer Press.

Schmuck, R.A. (2006) *Practical Action Research for Change*. 2nd edn. London: Sage.

Schon, D. (1983) *The Reflective Practitioner*. San Francisco, CA: Jossey-Bass.

Schum, T., Kolb, T., McAuliffe, T., Simms, M., Underhill, R. and Lewis, M. (2002) 'Sequential acquisition of toilet training skills: a descriptive study of gender and age differences in normal children', *Pediatrics*, 109(3): 48. http://pediatrics.aappublications.org (accessed 22 March 2008).

Science and Technology Facilities Council (STFC) (2008) www.lhc.ac.uk/ (accessed 1 November 2008).

Sheridan, M., Sharma, A. and Cockerill, H. (2008) *Children's Developmental Progress*. London: Routledge.

Silverman, D. (1993) *Interpreting Qualitative Data: Strategies for Analysing Talk, Text and Interaction*. London: Sage.

Silverman, D. (2005) *Doing Qualitative Research*. 2nd edn. London: Sage.

Silverman, D. (2006) *Interpreting Qualitative Data: Strategies for Analysing Talk, Text and Interaction*. 3rd edn. London: Sage.

Simmons, R. (2008) 'Questionnaires', in N. Gilbert (ed.), *Research Social Life*. 3rd edn. London: Sage.

Siraj-Blatchford, I. and Siraj-Blatchford, J. (2001a) 'Surveys and questionnaires: an evaluative case study', in G. MacNaughton, S. Rolfe and I. Siraj-Blatchford (eds), *Doing Early Childhood Research: International Perspectives on Theory and Practice*. Buckingham: Open University Press.

Siraj-Blatchford, I. and Siraj-Blatchford J. (2001b) 'An ethnographic approach to researching young children's learning', in G. MacNaughton, S. Rolfe and I. Siraj-Blatchford (eds), *Doing Early Childhood Research. International Perspectives on Theory and Practice*. Buckingham: Open University Press.

Soto, L. and Swadener, B. (2002) 'Toward liberatory early childhood theory, research and praxis: decolonizing a field', *Contemporary Issues in Early Childhood*, 3(1): 38–66.

Soto, D.S. and Swadener, B.B. (eds) (2005) *Power and Voice in Research with Children*. New York: Peter Lang.

Stake, R.E. (1995) *The Art of Case Study Research*. Thousand Oaks, CA: Sage.

Stake, R.E. (2000) 'Case studies', in N.K. Denzin and Y.S. Lincoln (eds), *Handbook of Qualitative Research*. 2nd edn. London: Sage.

Standing, K. (1998) 'Writing the voices of the less powerful: research on lone mothers', in J. Ribbens and R. Edwards (eds), *Feminist Dilemmas in Qualitative Research: Public Knowledge and Private Lives*. London: Sage.

Statistics on line, http://www.statistics.gov.uk/default.asp (accessed 23 March 2008).

Stewart, D. and Shamdasani, P. (1998) 'Focus group research', in L. Bickman and D. Roj (eds), *Handbook of Applied Research Methods*. Los Angeles, CA: Sage.

Swantz, M.L. (2008) 'Participatory action research as practice', in P. Reason and H. Bradbury (eds), *The Sage Handbook of Action Research*. 2nd edn. London: Sage.

Sylva, K. (1999) 'The role of research in explaining the past and shaping the future', in L. Abbott and H. Moylett (eds), *Early Education Transformed*. London: Falmer Press.

Sylva, K., Melhuish, E., Sammons, P., Siraj-Blatchford, I., Taggart, B. and Elliot, K. (2003) *The Effective Provision of Pre-School Education (EPPE) Project: Findings from the Pre-school Period Summary of Findings*. London: Institute of Education. www.ioe.ac.uk/cdl/eppe/pdfs/eppe_brief2503.pdf (accessed 11 November 2008).

Sylva, K., Roy, C. and Painter, M. (1980) *Childwatching at Playgroup and Nursery School*. London: Grant McIntyre.

Taylor, A.S. (2000) 'The UN Convention on the Rights of the Child: giving children a voice', in A. Lewis and G. Lindsay (eds), *Researching Children's Perspectives*. Buckingham: Open University Press.

Tobin, J., Wu, D. and Davidson, D. (1989) *Preschool in Three Cultures. Japan, China and the United States.* New Haven, CT: Yale University Press.

Towers, J. (1997) 'The neglect of playtime: a review of the literature', *Early Child Development and Care,* 131: 31–43.

Townsend, P. (1979) *Poverty in the United Kingdom.* Harmonsdworth: Penguin.

Tripp, D. (1993) *Critical Incidents in Teaching: Developing Professional Judgement.* Abingdon: Routledge.

Trivers, R. and Willard, D. (1973) 'Natural selection of parental ability to vary the sex ratio of offspring', *Science,* 179(4068): 90–2.

Veale, A. (2005) 'Creative methodologies in participatory research with children', in S. Greene and D. Hogan (eds), *Researching Children's Experience: Approaches and Methods.* London: Sage.

Viruru, R. (2001) *Early Childhood Education: Post colonial perspectives from India.* London: Sage.

Wadsworth, B. (1996) *Piaget's Theory of Cognitive and Affective Development: Foundations of Constructivism.* 5th edn. London: Longman.

Walliman, N. (2001) *Your Research Project: A Step-by-Step Guide for the First-time Researcher.* London: Sage.

Walsh, G. and Gardner, J. (2005) 'Assessing the quality of early years learning environments', *Early Childhood Research and Practice,* 7(1). http://ecrp.uiuc.edu/v7n1/walsh.html (accessed 30 November 2008).

Warming, H. (2005) 'Participant observation: a way to learn about children's perspectives', in A. Clark, A.T. Kjorholt and P. Moss (eds), *Beyond Listening: Children's Perspectives on Early Childhood Services.* Bristol: Policy Press.

Warnock Committee (1978) *Special Educational Needs: the Warnock Report.* London: DES.

Wasserfall, R.R. (1997) 'Reflexivity, feminism, and difference', in R. Hertz (ed.), *Reflexivity and Voice.* London: Sage.

Wells, G. and Wells, J. (1984) 'Learning to talk and learning to learn', *Theory and Practice,* 23(3): 190–7.

Westcott, H. and Littleton, K. (2005) 'Exploring meaning in interviews with children', in S. Greene and D. Hogan (eds), *Researching Children's Experience: Approaches and Methods.* London: Sage.

Wicks, P.G., Reason, P. and Bradbury, H. (2008) 'Living inquiry: personal, political and philosophical groundings for action research practice', in P. Reason and H. Bradbury (eds), *The Sage Handbook of Action Research.* 2nd edn. London: Sage.

Willow, C. and Hyder, T. (1998) *It Hurts You Inside: Children Talking about Smacking.* London: NCB and Save the Children.

Woodhead, M. and Faulkner, D. (2008) 'Subjects, objects or participants? Dilemmas of psychological research with children', in P. Christensen and A. James (eds), *Research with Children: Perspectives and Practices.* 2nd edn. Abingdon: Routledge.

Woolfitt, R. (2008) 'Conversation analysis and discourse analysis', in N. Gilbert (ed.), *Researching Social Life.* 3rd edn. London: Sage.

INDEX

Added to a page number 'f' denotes a figure; 'g' denotes glossary and 't' denotes a table.